Evaluation and Assessment in Educational Information Technology

Evaluation and Assessment in Educational Information Technology has been co-published simultaneously as *Computers in the Schools*, Volume 18, Numbers 2/3/4 2001.

The *Computers in the Schools* Monographic "Separates"

Below is a list of "separates," which in serials librarianship means a special issue simultaneously published as a special journal issue or double-issue *and* as a "separate" hardbound monograph. (This is a format which we also call a "DocuSerial.")

"Separates" are published because specialized libraries or professionals may wish to purchase a specific thematic issue by itself in a format which can be separately cataloged and shelved, as opposed to purchasing the journal on an on-going basis. Faculty members may also more easily consider a "separate" for classroom adoption.

"Separates" are carefully classified separately with the major book jobbers so that the journal tie-in can be noted on new book order slips to avoid duplicate purchasing.

You may wish to visit Haworth's website at . . .

http://www.HaworthPress.com

. . . to search our online catalog for complete tables of contents of these separates and related publications.

You may also call 1-800-HAWORTH (outside US/Canada: 607-722-5857), or Fax 1-800-895-0582 (outside US/Canada: 607-771-0012), or e-mail at:

getinfo@haworthpressinc.com

Evaluation and Assessment in Educational Information Technology, edited by Leping Liu, PhD, D. LaMont Johnson, PhD, Cleborne D. Maddux, PhD, and Norma J. Henderson, MS (Vol. 18, No. 2/3 and 4, 2001). *Explores current trends, issues, strategies, and methods of evaluation and assessment in educational information technology.*

Using Information Technology in Mathematics Education, edited by D. James Tooke, PhD, and Norma Henderson, MS (Vol. 17, No. 1/2 2001). *"Provides thought-provoking material on several aspects and levels of mathematics education. The ideas presented will provide food for thought for the reader, suggest new methods for the classroom, and give new ideas for further research." (Charles E. Lamb, EdD, Professor, Mathematics Education, Department of Teaching, Learning, and Culture, College of Education, Texas A&M University, College Station)*

Integration of Technology into the Classroom: Case Studies, edited by D. LaMont Johnson, PhD, Cleborne D. Maddux, PhD, and Leping Liu, PhD (Vol. 16, No. 2/3/4, 2000). *Use these fascinating case studies to understand why bringing information technology into your classroom can make you a more effective teacher, and how to go about it!*

Information Technology in Educational Research and Statistics, edited by Leping Liu, PhD, D. LaMont Johnson, PhD, and Cleborne D. Maddux, PhD (Vol. 15, No. 3/4, and Vol. 16, No. 1, 1999). *This important book focuses on creating new ideas for using educational technologies such as the Internet, the World Wide Web and various software packages to further research and statistics. You will explore on-going debates relating to the theory of research, research methodology, and successful practices.* Information Technology in Educational Research and Statistics *also covers the debate on what statistical procedures are appropriate for what kinds of research designs.*

Educational Computing in the Schools: Technology, Communication, and Literacy, edited by Jay Blanchard, PhD (Vol. 15, No. 1, 1999). *Examines critical issues of technology, teaching, and learning in three areas: access, communication, and literacy. You will discover new ideas and practices for gaining access to and using technology in education from preschool through higher education.*

Logo: A Retrospective, edited by Cleborne D. Maddux, PhD, and D. LaMont Johnson, PhD (Vol. 14, No. 1/2, 1997). *"This book–honest and optimistic–is a must for those interested in any aspect of Logo: its history, the effects of its use, or its general role in education." (Dorothy M. Fitch, Logo consultant, writer, and editor, Derry, New Hampshire)*

Using Technology in the Classroom, edited by D. LaMont Johnson, PhD, Cleborne D. Maddux, PhD, and Leping Liu, MS (Vol. 13, No. 1/2, 1997). *"A guide to teaching with technology that emphasizes the advantages of transitioning from teacher-directed learning to learner-centered learning–a shift that can draw in even 'at-risk' kids." (Book News, Inc.)*

Multimedia and Megachange: New Roles for Educational Computing, edited by W. Michael Reed, PhD, John K. Burton, PhD, and Min Liu, EdD (Vol. 10, No. 1/2/3/4, 1995). *"Describes and analyzes issues and trends that might set research and development agenda for educators in the near future." (Sci Tech Book News)*

Language Minority Students and Computers, edited by Christian J. Faltis, PhD, and Robert A. DeVillar, PhD (Vol. 7, No. 1/2, 1990). *"Professionals in the field of language minority education, including ESL and bilingual education, will cheer this collection of articles written by highly respected, research-writers, along with computer technologists, and classroom practitioners." (Journal of Computing in Teacher Education)*

Logo: Methods and Curriculum for Teachers, by Cleborne D. Maddux, PhD, and D. LaMont Johnson, PhD (Supp #3, 1989). *"An excellent introduction to this programming language for children." (Rena B. Lewis, Professor, College of Education, San Diego State University)*

Assessing the Impact of Computer-Based Instruction: A Review of Recent Research, by M. D. Roblyer, PhD, W. H. Castine, PhD, and F. J. King, PhD (Vol. 5, No. 3/4, 1988). *"A comprehensive and up-to-date review of the effects of computer applications on student achievement and attitudes." (Measurements & Control)*

Educational Computing and Problem Solving, edited by W. Michael Reed, PhD, and John K. Burton, PhD (Vol. 4, No. 3/4, 1988). *Here is everything that educators will need to know to use computers to improve higher level skills such as problem solving and critical thinking.*

The Computer in Reading and Language Arts, edited by Jay S. Blanchard, PhD, and George E. Mason, PhD (Vol. 4, No. 1, 1987). *"All of the [chapters] in this collection are useful, guiding the teacher unfamiliar with classroom computer use through a large number of available software options and classroom strategies." (Educational Technology)*

Computers in the Special Education Classroom, edited by D. LaMont Johnson, PhD, Cleborne D. Maddux, PhD, and Ann Candler, PhD (Vol. 3, No. 3/4, 1987). *"A good introduction to the use of computers in special education. . . . Excellent for those who need to become familiar with computer usage with special population students because they are contemplating it or because they have actually just begun to do it." (Science Books and Films)*

You Can Do It/Together, by Kathleen A. Smith, PhD, Cleborne D. Maddux, PhD, and D. LaMont Johnson, PhD (Supp #2, 1986). *A self-instructional textbook with an emphasis on the partnership system of learning that introduces the reader to four critical areas of computer technology.*

Computers and Teacher Training: A Practical Guide, by Dennis M. Adams, PhD (Supp #1, 1986). *"A very fine . . . introduction to computer applications in education." (International Reading Association)*

The Computer as an Educational Tool, edited by Henry F. Olds, Jr. (Vol. 3, No. 1, 1986). *"The category of tool uses for computers holds the greatest promise for learning, and this . . . book, compiled from the experiences of a good mix of practitioners and theorists, explains how and why." (Jack Turner, Technology Coordinator, Eugene School District 4-J, Oregon)*

Logo in the Schools, edited by Cleborne D. Maddux, PhD (Vol. 2, No. 2/3, 1985). *"An excellent blend of enthusiasm for the language of Logo mixed with empirical analysis of the language's effectiveness as a means of promoting educational goals. A much-needed book!" (Rena Lewis, PhD, Professor, College of Education, San Diego State University)*

Humanistic Perspectives on Computers in the Schools, edited by Steven Harlow, PhD (Vol. 1, No. 4, 1985). *"A wide spectrum of information." (Infochange)*

Evaluation and Assessment in Educational Information Technology

Leping Liu, PhD
D. LaMont Johnson, PhD
Cleborne D. Maddux, PhD
Norma J. Henderson, MS
Editors

Evaluation and Assessment in Educational Information Technology has been co-published simultaneously as *Computers in the Schools*, Volume 18, Numbers 2/3/4 2001.

The Haworth Press, Inc.
New York • London • Oxford

Evaluation and Assessment in Educational Information Technology
has been co-published simultaneously as *Computers in the Schools*™,
Volume 18, Numbers 2/3/4 2001.

The development, preparation, and publication of this work has been undertaken with great care. However, the publisher, employees, editors, and agents of The Haworth Press and all imprints of The Haworth Press, Inc., including The Haworth Medical Press® and Pharmaceutical Products Press®, are not responsible for any errors contained herein or for consequences that may ensue from use of materials or information contained in this work. Opinions expressed by the author(s) are not necessarily those of The Haworth Press, Inc. With regard to case studies, identities and circumstances of individuals discussed herein have been changed to protect confidentiality. Any resemblance to actual persons, living or dead, is entirely coincidental.

The Haworth Press, Inc., 10 Alice Street, Binghamton, NY 13904-1580 USA

Cover design by Thomas J. Mayshock Jr.

Library of Congress Cataloging-in-Publication Data

Evaluation and assessment in educational information technology / Leping Liu . . . [et al.], editors.
     p. cm.
    "Co-published simultaneously as Computers in the schools, volume 18, numbers 2/3/4, 2001."
    Includes bibliographical references and index.
      ISBN 0-7890-1938-8 (hardback : alk. paper) – ISBN 0-7890-1939-6 (pbk. : alk. paper)
    1. Educational technology. 2. Information technology. 3. Education–Effect of technological innovations on. I. Liu, Leping.
    LB1028.3 .E963 2002
    371.33′4–dc21   2002001522

Indexing, Abstracting & Website/Internet Coverage

This section provides you with a list of major indexing & abstracting services. That is to say, each service began covering this periodical during the year noted in the right column. Most Websites which are listed below have indicated that they will either post, disseminate, compile, archive, cite or alert their own Website users with research-based content from this work. (This list is as current as the copyright date of this publication.)

(continued)

(continued)

Special Bibliographic Notes related to special journal issues (separates) and indexing/abstracting:

- indexing/abstracting services in this list will also cover material in any "separate" that is co-published simultaneously with Haworth's special thematic journal issue or DocuSerial. Indexing/abstracting usually covers material at the article/chapter level.
- monographic co-editions are intended for either non-subscribers or libraries which intend to purchase a second copy for their circulating collections.
- monographic co-editions are reported to all jobbers/wholesalers/approval plans. The source journal is listed as the "series" to assist the prevention of duplicate purchasing in the same manner utilized for books-in-series.
- to facilitate user/access services all indexing/abstracting services are encouraged to utilize the co-indexing entry note indicated at the bottom of the first page of each article/chapter/contribution.
- this is intended to assist a library user of any reference tool (whether print, electronic, online, or CD-ROM) to locate the monographic version if the library has purchased this version but not a subscription to the source journal.
- individual articles/chapters in any Haworth publication are also available through the Haworth Document Delivery Service (HDDS).

Evaluation and Assessment in Educational Information Technology

Contents

CURRENT TRENDS AND PRACTICES

ABOUT THE EDITORS

Leping Liu, PhD, is Assistant Professor of Education in the Department of Reading, Special Education and Instructional Technology at Towson University. She received her PhD in information technology in education and statistics from the University of Nevada, Reno. She teaches courses on the application of technology in education. Her research interests focus on integration of technology in classroom teaching/learning, technology and mathematical thinking, multimedia learning environment and cognitive development, and computer achievement modeling. She has authored or co-authored several professional articles and co-edited two books.

D. LaMont Johnson, PhD, is Professor of Education in the Department of Counseling and Educational Psychology at the University of Nevada, Reno. He is also Program Coordinator of the Information Technology in Education Program. He teaches courses on the application of technology in education and trains teachers across the state of Nevada in using the Internet and other technologies in their classrooms. Co-author of the textbook *Educational Computing: Learning with Tomorrow's Technologies*, now in its third edition, Professor Johnson has authored or co-authored numerous books and articles on educational computing and information technology in education.

Cleborne D. Maddux, PhD, is Professor of Education in the Department of Counseling and Educational Psychology at the University of Nevada, Reno, where he teaches courses on statistics and on integrating technology into education. He trains elementary and high school teachers in the state of Nevada on how to make the Internet a regular feature of their classroom agendas. Senior author of *Educational Computing: Learning with Tomorrow's Technologies*, a textbook now in its third edition, Professor Maddux has authored or co-authored numerous professional articles and books on information technology in education and educational technology.

Norma J. Henderson, MS, is Doctoral Candidate in Counseling and Educational Psychology with an emphasis in educational technology at the University of Nevada, Reno. She received her BS in civil engineering and an MS in information technology in education from the University of Nevada, Reno. She teaches courses on the integration of technology in education. Her research interests focus on the integration of technology in the classroom, program evaluation and assessment, distance education, Web page development, and statistical modeling. She has authored or co-authored several professional articles and co-edited a book.

EDITORIAL

Leping Liu
D. LaMont Johnson
Cleborne D. Maddux
Norma J. Henderson

Assessing Learning in the New Age of Information Technology in Education

This collection of articles is devoted to issues and trends in assessment relating to information technology in education. We believe an examination of such issues and trends is important because of the increased emphasis information technology in education is receiving at

LEPING LIU is Assistant Professor, Department of Reading, Special Education and Instructional Technology, College of Education, Towson University, Towson, MD 21252 (E-mail: lliu@towson.edu).
D. LAMONT JOHNSON is Professor, Department of Counseling and Educational Psychology, University of Nevada, Reno, NV 89557 (E-mail: ljohnson@unr.edu).
CLEBORNE D. MADDUX is Professor, Department of Counseling and Educational Psychology, University of Nevada, Reno, NV 89557 (E-mail: maddux@unr.edu).
NORMA J. HENDERSON is doctoral candidate, Department of Counseling and Educational Psychology, University of Nevada, Reno, NV 89557 (E-mail: normah@unr.edu).

[Haworth co-indexing entry note]: "Assessing Learning in the New Age of Information Technology in Education." Liu et al. Co-published simultaneously in *Computers in the Schools* (The Haworth Press, Inc.) Vol. 18, No. 2/3, 2001, pp. 1-3; and: *Evaluation and Assessment in Educational Information Technology* (ed: Leping Liu et al.) The Haworth Press, Inc., 2001, pp. 1-3. Single or multiple copies of this article are available for a fee from The Haworth Document Delivery Service [1-800-HAWORTH, 9:00 a.m. - 5:00 p.m. (EST). E-mail address: getinfo@haworthpressinc.com].

national, state, and local levels. The emphasis on using information technology in teaching and learning cuts across all levels of education from pre-school to higher education. Consequently, in an age of ever-increasing demand for accountability, those who advocate using technology in education are being asked to demonstrate results using valid and relevant assessment procedures. The bottom line is that those of us who advocate for integrating information technology into teaching and learning promise more efficient and effective education. Questions are being asked now and will be asked more forcefully in the near future regarding our ability to deliver on this promise. This collection of articles addresses ways and means of demonstrating our success.

In 1988, *Computers in the Schools* devoted a theme issue to assessing the impact of information technology (Maddux, 1988). A lot has changed since that issue was published. The technology has certainly changed, the way we use the technology has changed, and we propose that the methods for evaluating our efforts have changed. Therefore, we believe this volume provides a timely reexamination of this important topic.

Since 1988, the number of master's and doctoral programs focusing on information technology in education has increased dramatically. This trend is one sign of the steady maturation of the field of information technology in education. As the field matures, the need for appropriate assessment methods becomes more urgent. As faculty members, administrators, and classroom teachers deal with meeting this need, three assumptions are emerging:

1. Instruction on learning to use, and learning to apply, information technology in education differs significantly from instruction in other curricular areas (Grin & van de Graaf, 1996; Hargreaves, 1997).
2. As the technology has changed, and the applications have changed, courses dealing with information technology in education have changed, thereby creating a need to reevaluate assessment methods for these courses (Johnson & Liu, 2001; Liu & Cheeks, 2001).
3. In most well-developed graduate programs emphasizing information technology in education, assessment is a core course. There is presently a serious paucity of texts and readings on this subject.

The articles within this volume address a broad range of issues relating to assessing the use of information technology in education. The articles fit into four broad categories:

1. The impact of using information technology in schools (How do we measure the effects information technology is having on teaching and learning?)
2. Learning to use technology (How effective are the instructional methods for teaching students to use new technology?)
3. Integrating technology (To what extent is technology being integrated into the curriculum as teaching and learning tools?)
4. Faculty development (How well are faculty members mastering the use of technology and using it in their teaching?)

The articles herein espouse the use of both quantitative and qualitative methods of assessment. Qualitative methods include portfolio analysis, observations, team assessment/evaluations, content analysis, and case studies. Quantitative methods include individual exams, group exams, questionnaires, self-evaluations, and project-based assessment/evaluations.

While the theme of this issue is assessment, we believe the articles provide a wealth of more general information. In addressing the ways and means of assessing the use of information technology in education, authors have shared experiences where technology has been successfully used. They also share a perspective on the overall positive impact information technology has had on education.

REFERENCES

Grin, J., & van de Graaf, H. (1996). Technology assessment as learning. *Science, Technology & Human Values, 21*(1), 72-101.

Hargreaves, D. J. (1997). Student learning and assessment are inextricably linked. *European Journal of Engineering Education, 22*(4), 401-410.

Johnson, L., & Liu, L. (2001). *Current issues and trends in assessing the use of information technology in education.* Paper presented and discussed at the Society for Information Technology & Teacher Education annual conference, Orlando, FL.

Liu, L., & Cheeks, C. (2001). *Assessing technology-assisted use of information.* Paper presented at the Society for Information Technology & Teacher Education annual conference, Orlando, FL.

Maddux, C. D. (1988). Preface: Assessing the impact of computer-based instruction. *Computers in the Schools, 5*(3/4), 1-10.

INSTRUMENTS AND TESTING

Rhonda Christensen
Gerald Knezek

Instruments for Assessing the Impact of Technology in Education

SUMMARY. Ten years of instrument development are summarized and placed within a framework for assessing the impact of technology in education. Seven well-validated instruments spanning the areas of attitudes, beliefs, skills, competencies, and technology integration proficiencies are presented, along with data analysis examples. These instruments are proposed for use in modeling the process of technology integration, which is believed to be an important intermediary step in effective use of technology in teaching and learning. *[Article copies available for a fee from The Haworth Document Delivery Service: 1-800-HAWORTH. E-mail address: <getinfo@haworthpressinc.com> Website: <http://www.HaworthPress.com> © 2001 by The Haworth Press, Inc. All rights reserved.]*

RHONDA CHRISTENSEN is Instructor, Institute for the Integration of Technology into Teaching and Learning (IITTL), University of North Texas, P.O. Box 311337, Denton, TX 76203 (E-mail: rhondac@tenet.edu).
GERALD KNEZEK is Professor of Technology and Cognition, University of North Texas, P.O. Box 311337, Denton, TX 76203 (E-mail: gknezek@tenet.edu).

[Haworth co-indexing entry note]: "Instruments for Assessing the Impact of Technology in Education." Christensen, Rhonda, and Gerald Knezek. Co-published simultaneously in *Computers in the Schools* (The Haworth Press, Inc.) Vol. 18, No. 2/3, 2001, pp. 5-25; and: *Evaluation and Assessment in Educational Information Technology* (ed: Leping Liu et al.) The Haworth Press, Inc., 2001, pp. 5-25. Single or multiple copies of this article are available for a fee from The Haworth Document Delivery Service [1-800-HAWORTH, 9:00 a.m. - 5:00 p.m. (EST). E-mail address: getinfo@haworthpressinc.com].

KEYWORDS. Technology, assessment, teachers, instruments, pre-service, in-service, attitudes, competencies, stages, integration

CALL FOR ACCOUNTABILITY

Significant resources have been expended to place computers in the schools over the past two decades. Recently, the call for accountability has become strong. According to a study by the Educational Testing Service, the total cost of technology in U.S. schools as of the late 1990s was about $3 billion, or $70 per pupil (Coley, Cradler, & Engal, 1998). Many educators have reported their opinions concerning the effects of this influx of technology on student learning; and, especially since the early 1990s, scholars in the field have pointed out the need to address the issue of accountability. As plans are made for the increased use of technology, it is important for policymakers, educators, and researchers to understand how teachers and children relate to this technology (Martin, Heller, & Mahmoud, 1992).

Small Allocation for Teacher Training

A major corollary of the accountability issue has to do with the proportion of technology funds that should be spent on training. Data from a 1995 national survey of school district technology budget allocations revealed that approximately 55% of technology money was being spent on hardware and 30% on software. Teacher education accounted for only 15% of the allocated funds (U.S. Congress, 1995). The U.S. Department of Education has recommended that districts allocate 30% of their technology budgets to staff development activities (U.S. Congress, 1995), but a CEO Forum report suggests that, as of 1998-99, schools were still spending less than 10% of their budget on training (CEO Forum, 1998).

Projected Training Needs

The 1998 CEO Forum study also estimated that the $3 billion spent on technology in U.S. schools represents just over 1% of total education spending, and that it will cost about $15 billion to make all our schools "technology rich." This is about $300 per student, or about 5% of total education spending, and about five times what we now spend on technology (CEO Forum, 1998). If the recommended 30% of this $300 per student is allocated to teacher training, then about $90 per pupil, or $1,800 per elementary school teacher with a class of 20, should be budgeted for training. This large proposed increase in funds for technology staff development necessitates studies to determine what types of teacher education and re-education lead to effective use of technology in the classroom.

Indicators of Success

Although there is a demonstrated need for investment in teacher training to make effective use of information technology in the classroom, there are no clear indicators of which prescribed training produces the desired outcomes. This paper focuses on indicators of technology integration and the association of these indicators with positive student learning outcomes.

The Search for Positive Impact on Students

Much recent research in educational technology has focused on impact. Researchers have been generally successful in demonstrating the positive impact of technology infusion with appropriate teacher training on teacher attitudes toward information technology, student attitudes toward information technology, and other learning-related student dispositions such as motivation (Christensen, 1997; Collis, Knezek, Lai, Miyashita, Pelgrum, Plomp, & Sakamoto, 1996; Woodrow, 1992). Instruments have been developed by several researchers to aid in this process (Christensen & Knezek, 1998; Knezek & Christensen, 1998; Knezek & Christensen, 2000; Ropp, 1999). Researchers have been less successful in identifying positive effects of technology infusion on student achievement, although some studies have met with success. For example, a review of 130 studies by Bailo and Sivin-Kachla (1995) concluded that using technology to support instruction improves student outcomes in language arts, math, social studies, and science. An evaluation of the West Virginia Basic Skills/Computer Education Program concluded that "the effective use of learning technology has led directly to significant gains in math, reading, and language arts skills in West Virginia" (Mann, Shakeshaft, Becker, & Kottkamp, 1999). More commonly, however, findings are mixed. For example, Pierce (1998) summarized a large-scale study of the impact of technology on mathematics achievement, conducted by the Educational Testing Service (ETS) and sponsored by the Milken Exchange on Education Technology and Education Week:

> Students who spent the most time at a computer in school actually scored lower than their peers on a national math test, the study found. Students who used "drill and practice" software also scored lower. But students who used computers for simulations and real-life applications of math concepts scored higher, especially those students in middle school. The study suggests that school districts should focus attention on professional development for teachers to make sure they know how to use computers with their students effectively. (p. 1)

Apparently, positive impacts of technology on achievement require wide-scale, long-term initiatives that include sufficient access to technology for students and teachers, and teacher training in appropriate technology integration techniques to be used in the classroom. Effective study of this kind of initiative could benefit from longitudinal data, and would likely be multivariate in nature. A research method that is believed to be well suited to these constraints is described in the following section.

TECHNIQUES, PROCEDURES AND INSTRUMENTS

Two theoretical approaches that form a logical basis for selecting assessment instruments of technology integration are presented in this paper. The first is diffusion of innovation, while the second is a structural model of technology integration.

Early research by Rogers (1983) found that adoption of innovations is an active process that involves much reinvention. Adopters must reinvent the innovation and make it their own if they are to continue using it. Hall and Rutherford (1974) developed the Concerns-Based Adoption Model (CBAM) in the early 1970s for the study of adoption of any educational innovation. CBAM Stages of Concern (1974) and Levels of Use of the Innovation (Loucks, Newlove, & Hall, 1975) classifications have been adapted for information technology innovations and used by researchers on several continents over the past three decades. The Levels of Use form, which is described in more detail in the following section, is based on CBAM work.

The second approach is a structural model of technology integration developed by Knezek and Christensen (Knezek, Christensen, Hancock, & Shoho, 2000). This model is based on the assumption that educator *will* (positive attitude), *skill* (competency, ability to perform tasks), and access to technology *tools* are all required for successful technology integration. The model is grounded in educational psychology principles that determine key variables influencing the school learning environment (Klausmeir & Goodwin, 1975), and it relies on the multivariate technique of Structured Equation Modeling (Schumacker, 1996) to guide measurement techniques. The instruments presented in the booklet *Instruments for Assessing Educator Progress in Technology Integration* are generally organized along these lines (Knezek, Christensen, Miyashita, & Ropp, 2000). Descriptions of key instruments from this book, and related instruments relevant to the content of this paper, follow.

Selected Instruments for Assessing the Impact of Technology in Education

Attitude Instruments

1. The Teachers' Attitudes Toward Computers Questionnaire (TAC version 5.1) (Christensen & Knezek, 1998) measures seven major indices regarding teacher attitudes. These scales are: F1-Enthusiasm/Enjoyment, F2-Anxiety, F3-Avoidance/Acceptance, F4–E-mail for Classroom Learning, F5-Negative Impact on Society, F6-Productivity, and F7-Semantic Perception of Computers. The reliabilities for these subscales typically range from .87 to .95 with K-12 teacher data.
2. Teachers' Attitudes Toward Information Technology Questionnaire (TAT version 2.0) (Knezek & Christensen, 1998) is a semantic differential instrument that measures attitudes toward new information technologies including e-mail (variable coded as EMAILT), the World Wide Web (WWWT), multimedia (MMT), technology for teacher productivity (PRODT), and technology for classroom learning (PRODCL). Reliabilities for these scales typically range from .91 to .98 for K-12 teachers.

Beliefs and Needs

The Snapshot Survey by Norris and Soloway (Norris, Box, & Soloway, 1999; Norris, Soloway, Knezek, Topp, Young, & Box, 2000) addresses how prevalent technology is in education today, and what an educator believes about the technology. This survey includes scales for beliefs and needs of the educators as well as classroom use of computers.

Skill/Competency

1. Technology Proficiency Self-Assessment (Ropp, 1999) measures educator proficiency in e-mail, the World Wide Web (WWW), Integrated Applications (IA), and Teaching with Technology (TT).
2. Technology in Education Competency Survey (Christensen, 1999) is a self-assessment rating form covering teacher competencies in nine major areas addressed by the National Council for the Accreditation of Teacher Education (NCATE) standards for the United States.

Level of Proficiency

1. Stages of Adoption of Technology (Christensen, 1997) is a self-assessment instrument of a teacher's level of adoption of technology, based on earlier work by Russell (1995).
2. Level of Use (Griffin & Christensen, 1999) is a self-assessment instrument adapted from the Concerns-Based Adoption Model (CBAM) designations for adoption of an educational innovation.

EVIDENCE OF SUCCESSFUL USE OF INSTRUMENTS

Relationship of Attitudes to Stages of Adoption

Data were gathered from 1,135 K-12 teachers from 13 school districts in north central Texas during 1998. This region of Texas contains predominantly rural schools. Educators were asked to complete the Stages of Adoption of Technology form (see Appendix A), the TAC, and the TAT during March 1998.

The average Stage of Adoption value across these 1,135 educators was 4.13. High correlations were found between stages of adoption and computer anxiety ($r = .67, p < .0005, N = 973$), in the direction of higher stages being associated with reduced anxiety. Higher stages of adoption were also strongly associated with increased computer enjoyment ($r =$

.60, $p < .0005$, $N = 973$). Background information was gathered regarding home access to computers and the Internet. To determine whether use of a computer at home or access to the WWW at home made a difference in teachers' stage of adoption, t-tests were carried out. Findings were that both home use of a computer and home access to the Internet were very strong discriminators for high or low stages of adoption (Knezek & Christensen, 1999). The nature of the relationship appears to be that home access makes a large contribution to technology integration advancement at the higher stages.

A discriminant function analysis, which is a form of regression analysis in which the dependent variable (stage of adoption) is assumed to be only categorical, was carried out on the data to determine if teacher attitudes toward information technology are sufficiently strongly related to advances in stages of adoption to be useful as predictors of stage. The seven major attitude subscales on the TAC, plus computer enjoyment and anxiety subscales that were completed by teachers and students in the study, were used as predictors for stage of adoption. Based on their reported attitudes toward information technology, 46% of the teachers in the sample could be correctly classified into their own reported stage. The expectation for correct classification would be $1/6 = 16.7\%$ by chance. Roughly 90% accuracy is possible if one is willing to accept plus or minus one stage as a success. This is often acceptable in a situation where the average stage of an entire school, rather than that of an individual teacher, is the goal (Knezek & Christensen, 1999).

Reliability of Stages of Adoption as an Outcome Measure

Because the Stages of Adoption instrument is a single-item survey, internal consistency reliability measures cannot be calculated. However, a high test-retest reliability estimate (.91) was obtained from a sample of 525 K-12 teachers from a metropolitan north Texas public school district for the period of August through November 1999. The Stages of Adoption form was included on two attitudinal questionnaires that were completed by educators as near to each other in time as within the same hour, or separated in time by as much as several days. During this process, educators never had access to the information provided on one survey while completing the other. A Pearson Product-Moment Correlation Coefficient was calculated between the two reported stage measures as a form of test-retest reliability. The resulting value of .91 indicates high consistency for these educators on reported stages within the recognized limitations (remembering and contextual cues) that undoubtedly inflated the estimate, compared to a standard reliability index.

Relationship to CBAM Level of Use

A study was conducted from August through September 1999 to determine if ratings on the CBAM Levels of Use of an Innovation scale (see Appendix B) were closely related to the ordered categories on the Stages of Adoption of Technology instrument. Responses from the same 525 educators cited in the previous section indicate that these two scales are related ($r = .64$). Future research is needed to determine if certain levels of use correspond with precise stages of adoption.

Validation of Association with Curricular Sequence

The first three University of North Texas courses listed in Table 1 have for more than a decade been approved for a Texas Education Agency Information Processing Technologies (IPT) endorsement, which can be added to a teaching certificate. Beginning in 1997, the third course (CECS 4100) was modified to include a major module on the Texas Essential Knowledge and Skills (TEKS), and funds awarded through a U.S. Department of Education Preparing Tomorrow's Teachers to Use Technology (PT[3]) grant were used to add the fourth course beginning in spring 1999-2000.

Completion of this four-course sequence entitles undergraduates to a University of North Texas certificate in curriculum and technology integration.

During fall semester 1998, participants in the first course of the sequence (CECS 1100–Computer Applications) began on the average at stage 3.1 and exited the course on the average at stage 3.9. Students in the second course in the sequence (CECS 3440–Teacher Productivity Tools) began on the average at stage 4.1 (posttest data were not available), while students in the third course (CECS 4100) began on the average at stage 4.4 and exited from the course at stage 5.2. This can be compared to a typical teacher, as measured by a sample of more than 1,000 from the same geographic area, during the same period. The average rating across practicing teachers was 4.13, a value lying near the center of the indices reported across the three-course technology integration sequence. These results are graphically displayed in Figure 1 (Christensen & Knezek, 2000a).

TABLE 1. Computer Education and Cognitive Systems (CECS) Courses in the Technology Applications Sequence

Course Number	Course Title	Course Description
CECS 1100	Computer Applications in Education	This is a tool-based course in which students learn to use an integrated word processing, spreadsheet, and database package.
CECS 3440	Technology and the Teacher	This course includes the use of presentation software and theories as well as the instructional design of presentation materials.
CECS 4100	Computers in the Classroom	Students in this class learn to find appropriate instructional software for the classroom, develop a multimedia project, find Internet resources for classroom use, develop a technology-infused lesson plan, and make a Web page to link to their instructional resources.
CECS 4800	Technology Integration Mentoring	This course provides field-based technology integration experiences to pre-service educators.

FIGURE 1. Stages of Adoption of Technology for Three Classes of Pre-Service Teachers versus In-Service Teachers (1998)

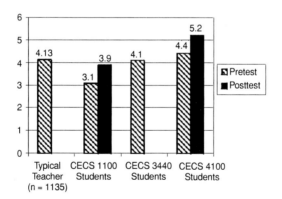

Profiles of Attitudes Toward Information Technology Among Educators at Various Stages of Adoption

Results of analysis of the data from 1,135 rural Texas educators are presented in Table 2 and graphically illustrated in Figure 2 (Christensen & Knezek, 2000b). Based on analysis of data, it appears that teachers who are in Stage One (awareness) also rated themselves lower in computer enjoyment, computer avoidance, e-mail, productivity, and overall per-

TABLE 2. Means, Standard Deviations, and Levels of Significance for Profile of Rural Educators' Attitudes Toward Technology by Stages of Adoption (1998 Data)

Factor	Stage 1	Stage 2	Stage 3	Stage 4	Stage 5	Stage 6	Sig F
F1-Enjoyment	2.97 (.51)	3.15 (.59)	3.39 (.52)	3.62 (.51)	3.85 (.50)	4.12 (.51)	.0000
F2-Anxiety (lack of)	2.59 (.65)	2.67 (.69)	3.22 (.60)	3.58 (.63)	4.01 (.52)	4.44 (.47)	.0000
F3-Avoidance (acceptance)	3.36 (.41)	3.62 (.39)	3.79 (.34)	3.93 (.39)	4.08 (.37)	4.28 (.32)	.0000
F4-E-mail	3.14 (.50)	3.08 (.57)	3.13 (.44)	3.23 (.61)	3.30 (.59)	3.62 (.80)	.0000
F5-Negative Impact (lack of)	3.13 (.66)	3.11 (.58)	3.40 (.50)	3.62 (.60)	3.70 (.52)	3.96 (.55)	.0000
F6-Productivity	2.88 (.42)	2.98 (.44)	3.10 (.37)	3.28 (.38)	3.39 (.37)	3.62 (.37)	.0000
F7-Semantic Perception	4.58 (.98)	4.55 (1.03)	5.02 (1.03)	5.44 (1.03)	5.77 (.82)	6.13 (1.10)	.0000
E-mailT	4.18 (1.22)	4.73 (1.30)	4.77 (1.18)	5.18 (1.17)	5.51 (1.12)	5.90 (1.28)	.0000
WWWT	4.64 (1.34)	5.17 (1.22)	5.30 (1.28)	5.60 (1.22)	5.93 (1.04)	6.33 (1.01)	.0000
MMT	4.93 (1.11)	5.31 (1.06)	5.52 (1.00)	5.84 (1.02)	6.02 (.99)	6.44 (.88)	.0000
ProdT	4.73 (1.40)	5.00 (1.20)	5.55 (1.09)	5.95 (.93)	6.18 (.83)	6.56 (.79)	.0000
ProdCL	4.89 (1.47)	5.63 (1.05)	5.96 (.96)	6.02 (1.06)	6.26 (.86)	6.62 (.73)	.0000
N	18	72	120	248	217	127	

Note. Anxiety, Avoidance and Negative Impact are coded in a positive direction. Higher means represent a lack of anxiety, lack of avoidance and lack of perceived negative impact.

ception of computers. They rated themselves as being more anxious toward computers and more negative in their feelings about the impact of computers.

Teachers who reported being in the sixth stage of technology adoption had the highest mean scores among the six stages of adoption category groupings in computer enjoyment, e-mail, productivity, semantic perception of computers, e-mail for teachers, WWW for teachers, multimedia for teachers, productivity for teachers, and productivity for classroom use. This subset of teachers also rated themselves the lowest of all the groups of teachers in anxiety, computer avoidance, and a negative feeling toward the impact of computers.

FIGURE 2. Profile of Attitude by Stage of Adoption for Rural Texas Educator Data (1998)

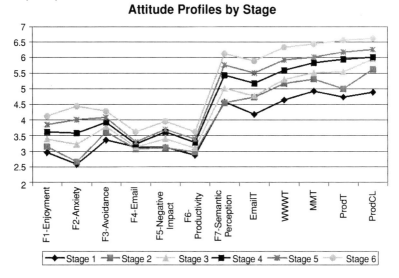

Associations Between Increased Technology Proficiency and Self-Reported Level of Technology Integration

Teachers from a suburban metropolitan area in north Texas received weekly local site training with the technology purchased through a school district bond election. Educators were invited to complete pretest and posttest online assessments of their technology skills and perceived needs during the fall 1999. One hundred eight (108) teachers responded to the request for pretest data, while 262 provided online posttest data.

The Technology Proficiency Self-Assessment Instrument (TPSA) was included to gather data on teacher competencies (Ropp, 1999). This instrument was selected because it has high reliability and measures skills recommended by the International Society for Technology in Education for all K-12 teachers. Four of Ropp's measurement scales (with five items each) were included: E-mail, Integrated Applications (IA), Teaching with Technology (TT), and the World Wide Web (WWW).

On a scale of 1 (little knowledge) to 5 (great knowledge), e-mail proficiency increased from a group mean average of 3.34 at the time of the pretest in early fall, to 4.20 at the time of the posttest in December 1999. Proficiency with integrated applications increased from a group mean average of 2.85 on the pretest to 4.18 by the posttest. Teachers' perceived proficiency in teaching with technology improved from an average rating of 3.25 at the time of the pretest to 4.16 at posttest time. Proficiency with the World Wide Web improved from 3.60 at the pretest to 4.53 at the posttest. All of these changes are highly significant in the statistical sense ($p < .0005$).

Furthermore, as shown in Figure 3, technology skill profiles for the groups with different reported stages of adoption were quite distinct, for all groups except Stage Five versus Stage Six. This implies that some other attributes besides technology skills (such as teacher attitudes) may be the distinguishing factor for Stage Five versus Stage Six level of technology integration.

Changes in Pre-Service Educator Skills

Data were gathered from UNT pre-service teachers using the Technology Proficiency Skills Assessment (TPSA) for the first time during fall 1999. Initial findings, based on one CECS 4100 class of 21 students, are graphically displayed in Figure 4. Students enrolled in the Computers in the Classroom course reported significant skill gains ($p < .001$)

FIGURE 3. Profile of Confidence in Skills by Stage of Adoption for Suburban Texas Educator Data (1999)

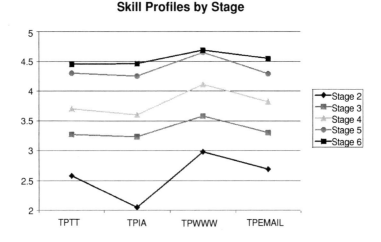

Skill Profiles by Stage

FIGURE 4. Pre- and Posttest Technology Integration Skills Comparison for CECS 4100 Pre-Service Students

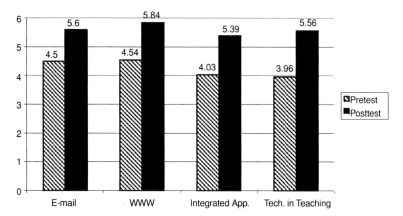

TPSA Pre-Service Gains

in four areas measured by the TPSA. The effect sizes of these gains ranged from .86 to 1.39. The average gain in level of technology proficiency was approximately one standard deviation.

Pre-post changes in ISTE competencies gathered from a class of pre-service teacher education students during fall 1999 are shown in Figure 5. This direct appraisal, nine-item form developed by Christensen, has yielded an internal consistency reliability estimate of .92 across 188 pre-service educators and 40 university faculty (Christensen & Knezek, 2000c). Items for this instrument are listed in Appendix C.

WST Model

Collaborative work by the authors dating back to 1991 has recently been consolidated into a new model for integrating technology into the classroom. This model relies on multiple indicators to show that technology investment can contribute to student achievement (see Figure 6). The Will, Skill, Tool *(WST)* Model includes three key elements for successful integration of technology: *will* (attitude) of the teacher, *skill* (technology competency), and technology *tools* (access to technology tools). The model also postulates that technology integration in the classroom contributes to higher student achievement. Preliminary analysis of this model has yielded promising results. Two studies based on this approach are summarized in the following section.

FIGURE 5. Pre- and Post-Competencies for CECS 4100 Pre-Service Students

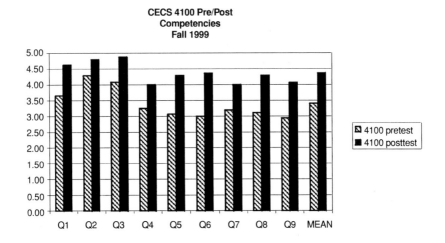

IMPACT OF WILL, SKILL, AND TOOLS
ON TECHNOLOGY INTEGRATION

Survey responses gathered during fall 1999 from teachers in a public high school in the Dallas/Fort Worth metroplex area of northern Texas were used to test some components of this model (Knezek, Christensen, Hancock, & Shoho, 2000). Regression analyses were carried out on data from 39 teachers who completed a battery of instruments. A brief summary of the findings follows.

Impact of Will. Approximately 40% of the variance in stage of adoption was found to be attributable to "will" measures for these teachers. The R-squared for Stage of Adoption predicted from the TAT attitude scales (E-mailT, WWWT, MMT, ProdT, ProdCL) was .39.

Impact of Will and Skill Combined. Adding skill measures to the equation increased the predictability of Stages of Adoption of Technology from roughly 40% to 70%. The R-squared for stages predicted from TAT attitude measures and TPSA skill measures was .69.

Combined Impact of Will, Skill and Access to Technology Tools. Adding measures of access to technology tools for teachers increased the predictability of Stages of Adoption from 70% to 84% for this set of data. The R-squared for TAT attitudes, TPSA skills, and the three tool variables of current hours per week using technology in the classroom

FIGURE 6. Will, Skill, Tool (WST) Model of Technology Integration

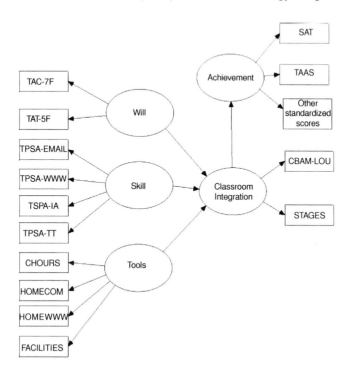

(CHOURS), access to a computer at home (HOMECOM) and access to the WWW at home (HOMEWWW) was .84.

Goodness of Fit for Individual Educators. Ideally, structured equation modeling (Joreskog & Sorbom, 1998; Schumacker, 1996) would have been employed to determine how well the model fit the data, but its use was not attempted in the spring 2000 analysis due to the small data set and large number of degrees of freedom in the model (Schumacker, 1999). Instead, discriminant function analysis was chosen to explore how well will, skill, and technology tools could place an individual in the proper Stage of Adoption. Twenty-five of 39 secondary school teachers provided complete data and were used in the analysis. The self-reported Stage of Adoption for these 25 ranged from Stage 2 (learning the process) to Stage 6 (creative applications to new contexts). The combined prediction abilities of the four discriminant functions derived for the data set yielded 100% accuracy in placing educators into proper stages of adoption, based solely on the will, skill, and tool parameters indicated in the model (Knezek, Christensen, Hancock, & Shoho, 2000).

Impact of Technology Investment on Student Achievement. In a related test of the WST Model focused on student achievement, Hancock (Knezek, Christensen, Hancock, & Shoho, 2000) randomly selected 100 of approximately 1,046 Texas school districts for detailed study of available variables representing both ends of the technology infusion-to-student-achievement continuum. The Texas Assessment of Academic Skills (TAAS) test pass rate and district-wide average SAT score were used as dependent variables in a regression analysis. District-wide hardware expenditures and district-wide expenditures on software and technology supplies were the two independent variables used to indicate extent of support for information technology (tool) facilities. Major findings were that hardware and software expenditures together accounted for approximately 11% of the variance in SAT scores across the sample of school districts (R squared = .11498). This relationship was found to be significant at the .05 level ($F = 3.25, 2 \times 50$ $df, p = .0472$). In addition, hardware and software expenditures together accounted for approximately 11% of the variance in TAAS pass rates across school districts (R squared = .11). This relationship was also significant at the .05 level ($F = 3.70, 2 \times 58$ $df, p = .03$). In summary, approximately 11% of Texas schools districts' standardized student achievement scores could be predicted from level of investment in technology (Knezek, Christensen, Hancock, & Shoho, 2000). These findings should certainly be interpreted with caution due to the small sample sizes and other limitations of the analyses. Nevertheless, they serve to illustrate the potential utility of the model.

CONCLUSION

Seven well-validated instruments spanning the areas of attitudes, beliefs, skills, competencies, and technology integration proficiencies have been developed by the authors and their colleagues over the past decade and assembled within a framework for technology integration. Research related to the development of these instruments, and findings resulting from the instruments themselves, has lead to the conclusion that *will* (motives, positive attitudes), *skill* (ability to use software applications), and *tools* (access to hardware and software systems) are all essential ingredients for a teacher to effectively integrate information technology into his/her daily classroom practices. The authors conjecture that effective technology integration at the classroom level will then lead to a positive impact on student learning and achievement. Future research is planned to more fully explore parameters influencing level of technology integration, and to test the extent to which classroom technology integration influences student achievement.

REFERENCES

Bailo, E. R., & Sivin-Kachla, J. (1995). *Effectiveness of technology in schools, 1990-1994.* Washington, DC: Software Publishers Association.

CEO Forum. (1998). Year 2 STaR report: *Professional development: A link to better learning.* [Online]. Available: *http://www.ceoforum.org*

Christensen, R. (1997). *Effect of technology integration education on the attitudes of teachers and their students.* [Online]. Unpublished doctoral dissertation, University of North Texas, Denton, Texas. Available: *http://courseweb.tac.unt.edu/rhondac*

Christensen, R. (1999). Technology in Education Preservice Competency Survey. [Online]. Available: *http://www.iittl.unt.edu/unt/students/tpsa2.htm*

Christensen, R., & Knezek, G. (1998). Parallel forms for measuring teachers' attitudes toward computers. In S. McNeil, J. Price, S. Boger-Mehall, B. Robin, & J. Willis (Eds.), *Technology and teacher education annual 1998* (Vol. 2, pp. 820-824). Charlottesville, VA: Association for the Advancement of Computing in Education.

Christensen, R., & Knezek, G. (1999). Stages of adoption for technology in education. *Computers in New Zealand Schools, 11*(3), 25-29.

Christensen, R., & Knezek, G. (2000a). Advancement of student technology integration skills through university preservice coursework. In D. Willis, J. Price, & J. Willis (Eds.), *Technology and teacher education annual 2000* (Vol. 2, pp. 1505-1510). Charlottesville, VA: Association for the Advancement of Computing in Education.

Christensen, R., & Knezek, G. (2000b). *Strategies for integrating technology into the classroom.* [Online]. Pre-conference symposium paper presented at the Society for Information Technology in Teacher Education Annual Conference, San Diego, CA. Available: *http://www.iittl.unt.edu/IITTL/presentations*

Christensen, R., & Knezek, G. (2000c, April 25). *Internal consistency reliability for the Technology in Education Competency Survey.* Paper presented to the Preparing Tomorrow's Teachers Evaluator's Workshop, American Educational Research Association Annual Meeting, New Orleans, LA.

Coley, R. J., Cradler, J., & Engal, P.K. (1998). *Computers and classrooms: The status of technology in U.S. schools* (Policy Information Report). Princeton, NJ: Policy Information Center, Educational Testing Service.

Collis, B. A., Knezek, G. A., Lai, K. W., Miyashita, K. T., Pelgrum, W. J., Plomp, T., & Sakamoto, T. (1996). *Children and computers in school.* Mahwah, NJ: Erlbaum.

Griffin, D., & Christensen, R. (1999). *Concerns-Based Adoption Model (CBAM) Levels of Use of an Innovation* (CBAM-LOU). Denton, TX: Institute for the Integration of Technology into Teaching and Learning.

Hall, G. E., & Rutherford, W. L. (1974). *Concerns questionnaire*. Procedures for Adopting Educational Innovations/CBAM Project, R&D Center for Teacher Education, University of Texas at Austin.

Joreskog, K. G., & Sorbom, D. (1998). *Lisrel 8: Structural equation modeling with the Simplis command language*. Mahwah, NJ: Erlbaum.

Klausmeir, H. J., & Goodwin, W. (1975). *Learning and human abilities: Educational psychology* (4th ed.). New York: Harper & Row.

Knezek, G., Christensen, R., Hancock, R., & Shoho, A. (2000, February). *Toward a structural model of technology integration*. Paper presented to the Annual Hawaii Educational Research Association, Honolulu, Hawaii.

Knezek, G., & Christensen, R. (2000). Attitudinal differences among integrated computing and traditional computer literacy students in the USA. In C. Morales, G. Knezek, R. Christensen, & P. Avila (Eds.), *Impact of new technologies on teaching and learning* (pp. 85-97). Mexico City, Mexico: Institute of the Educative Communication.

Knezek, G., & Christensen, R. (1998). Internal consistency reliability for the Teachers' Attitudes Toward Information Technology (TAT) questionnaire. In S. McNeil, J. Price, S. Boger-Mehall, B. Robin, & J. Willis (Eds.), *Technology and teacher education annual 1998* (Vol. 2, pp. 831-832). Charlottesville, VA: Association for the Advancement of Computing in Education.

Knezek, G., Christensen, R., Miyashita, K., & Ropp, M. (2000). *Instruments for assessing educator progress in technology integration*. [Online]. Available: *http://www.iittl.unt.edu*

Loucks, S. F., Newlove, B. W., & Hall, G. E. (1975). *Measuring levels of use of the innovation: A manual for trainers, interviewers, and raters*. Austin, TX: The University of Texas.

Mann, D., Shakeshaft, C., Becker, J., & Kottkamp, R. (1999) *West Virginia story: Achievement gains from a statewide comprehensive instructional technology program 1999: What impact does technology have on learning?* [Online]. Available: *http://www.mff.org/edtech*

Martin, C. D., Heller, R. S., & Mahmoud, E. (1992). American and Soviet children's attitudes toward computers. *Journal of Educational Computing Research, 8*(2), 155-185.

Norris, C., Box, K., & Soloway, E. (1999, June 20). *Technology in the classroom: What do teachers do, believe, need? Snapshots from around the U.S.A.* Paper presented at the International Society for Technology in Education Leadership Symposium, National Education Computer Conference, Atlantic City, NJ.

Norris, C. A., Soloway, E., Knezek, G., Topp, N. W., Young, J., & Box, K. (2000). Snapshot survey: What do your administrators and teachers really need? *Electronic School: The School Technology Authority, 187*(6), 32-34.

Pierce, D. (1998 October 5). ETS study shows how computers can help or hurt math achievement. *eSchool News*. [Online]. Available: *http://eschoolnews.com*.

Rogers, E. M. (1983). *Diffusion of innovations* (3rd ed.) New York: The Free Press.

Ropp, M. M. (1999). Exploring individual characteristics associated with learning to use computers in preservice teacher preparation. *Journal of Research on Computing in Education, 31*(4), 402-424.

Russell, A. L. (1995). Stages in learning new technology: Naive adult email users. *Computers in Education*, 25(4), 173-178.

Schumacker, R. E. (1996). *A beginner's guide to structural equation modeling*. Mahwah, NJ: Erlbaum.

U.S. Congress, Office of Technology Assessment. (1995, April). *Teachers and technology: Making the connection* (OTA-EHR-616). Washington, DC: U.S. Government Printing Office.

Woodrow, J. E. (1992). The influence of programming training on the computer literacy and attitudes of preservice teachers. *Journal of Research on Computing in Education*, 25(2), 200-218.

APPENDIX A
Stages of Adoption of Technology

Name: _____   Date: _____

Instructions: Please read the descriptions of each of the six stages related to adoption of technology. Choose the stage that best describes where you are in the adoption of technology.

Stage 1: Awareness

I am aware that technology exists but have not used it–perhaps I'm even avoiding it.

Stage 2: Learning the process

I am currently trying to learn the basics. I am often frustrated using computers. I lack confidence when using computers.

Stage 3: Understanding and application of the process

I am beginning to understand the process of using technology and can think of specific tasks in which it might be useful.

Stage 4: Familiarity and confidence

I am gaining a sense of confidence in using the computer for specific tasks.
I am starting to feel comfortable using the computer.

Stage 5: Adaptation to other contexts

I think about the computer as a tool to help me and am no longer concerned about it as technology. I can use it in many applications and as an instructional aid.

Stage 6: Creative application to new contexts

I can apply what I know about technology in the classroom. I am able to use it as an instructional tool and integrate it into the curriculum.

From: Christensen, R. (1997). *Effect of technology integration education on the attitudes of teachers and their students*. Doctoral dissertation, University of North Texas. Based on Russell, A. L. (1995). Stages in learning new technology. *Computers and Education, 25*(4), 173-178.

APPENDIX B
Concerns-Based Adoption Model (CBAM)
Levels of Use of an Innovation

Level 0 Non-use

I have little or no knowledge of information technology in education, no involvement with it, and I am doing nothing toward becoming involved.

Level 1 Orientation

I am seeking or acquiring information about information technology in education.

Level 2 Preparation

I am preparing for the first use of information technology in education.

Level 3 Mechanical Use

I focus most effort on the short-term, day-to-day use of information technology with little time for reflection. My effort is primarily directed toward mastering tasks required to use the information technology.

Level 4 A Routine

I feel comfortable using information technology in education. However, I am putting forth little effort and thought to improve information technology in education or its consequences.

Level 4 B Refinement

I vary the use of information technology in education to increase the expected benefits within the classroom. I am working on using information technology to maximize the effects with my students.

Level 5 Integration

I am combining my own efforts with related activities of other teachers and colleagues to achieve impact in the classroom.

Level 6 Renewal

I reevaluate the quality of use of information technology in education, seek major modifications of, or alternatives to, present innovation to achieve increased impact, examine new developments in the field, and explore new goals for myself and my school or district.

I best fit into Level _____.

APPENDIX C
Technology in Education Competency Survey

1 = Strongly Disagree (SD)
2 = Disagree (D)
3 = Undecided (U)
4 = Agree (A)
5 = Strongly Agree (SA)

	SD	D	U	A	SA
1. I feel competent using a word processor and graphics to develop lesson plans.	1	2	3	4	5
2. I feel competent using e-mail to communicate with colleagues.	1	2	3	4	5
3. I feel competent using the World Wide Web to find educational resources.	1	2	3	4	5
4. I feel competent using an electronic grade book.	1	2	3	4	5
5. I feel competent constructing and implementing project-based learning lessons in which students use a range of information technologies.	1	2	3	4	5
6. I feel competent to help students learn to solve problems, accomplish complex tasks, and use higher order thinking skills in an information technology environment.	1	2	3	4	5
7. I feel competent in recognizing when a student with special needs may benefit significantly by the use of adaptive technology.	1	2	3	4	5
8. I feel competent about teaching K-12 students age-appropriate information technology skills and knowledge.	1	2	3	4	5
9. I feel competent working with students in various IT environments (such as stand-alone and networked computers, on-computer classrooms, labs, etc.).	1	2	3	4	5

Adapted from *Preparedness of graduates* (pp. 41-43), International Society for Technology in Education (1999). *Will new teachers be prepared to teach in a digital age? A national survey on information technology in teacher education.* Santa Monica, CA: Milken Family Foundation, Milken Exchange on Education Technology.

Baruch Offir
Yossi Lev
Yael Lev
Ingrid Barth

Using Interaction Content Analysis Instruments to Assess Distance Learning

SUMMARY. Utilizing the full potential of distance education requires an understanding of how the absence of face-to-face communication affects the relationship between teaching behaviors and learning outcomes. Teachers' awareness of how their teaching behaviors change across distance and conventional contexts can assist them in overcoming the limitations of distance learning. This paper describes the development of two content analysis instruments for analyzing teacher-learner interaction patterns in order to enable educators to (a) identify the effect of separation from learners by space and/or time, (b) examine the relationship between interaction patterns and learning outcomes, (c) identify teacher-learner interactions which comprise essential elements of effective distance education, (d) increase the effectiveness of the instructional

BARUCH OFFIR is Senior Lecturer, School of Education, Bar-Ilan University, 52900 Ramat-Gan, Israel (E-mail: veliksd@mail.biu.ac.il).
YOSSI LEV is a doctoral student, School of Education, Bar-Ilan University, 52900 Ramat-Gan Israel.
YAEL LEV is a master's student, School of Education, Bar-Ilan University, 52900 Ramat-Gan, Israel.
INGRID BARTH is a doctoral student, School of Education, Bar-Ilan University, 52900 Ramat-Gan, Israel.

[Haworth co-indexing entry note]: "Using Interaction Content Analysis Instruments to Assess Distance Learning." Offir, Baruch et al. Co-published simultaneously in *Computers in the Schools* (The Haworth Press, Inc.) Vol. 18, No. 2/3, 2001, pp. 27-41; and: *Evaluation and Assessment in Educational Information Technology* (ed: Leping Liu et al.) The Haworth Press, Inc., 2001, pp. 27-41. Single or multiple copies of this article are available for a fee from The Haworth Document Delivery Service [1-800-HAWORTH, 9:00 a.m. - 5:00 p.m. (EST). E-mail address: getinfo@haworthpressinc.com].

design, (e) plan more effective staff development programs, and (f) enable decision makers to assess the effectiveness of distance learning programs. *[Article copies available for a fee from The Haworth Document Delivery Service: 1-800-HAWORTH. E-mail address: <getinfo@haworthpressinc.com> Website: <http://www.HaworthPress.com> © 2001 by The Haworth Press, Inc. All rights reserved.]*

KEYWORDS. Distance learning, content analysis, verbal interaction, nonverbal interaction, social (negative and positive) interaction, procedural interaction, expository interaction, explanatory interaction, in-depth processing

One of the main advantages of distance learning is the high degree of flexibility resulting when teachers and learners no longer have to be in the same place at the same time. However, this advantage may also be a disadvantage, unless we understand how the lack of face-to-face communication can affect teaching behaviors and learning outcomes. Our studies have focused on analyzing how teacher-learner interactions differ between conventional and distance contexts. The use of content analysis as a means of assessing teacher-learner interactions will be described, as well as the development of two models for analyzing verbal and nonverbal teacher-learner interactions. We will indicate how interaction content analysis instruments can be used to map key variables that determine the effectiveness of distance learning. Finally, a discussion of possible implications and applications of interaction content analysis research will be presented.

RATIONALE BEHIND A CONTENT ANALYSIS APPROACH TO DISTANCE EDUCATION ASSESSMENT

The quality of teacher-learner interactions has always been considered a key variable determining the effectiveness of both conventional and distance education. Several attempts have been made (Flanders, 1970; Hargreaves, 1975; Cazden, 1988) to construct instruments for analyzing teacher-learner interactions in the conventional classroom.

Distance learning is characterized by a separation in space and sometimes in time between teachers and learners. Many educators and parents consequently fear that the medium may lack some of the social and psychological conditions necessary for learning. Several studies on distance learning have therefore focused on the relationship between teacher-learner interactions and learning outcomes. For example, Holmberg's (1989) theory of guided didactic conversation indicates that a significant relationship exists between the teacher's interactions and student performance. This theory forms one of the central theoretical bases of our research.

Moore and Kearsley (1996) also focus on the importance of teacher-learner interactions, and use the concept of *transactional distance* to emphasize that distance is pedagogical, not geographic. Transactional distance refers to a communications gap–a psychological space of potential misunderstandings between the behaviors of instructors and those of the learners. These gaps can exist in both conventional and distance educational contexts, since the amount of transactional distance between the teacher and the learner is determined not by geographical distance but by the quality and amount of dialogue between the teacher and the learner. Both the extent and nature of this dialogue are determined by the educational philosophy, personalities, and attitudes of the teacher and the learner; the subject matter of the course; and environmental variables such as the learning group size.

Not all teacher-learner interactions have the same effect on learning outcomes. In their survey of the literature, Moore and Kearsley (1996) observed that the effectiveness of any medium depends more on the quality of the interaction that the instructor is capable of than on the characteristics of the medium. The aim of interaction content analysis is to dissect the types and frequencies of teacher-learner interactions occurring during distance learning.

Interaction content analysis can thus be used to establish:

1. How intra-individual teaching behaviors compare across conventional and distance education contexts.
2. How the lack of direct communication and immediate feedback affect the teaching process.
3. The relationship between specific teacher-learner interaction patterns and learning outcomes.
4. The types of teacher-learner interactions that represent essential elements for effective learning in a distance education context.

Since one of our main purposes is to accumulate knowledge in order to inform and improve distance education practices, we have adopted a content analysis methodology as a means for finding answers to items one through four.

BASIC ASSUMPTIONS OF THE RESEARCH

The basic construct underlying our research is that a direct interrelationship exists between teachers' attitudes, their teaching behaviors, and learning outcomes. The cyclical nature of this relationship forms the basis of the following three assumptions:

1. Advanced delivery systems represent a necessary but not sufficient condition for interactive learning. Technology is merely a tool: Learning outcomes are directly affected by teachers' attitudes and interaction patterns.
2. A direct relationship exists between learners' active engagement in the learning process and learning outcomes.
3. Teachers' attitudes and teaching behaviors are dynamic variables that can be modified by means of formative feedback.

Since the above assumptions form the basis of our assessment instruments, they will be explained briefly, before we describe the instruments.

1. Advanced delivery systems represent a necessary but not sufficient condition for interactive learning.

Teachers' attitudes and interaction patterns directly affect the extent to which learners will actively engage in the learning process, or remain passive observers of the teacher. This means that teachers who have a constructivist approach to education (Duffy & Cunningham, 1996) will consider active participation of their students as a main objective of the teaching process. In contradistinction, teachers working according to a knowledge transmission paradigm will tend to focus on knowledge supply rather than on knowledge facilitation. These teachers usually do not regard helping students transform information into personal knowledge as a key aspect of their role as teachers. One of our basic working hypotheses is that these attitudes and values drive teacher-learner interaction patterns, thus affecting learning outcomes and determining the effectiveness of the learning context.

2. *A direct relationship exists between learners' active engagement in the learning process and learning outcomes.*

In their review of the literature, Moore and Kearsley (1996) observed that increasing the level of participation in a class increases motivation as well as learning. They therefore concluded that the single most important skill that all distance educators must develop is turning their students into active participants in the educational program. This represents a conservatively constructivist approach to education which views learning as an active process of constructing rather than acquiring knowledge, and views instruction as a process of supporting that construction rather than a process of communicating knowledge (Duffy & Cunningham, 1996).

Supporting construction, according to cognitive psychologists such as Perkins (1992), refers to helping the student "learn by doing" (i.e., actively use the information given in order to solve a problem that is relevant to him or her, or adopt and defend a position). According to Perkins, "learning by doing" requires a high degree of in-depth cognitive processing that results in more effective long-term memory storage and retrieval. As we will describe later, identification of teacher-learner interactions that support learners' in-depth cognitive processing form one of the five central categories in our instrument for assessing distance education lessons.

3. *Teachers' attitudes and teaching behaviors are dynamic and modifiable rather than permanent variables.*

According to Zimbardo and Leippe (1991), attitudes are evaluative dispositions that organize or provide direction to observable behaviors Attitudes consist of four components: (a) affective responses, (b) cognitions, (c) past overt behaviors and (d) behavioral intentions. These four components are interrelated, so that a change in one component (for example, added information in the form of performance feedback) can modify behavior. Both teachers' attitudes and teaching behaviors can be modified by formative feedback regarding the effectiveness of their interaction patterns. Teachers working in a distance education context can use content analysis to identify which interaction patterns should be maintained and which should be replaced. For example, information regarding positive learner outcomes or "islands of success" can serve to reinforce the teacher-learner interaction patterns that contributed to favorable results. Information regarding negative learning outcomes, on the other hand, may act as a catalyst encouraging teachers to try alternative interactions.

MODEL FOR ANALYZING CONTENT
OF DISTANCE EDUCATION LESSONS

Methodology Used to Design the Instruments

The research approach we developed is defined as "online" research. With this method, a limited scale research project is carried out in the field. As the study progresses, data are collected. The research data are then applied to directing the continuation of the project. With the accumulation of data, decision making becomes more accurate (Lind, 1999). Our research consisted of the following stages: (a) reviewing existing theories in the relevant literature in order to crystallize a theoretical basis, (b) running a field project based on the crystallized theory, (c) collecting research data in the field during the project, and (d) using the data to improve the project's learning outcomes.

THEORETICAL BASIS OF THE RESEARCH

Our focus on interaction content analysis is based mainly on Holmberg (1986, 1989, 1995), who selected the teacher-learner dialogue as the critical defining aspect of distance education. Effective distance teaching, according to Holmberg, should resemble a guided conversation aimed at learning. According to Holmberg (1986, 1989), creation of an effective learning environment depends on a clear understanding of the following issues:

1. The nature of the interactions between the teacher and the learner on the subject matter.
2. The impact of emotional involvement and personal relations on the learning process.
3. The relationship between the enjoyment of learning and motivation.
4. The relationship between student participation in decision making, motivation levels, and effective learning.
5. The relationship between the effectiveness of the teaching process and the level of learning outcomes.

As pointed out earlier, the crucial effect of different levels and kinds of teacher-learner interactions on learner outcomes was recognized long before the development of distance learning. Several studies have found that the quality of the interaction between teacher and learner in the distance learning context is an important factor in improving learning outcomes (Mason, 1994; Moore, 1989; Offir & Lev, 1999; Oliver & McLoughlin, 1996). Henri (1992) followed this direction in order to analyze the verbal interaction in the computerized discourse content. He chose to develop an analytical method focusing on the learning process and not on its products. The analysis is performed on three levels: (a) what was said on the discussed subject; (b) how it was said; and (c) the process and the strategies adopted for the discussion. Emphasis was placed on the latter two levels.

Henri's scheme is valuable, since it is based on numerous studies in the field of learning. For example, Henri used the Taxonomy of Critical Thinking Dispositions and Abilities developed by Ennis (1986) to identify different cognitive levels. Based on Schmeck (1983) and Entwistle and Waterston (1988), Henri also differentiated between "surface" and "in-depth" cognitive processing levels.

Henri recognized that, in order to maximize the full potential of computer-mediated learning, a finer-grained content analysis is necessary for identifying the elements which give rise to learning (i.e., "the scenarios of how learning occurs" in a distance education context). Subsequent studies (Doron, 1999; Oliver & McLoughlin, 1996; Shapira, 1995) found that although Henri's model is effective, some of his categories are inconvenient, sometimes irrelevant, and often not clearly defined. In response to Henri's call for a finergrained analysis, these studies suggested a number of modifications to Henri's work. Several of these changes were incorporated in the construction of our instruments (Offir & Lev, 1999).

DESCRIPTION OF THE FIELD PROJECT

For the past few years, Bar-Ilan University has used video-conferencing and satellite systems to deliver academic courses. To date, we have recorded approximately 75 hours of lessons delivered via video-conferencing. The five teachers who taught in a distance learning context ($n = 5$) were also filmed when teaching in a conventional classroom in front of the students. This large pool of videotaped lessons enabled us to study both verbal and nonverbal teacher-learner interactions across different learning contexts. A close analysis of the taped lessons, a survey of the relevant literature, and conclusions from the previously mentioned studies were used to construct two content analysis matrices for assessing verbal and nonverbal interactions in distance learning lessons.

DESCRIPTION OF THE MACINDEL
(MODEL FOR ANALYZING CONTENT OF INTERACTIONS
IN DISTANCE EDUCATION LESSONS)

Teacher interactions can be divided into verbal and nonverbal messages or units of meaning. The MACINDEL uses predefined criteria to classify the verbal messages of the distance lesson into one of five different categories: social positive or negative, procedural, expository, explanatory, or in-depth cognitive processing.

A message can be a single word or a complete sentence. A sentence can consist of two units of meaning: each message is divided into its units of meaning, where one unit of meaning is defined as containing the entire verbal message that has the same meaning (for example, a social discourse). The length of a unit of meaning can therefore range from one word to a complete and lengthy section. For example, "Sharon, your reaction is very interesting, but how does it complete your idea?" is a single sentence that contains two units of meaning: The first is a social positive interaction, whereas the second is an interaction that encourages the learner to engage in in-depth cognitive processing. The instrument's first criterion for analyzing verbal interactions divides messages, or units of meaning, into two groups:

1. Messages not directly related to the content to be learned.
2. Messages related to the subject content.

Group 1 messages that do not deal directly with content to be learned or subject matter are divided into two categories: social interactions and procedural interactions. Social interactions support learning by creating a personal connection between the teacher and the learner, offering emotional support, encouragement, and decreasing tension.

Following Cookson and Chang (1995), we subdivided the social interaction category into two parts: positive and negative. Social negative interactions, as opposed to social positive interactions that encourage learning, consist of negatively toned distant, formal, or critical messages that criticize or embarrass the learner. Cookson and Chang added another category of non-content related interactions, the procedural interactions. These interactions deal with "housekeeping," administrative issues arising during the lesson. Both positive social and procedural interactions have the same goal: creating a supportive atmosphere for the learner.

Group 2 messages, content-related interactions, are subdivided into three categories, according to whether the interaction requires surface or in-depth processing from the learner: expository interaction, explanatory interaction, and in-depth cognitive processing interaction. Schmeck (1983) defined *in-depth processing* as a process by which learners critically evaluate information. This occurs only when learners translate new information into their own terms and relate them to their personal experience. Entwistle and Waterston (1988) also distinguish between in-depth and superficial processing of information.

In the *expository interaction* the learner or the teacher demonstrates knowledge. For example, the teacher can ask when America was discovered, and the learner can answer. This does not involve in-depth processing of the learned material. This is an interaction involving only superficial processing, and no in-depth cognitive processing is required in order to go beyond the information given.

In the *explanatory interaction* the teacher explains the information and develops the content of the lesson. It can occur as follows: The teacher registers the learners' responses as feedback, which informs him how much the learners understood and what points require further comprehensive explanation. Explanatory interactions can include any pedagogic means used by the teacher to mediate between the content and the learner, such as adding more information or examples, drawing analogies, or using a graphic organizer to clarify the subject. This interaction is related to the expository interaction, since in both cases, the learner is not required to perform in-depth research or reflection on the subject content. Both interactions appear frequently within the framework of a lesson presented as a lecture, and teachers tend to pass naturally from one to the other.

The *in-depth cognitive processing interaction* refers to interactions that require the learner to reach conclusions using critical thinking. The difference between this category and expository and explanatory interactions is in the relative level of complexity of required cognitive processing. Expository and explanatory interactions include Bloom's (Bloom, 1956) first two levels, whereas the third category of cognitive interaction includes all higher order level thinking processes that require the learner to add something of his own to the knowledge he acquires, instead of merely re-formulating it in different words. This interaction encourages fundamental processing of content, and may increase the effectiveness of learning and the general satisfaction of the learners from the lesson. Additional criteria for identifying in-depth processing levels can be found in Bloom's (1956) Taxonomy (see Table 1).

When the MACINDEL matrix was used to analyze verbal interactions in videotaped lessons, the results shown in Table 2 were obtained.

The correlations in Table 2 indicate the high level of agreement reached among the six judges who used the MACINDEL model (see Table 1) to analyze interaction content. We interpreted the high degree of inter-rater consistency as evidence that the categories of the MACINDEL model are sufficiently differentiated and represent a reliable means of analyzing all the interaction varieties occurring during the lessons.

However, the verbal message does not present the entire picture. Human communication consists of two types of messages: verbal messages that contain information in the form of words and sentences and nonverbal messages containing information transferred by external appearance, posture, body movements, facial expressions and voice properties. Nonverbal communication has many functions, such as reinforcing, complementing, and emphasizing the verbal communication (Knapp, 1972; Schneller, 1992). In videoconferencing the teacher appears on a large screen in front of the class. This can enhance the influence of nonverbal interactions.

The nonverbal interaction is divided into two main parts: the vocal and the behavioral channels. The vocal channel consists of the paralanguage interaction, which covers various factors such as speed, fluency level, rhythm, volume, and flexibility of voice. These variables are

TABLE 1. MACINDEL Model Observation Form for Analyzing the Content of Verbal Interactions in Distance Learning Lessons

Non Content-Related Interactions (I)			Content-Related Interactions (II)		
Message #	Social interactions	Administrative procedures	Expository interactions (surface processing of content)	Explanatory interactions (surface processing of content)	In-depth processing of content

mainly technical. The connection between culture and voice is also included in this interaction.

The behavioral channel consists of proxemics (the authority given to a person's posture, the carriage or attitude of the body), gestures (hand or arm movement or a facial expression to show an idea or feeling or to emphasize what is being said), mimics (facial expressions inclined to copy or imitate or pretend), and eye gaze (Argil, 1977; Birdwistell, 1970; Davis, 1971; Hall, 1959; Knapp, 1972).

DESCRIPTION OF THE NONVERBAL INTERACTION MODEL

Since information on both the verbal and nonverbal interactions forms the basis for understanding the teaching process (Nussbaum, 1983), we developed an additional instrument for analyzing nonverbal interactions. The same method of literature reviews and close analysis of conventional and videotaped lessons used for developing the verbal interaction instrument was also used to develop the nonverbal instrument. Both verbal and nonverbal instruments use the same categories to analyze content of interactions (e.g., social interaction, explanatory interaction, etc.) (see Table 2). In addition to analyzing content, the nonverbal instrument also identifies the nonverbal means used to deliver the messages (e.g., changes in posture, gestures, teacher-learner proximity, etc.) (see Table 3).

The data collected by measuring nonverbal interactions have so far served two purposes: establishing the reliability of the verbal matrix, and obtaining a more complete picture of how interaction patterns change in distance learning (Offir & Lev, 2000). By using both instruments, we were able to identify:

1. How verbal and nonverbal interactions change across conventional and distance learning contexts.
2. How different verbal and nonverbal interaction patterns affect learning outcomes.
3. Which verbal and nonverbal interaction patterns represent essential components and necessary conditions of effective teaching and learning.
4. In which subject areas the degree of teacher-learner proximity during the teaching process has a major effect on learning outcomes. For example, one direction for our future research will

be how and to what extent can distance learning be used effectively in areas with a strong affective component, such as acquisition and assessment of attitudes and values clarification.

RESULTS

In their 1996 study of distance learning delivered via interactive television (satellite transmissions), Oliver and McLoughlin did not identify many in-depth interactions. Our results (Offir & Lev, 1999) present a similar picture, and can be summarized as follows:

1. Teachers working in an interactive distance learning environment made most frequent use of the procedural, expository, and explanatory interactions.
2. The effectiveness of distance learning increased when the teacher-learner interaction increased.
3. The effectiveness of distance learning depended mainly on social-positive, explanatory interactions that encourage learners to engage in in-depth processing.
4. Explicit training regarding effective teacher interactions can increase the teachers' use of different kinds of interactions.

INTERPRETATION OF RESULTS:
APPLICATIONS AND IMPLICATIONS

Analysis of the accumulated data has enabled our research team to build instruments that can systematically assess the teacher's contribution to the learning process. These instruments help analyze verbal and nonverbal interactions in order to identify the strong and weak points of various distance education contexts. Finding the strong and weak points of each learning context may enable educators to integrate technological systems to improve learner outcomes.

The results obtained with these instruments to date reinforce our position that any institutional, curricular, or instructional change is only as effective as the ability of the teaching staff to accommodate the change successfully.

The aims of distance education cannot be attained without the teachers' help. Human communication is of key importance during the teach-

TABLE 2. Analyzing Verbal Content of Distance Learning Lessons–Correlations Between Judges

		Judge #1	Judge #2	Judge #3	Judge #4	Judge #5	Judge #6
Judge #1	Pearson Correlation Sig. (2-tailed) N		.801** .000 40	.899** .000 40	.881** .000 40	.881** .000 40	.682** .000 40
Judge #2	Pearson Correlation Sig. (2-tailed) N	.801** .000 40		.815** .000 40	.800** .000 40	.697** .000 40	.593** .000 40
Judge #3	Pearson Correlation Sig. (2-tailed) N	.899** .000 40	.815** .000 40		.923** .000 40	.702** .000 40	.744** .000 40
Judge #4	Pearson Correlation Sig. (2-tailed) N	.881** .000 40	.800** .000 40	.923** .000 40		.709** .000 40	.789** .000 40
Judge #5	Pearson Correlation Sig. (2-tailed) N	.606** .000 40	.697** .000 40	.702** .000 40	.709** .000 40		.661** .000 40
Judge #6	Pearson Correlation Sig. (2-tailed) N	.682** .000 40	.593** .000 40	.744** .000 40	.789** .000 40	.661** .000 40	

** Correlation is significant at the 0.01 level (2-tailed).

TABLE 3. MACINDEL Model Observation Form for Analyzing Content of Nonverbal Interactions in Distance Learning Lessons

Observation Form for Nonverbal Interactions in the Classroom							Proximity to Pupil			
Sender	Obser-vation #	Changing posture	Changing head position	Changing facial expression	Using gestures	Contact	Hand's length	Forearm's length	Arm's length	Other changes
Teacher–class										
Teacher – single pupil										
Pupil–teacher										
Pupil–pupil										

ing process. Advanced interactive delivery systems do not stand alone. Teachers' attitudes and interaction patterns determine the extent to which the interactivity of the system will be fully utilized.

Content analysis can contribute to the effectiveness of staff development by identifying the interactions that increase learning outcomes. Formative feedback and coaching can be used to help teachers to increase interaction patterns that can improve learning outcomes in both the affective and cognitive domains. Understanding what constitutes effective instruction in a distance learning context represents a necessary condition for effective teaching, especially when teachers have no immediate feedback from their students. Content analysis can thus help teachers use the full potential of distance education.

REFERENCES

Argil, M. (1977). *Bodily communication*. New York: International University.

Birdwistell, R. (1970). *Kinesis and content*. Philadelphia: University of Pennsylvania.

Bloom, B.S. (Ed.) (1956). *Taxonomy of educational objectives–Handbook 1: Cognitive domain*. New York: Longman.

Cazden, C. (1988). *Classroom discourse*. Portsmouth: Heinemann.

Cookson, P.S., & Chang, Y. (1995). The multidimensional audioconferencing classification system. *The American Journal of Distance Education, 9*(3), 18-35.

Davis, F. (1971). *Inside intuition: What we should know about nonverbal communication*. New York: Melgrand.

Doron, O. (1999). Matrix for analyzing interactions in Distance Learning. Unpublished dissertation, Tel-Aviv University.

Duffy, T.M., & Cunningham, D.J. (1996). Constructivism: Implications for the design and delivery of instruction. In D.H. Jonassen (Ed.), *Handbook of research for education communications and technology* (pp. 170-198). New York: Macmillan.

Ennis, R. H. (1986). A taxonomy of critical thinking dispositions and abilities. In G. B. Baron & R.J. Sternberg (Eds.), *Teaching thinking skills: Theory and practice* (pp. 9-26). New York: Freeman.

Entwistle, N., & Waterston, S. (1988). Approaches to studying and levels of processing in university students. *Journal of Educational Psychology, 58*, 258-265.

Flanders, N. (1970). *Analyzing teaching behavior*. Reading, MA: Addison Wesley.

Hall, E. (1959). *The silent language*. Garden City, NY: Doubleday.

Hargreaves, D.H. (1975). *Interpersonal relations and education*. London: Routledge & Paul.

Henri, F. (1992). Computer conferencing and content analysis. In A. Kaye (Ed.), *Collaborative learning through computer conferencing* (pp. 117-136). Berlin: Springer Verlag.

Holmberg, B. (1986). *Theory and practice of distance education*. London: Routledge.

Holmberg, B. (1989). *Distance education*. London: Kogan Page.

Holmberg, B. (1995). The evolution of the character and practice of distance education. *Open Learning, 10*(2), 47-53.

Knapp, M.L. (1972). *Nonverbal communication in human interaction.* New York: Holt, Rinehart & Winston.

Lind, L. (1999). Editorial. *Education Media International, 36*(2), 1-2.

Mason, R. (1994). *Using communication media in open and flexible learning.* London: Kogan Page.

Miles, M.B., & Huberman, A.M. (1987). *Qualitative data analysis.* London: Sage.

Moore, M. (1989). Three types of interaction. *The American Journal of Distance Education, 3*(2), 1-7.

Moore, M.G., & Kearsley, G. (1996). *Distance education: A systems view.* London: Wadsworth.

Nussbaum, J.F. (1983). Systematic modification of teacher behavior. In R.N. Bostrom & B.H. Westley (Eds.), *Communication yearbook* (pp. 672-684). Beverly Hills: Sage.

Offir, B., & Lev, Y. (1999). Teacher-learner interaction in the process of operating DL (Distance Learning) systems. *Educational Media International, 36*(2), 132-138.

Offir, B., & Lev, Y. (2000). Constructing an aid for evaluating teacher-learner interaction in distance learning. *Educational Media International, 27*(2), 92.

Oliver, R., & McLoughlin, C. (1996). An investigation of the nature and form of interactions in live interactive television. (Eric Document Number 396738).

Perkins, D.N. (1992). *Smart schools.* New York: The Free Press.

Schmeck, R.R. (1983). Learning style of college students. In R. Dillon & R.R. Schmeck (Eds.), *Individual difference in cognition* (pp. 233-279). New York: Academic Press.

Schneller, R. (1992). Matrix for analyzing multicultural classroom. Bar-Ilan University. Unpublished.

Shapira, T. (1995). Examination of a model for text analysis in distance learning. Unpublished dissertation. Tel-Aviv University.

Zimbardo, P., & Leippe, M. (1991). *The psychology of attitude change and social influence.* Philadelphia: Temple University Press.

Anna C. McFadden
George E. Marsh II
Barrie Jo Price

Computer Testing in Education: Emerging Trends

SUMMARY. The rapid growth of the Internet and intranets supports the infrastructure necessary for computer-based testing (CBT). The parallel growth of sophisticated computer programming and powerful computers offers new possibilities in testing, such as Computerized Adaptive Testing (CAT), where the responses of the subject dictate the nature of the test items to be presented. This article considers research about the comparability of computerized tests to conventional tests, local uses of computerized testing, tests available in online delivery programs, public domain software, authoring languages, and commercial and shareware options. The article concludes with a discussion of formative assessment and how computerized tests may be used to meet daily instructional needs. *[Article copies available for a fee from The Haworth Document Delivery Service: 1-800-HAWORTH. E-mail address: <getinfo@haworthpressinc.com> Website: <http:// www.HaworthPress.com> © 2001 by The Haworth Press, Inc. All rights reserved.]*

ANNA C. MCFADDEN is Associate Professor, Instructional Technology, P.O. Box 870302, College of Education, The University of Alabama, Tuscaloosa, AL 35487 (E-mail: amcfadden@bamaed.ua.edu).
GEORGE E. MARSH II is Associate Professor, Instructional Technology, P.O. Box 870302, College of Education, The University of Alabama, Tuscaloosa, AL 35487 (E-mail: gemarsh@bamaed.ua.edu).
BARRIE JO PRICE is Associate Professor, Instructional Technology, P.O. Box 870302, College of Education, The University of Alabama, Tuscaloosa, AL 35487 (E-mail: bjprice@bamaed.ua.edu).

[Haworth co-indexing entry note]: "Computer Testing in Education: Emerging Trends." McFadden, Anna C. et al. Co-published simultaneously in *Computers in the Schools* (The Haworth Press, Inc.) Vol. 18, No. 2/3, 2001, pp. 43-60; and: *Evaluation and Assessment in Educational Information Technology* (ed: Leping Liu et al.) The Haworth Press, Inc., 2001, pp. 43-60. Single or multiple copies of this article are available for a fee from The Haworth Document Delivery Service [1-800-HAWORTH, 9:00 a.m. - 5:00 p.m. (EST). E-mail address: getinfo@haworthpressinc.com].

KEYWORDS. CBT, computer based testing, computer adaptive testing, CAT, assessment, instructional technology, tests, computers, education, evaluation

According to the National Center for Fair and Open Testing (FairTest: The National Center for Fair & Open Testing, n.d.), over 100 million standardized tests are administered annually in schools. The states will have spent $330 million on standardized achievement tests in 2000 and many individual students will pay for other examinations, such as the Scholastic Aptitude Test (SAT) and the Graduate Record Examination (GRE). Additionally, most states now require examinations for promotion and matriculation. Added to this number are numerous tests administered by state and national occupational and professional licensing and certification boards. Current intentions of the Bush administration to require testing for all grades annually could significantly increase testing in public education. The requirement for high-stakes testing programs in tracking, promotion, graduation, and entrance to post-secondary institutions and professions has increased the demand for computer-based testing (CBT). CBT promises greater efficiency, security, and immediacy of scoring.

Klein and Hamilton (1999) issued a report supporting CBT for K-12 schools, especially computer-adapted testing (CAT), and recommended Web-based testing in schools via the Internet, supplemented with open-ended and other types of items. Generally, computerized tests are of two types, linear or adaptive. A linear computerized test is a series of items presented one at a time, in the same order, to all students. Adaptive tests are individualized and account for differing abilities by changing the order and total number of items presented. The report concluded that numerous studies comparing CATs with traditional paper-and-pencil tests in the same subjects show that the two methods rank-order students in about the same way in less time. The number of test items needed for a given level of precision can be reduced by more than half (Bunderson, Inouye, & Olson, 1989). Other advantages of CATs include year-round testing, longer time per question, and immediate feedback or notice of standing. Klein and Hamilton (1999) extol the virtues of CAT, because it can be tailored to district or state educational goals, target each student's proficiency level, a "bank" of thousands of questions in each subject matter area can be used, which improves test security, new students can be tested quickly, and all students can be examined repeatedly throughout the school year.

ARE COMPUTERIZED TESTS COMPARABLE
TO CONVENTIONAL TESTS?

Although there is a clear trend to computerize test administration, there is relatively little research about differential effects of computer and printed versions and most of it is old. On the face of it, written tests and computerized versions appear to be identical. The items are the same and the requirements seem almost identical. Rather than filling in a small circle with a pencil, the subject clicks on a small circle with a mouse cursor. But to be assured tests are comparable they must be highly correlated, as would be required in parallel-form reliability, and the validity must be checked by establishing that the rank order of scores in both forms is closely approximated, and the means, dispersions, and shapes of the score distributions must be approximately the same. The first comprehensive review of research about computerized testing was conducted by Mazzeo and Harvey (1988), who offered these conclusions among others: (a) computer tests for speed differ from the paper form; (b) scores on computer tests are affected by graphics; and (c) reading passages on computerized tests is sometimes more difficult. Green (1988) reported that a number of variables affect validity: (a) Passively omitting (skipping items) may be impossible or distracting; (b) it may difficult or impossible to change previous answers; (c) screen capacity limits may require several continuations before a response can be made; (d) low-resolution graphics are not as clear as print; and, (e) pressing a key is faster than using a pencil on an answer sheet.

CAT differs from conventional test administration because items can be tailored from a large pool of equated items based on probes that estimate the subject's ability according to responses. On a conventional test all subjects get the same items in the same order. The CAT establishes a testing "floor" and "ceiling" quickly by presenting a subject with an item of medium difficulty that is followed by a simpler or more difficult item, depending upon the response. Dunkel (1999) describes the psychometric model underlying CAT as Item Response Theory (IRT), which is based on probabilistic theory, or the chances that a subject will succeed on a particular item. If a subject's ability is the same as the difficulty level of the item, the chance of succeeding is 50-50. Probabilities of success or failure on an item decrease or increase according to ability. Lawrence M. Rudner, of the ERIC Clearinghouse on Assessment and Evaluation, has provided an On-line, Interactive, Computer Adaptive Testing Mini-Tutorial that offers a description of CAT and a demonstration. As Rudner (1998) explains:

When an examinee is administered a test via the computer, the computer can update the estimate of the examinee's ability after each item and then that ability estimate can be used in the selection of subsequent items. With the right item bank and a high examinee ability variance, CAT can be much more efficient than a traditional paper-and-pencil test . . . With computer adaptive tests, the examinee's ability level relative to a norm group can be iteratively estimated during the testing process and items can be selected based on the current ability estimate. Examinees can be given the items that maximize the information (within constraints) about their ability levels from the item responses. Thus, examinees will receive few items that are very easy or very hard for them. This tailored item selection can result in reduced standard errors and greater precision with only a handful of properly selected items. (¶ 11)

Critics of testing programs, such as the National Center for Fair and Open Testing, argue that time and money for testing are misspent, because tests are poorly constructed, unreliable, and unevenly administered. A major contention is that multiple-choice questions cannot measure many traits, including thinking skills, creativity, the ability to solve real problems, or social skills; furthermore, many examinations are said to be biased racially, culturally, linguistically, and by class and gender. In another report, the National Center for Fair and Open Testing (Fair Test) questions the comparability of computerized tests: "Automating bad tests does nothing to solve their long-standing problems and may actually compound them" (n.d., ¶ 1). According to this report, there are several unresolved problems including:

1. Some studies show higher scores for paper-and-pencil exams.
2. Some respondents may still get lower scores even if the average score increases.
3. Some types of questions elicit different responses on the two types of tests.
4. Computerized tests constrain test-takers because they are unable to underline text, scratch out to eliminate choices, or work out problems.
5. Computer screens take longer to read than printed materials, and it is more difficult to detect errors on computer screens.
6. Most computerized tests show only one item on the screen at a time, preventing test-takers from easily checking previous items and the pattern of their responses.

7. Persons with prior experience using a computer keyboard have an advantage.
8. Computerized tests worsen test bias, affecting men and women, ethnic groups, and poor persons differently.

Federico (1992) reported no significant differences for comparable tests on reliability estimates of scores or degrees of confidence. Mead and Drasgow (1993), in a meta-analysis of relevant research, reported that computerized tests are comparable for *power* tests but there is an effect for *speed* tests. Bunderson, Inouye and Olsen (1989) reported that score differences are small and of little practical significance. Apparently the font typeface has an effect for some test-takers, as does the order of item presentation and the order of response options (Cizek, 1991).

Mourant, Lakshmanan, and Chantadisai (1981) discovered that fatigue is greater after reading computer text than a printed version. Haas and Hayes (1986) found that reading passages covering more than one page results in lower scores for computer tests than a paper-and-pencil version.

Students who use computers extensively write more and revise their work more (Daiute, 1985), and this is a factor in some forms of computer test performance. Owston, Wideman, Pacini, and Dodick (1999) note that students in classes where there is a 2:1 student to laptop ratio showed significantly greater improvement in their writing over time, compared to control groups and laptop classes with lower ratios. Russell and Haney (1997) found differences on performance among subjects with high and low typing speeds. In a follow-up study, Russell concluded that more research is necessary about computers and open-ended tests.

Sissel (n.d.) maintains that the most important factors warranting attention are reading multiple computer screens, interpreting graphics, and working quickly, all factors that seem to have implications for many kinds of tests. Some of Sissel's observations from a review of research are summarized as follows:

1. Students taught on computer or paper and then tested on computer or paper perform the same, regardless of the mode used during the assessment process.
2. At least with adult subjects, there is greater confidence with paper than computer, although results are equal.
3. For students with little or no computer experience, tests requiring rapid computer manipulation are more difficult.
4. Achievement tests on a wide range of subjects show no mode effect.

5. Studies with the GRE, including the Verbal section, found no mode effect.
6. Computer tests produce equivalent results on objective personality and ability tests.

The research on computerized tests is mixed. In some studies there is equivalence regardless of test mode; in others, there are differences. Reading tests, especially tests where a page extends over multiple screens, are more difficult on a computer. Computer versions of achievement tests and certain psychology and inventory tests are comparable, although there are obvious limitations (e.g., inability to underline, scratch out, and check previous items).

While the question about the equivalence of computer and printed tests draws attention to technical aspects, the need to match the medium of assessment with the medium of learning brings into question the use of paper-and-pencil tests for thousands of students who do most or all of their writing on computers. While a computerized version of a multiple-choice test requires scrolling and clicking a mouse, many students today are unaccustomed to using a pencil as a primary writing tool. Students who are required to write with a pencil for extensive testing, such as an essay examination, may be penalized due to cramping, fatigue, and lack of fine motor skills, something very noticeable among graduate students who take comprehensive examinations. Russell and Haney (1997) provide a unique perspective on extensive computer use by students.

> Increasingly, schools are encouraging students to use computers in their writing. Consequently, it is likely that increasing numbers of students are growing accustomed to writing on computers. Nevertheless, large-scale assessments of writing, at state, national and even international levels, are attempting to estimate students' writing skills by having them use paper-and-pencil. Our results, if generalizable, suggest that for students accustomed to writing on computer for only a year or two, such estimates of student writing abilities based on responses written by hand may be substantial underestimates of their abilities to write when using a computer. (¶ 56)

Bugbee (1996), who has discussed the advantages of computerized tests, reported that typically subjects do as well on computer-based tests, most students today enjoy computer-based tests, and students usually take more time on a computer test. However, there may be differences for students who have test anxiety and/or computer anxiety. There are conflicting findings on the impact of anxiety (Wise & Plake, 1989). Legg and Buhr (1992) found that computer anxiety is much more prevalent among females, especially African American females. Fatigue can be a factor affecting scores (Green, 1991; Mazzeo & Harvey, 1988), and the order that items are presented has differential effects (Mazzeo, Druesne, Raffeld, Checketts, & Muhlstein, 1991). These differences in examinee characteristics and mode effects are clearly inconclusive. While it seems certain that computerized testing will continue to grow, the research so far suggests that for certain persons there may be differing abilities between using a pencil and a keyboard. This brings into question the validity of tests and may overlook changes in instruction. The fact that many students now learn subject matter via technology, such as spreadsheets and word processors, traditional modes of assessment may fail to measure what students have learned (Russell & Haney, 1997, ¶ 57).

The electronic delivery system is expanding as distance education increases in popularity, and distance education stimulates a demand for electronic options in assessment to keep pace with electronic instructional innovations. This development, in addition to other trends in computerized testing, assures further growth of computer tests. However, research has not kept pace with technological innovations and their impact on testing. We should be cautious about conclusions based on a body of research where many of the studies are more than a decade old. Many studies should be replicated using modern computer screens with color and high resolution. Computers of the 1980s are not comparable to multimedia computers today. Moreover, new research will have to account for technological innovations in computing.

Emerging standards, such as eXtensible Markup Language (XML), affordable virtual reality, and other developments, make instruction and testing beyond the realm of anything previously experienced or even imagined. Common Gateway Interface (CGI), Perl, Java, Flash, Shockwave, high-resolution graphics, streaming video and audio, and animated graphics make current linear and adaptive tests seem primitive in appearance and function, especially simple migrations of print to a computerized format. Dynamic and powerful computer applications will alter the nature of examination entirely, far surpassing current paper-and-pencil tests or "paper tests" on a computer screen. For the Graduate Management Admission Test (GMAT), there is an "E-rater robot" that grades essays, replacing a human grader. Interactions of these new variables will create a major challenge for test developers, especially in addressing the traditional concerns of validity, reliability, and comparability. It is conceivable that print tests, at least in some applications, will disappear entirely. Some investigators have questioned the reliability of software's ability to interpret complex personality data (Honaker, 1988), but artificial neural network software and other advances may now make this more likely. Although some wild guesses could be made about the future, it would be imprudent to try. Any innovation in the next six months or a year could entirely alter any projections that might be made based on current understandings of the potential of technology.

LOCAL USE OF COMPUTERIZED TESTING

Professional organizations and corporate bodies are computerizing tests and making them available primarily in proctored testing centers. The major testing programs of professional organizations and state and federal governments account for most of the growth in computer-based testing. With millions of dollars to spend on test development, the major players like the Educational Testing Service, Harcourt Educational Measurement, Riverside Publishing, and McGraw-Hill are investing in adaptive testing for greater efficiency, security control, and profits. For most educators the testing programs of corporations, state governments, or professional licensure groups are unrelated to formative assessment or daily instructional activities.

Most states and institutions will not have the resources to invest in developing their own CAT programs or purchase them from vendors, but with the infrastructure of local-area networks and the Internet, many school districts, schools, and individual teachers find computerized testing appealing. Some states and districts may contract vendors for CAT services, but for those who cannot or will not, there are other possibilities: (a) Teachers can computerize a test and put it on a classroom computer; (b) an individual school, district, college, or university can put tests on local servers for access by classrooms; and (c) tests can be available on the Internet (World Wide Web). Web-Based Testing (WBT) enables schools, teachers, and professors to expand their testing capabilities for instructional needs, mainly formative assessment, by making tests available over the Web. Schools with wide-area and local-area networks can restrict tests to local levels, of course, but as more institutions are becoming engaged in distance education there is a need to migrate tests, summative and formative, to the Web.

Brewer, Dholakia, Vouk, and Bitzer (n.d.) point out that an important characteristic of an advanced learning environment, such as the World Wide Web, is the ability to evaluate the knowledge and retention of students. Testing can come in many forms: (a) online delivery programs, (b) public domain software/online testing systems, (c) programs available in authoring languages/programming; and (d) commercial, shareware, and freeware software.

Online Delivery Programs

The expansion of distance education, in particular Web courses, has spawned the growth of many commercial products to make it possible for teachers to put courses online, which often include support for testing. Several examples are described by Marsh, McFadden, and Price (1999). Perhaps the most popular are Blackboard and WebCT, both of which include conferencing systems, chat capability, student progress tracking, group project organization, student self-evaluation, grade maintenance and distribution, auto-marked quizzes, electronic mail, and other electronic tools.

Public Domain Software/Online Testing Systems

Examples in the public domain software/online testing systems category include Tutorial Gateway and the Open Learning Agency of Australia's (OLAA) system. Brewer, Dholakia, Vouk, and Bitzer (n.d.) examined these and other programs. Programs of this type do not always have the extent of tutorial assistance and support of a commercial product, but with some persistence they can be established. The teacher can either download or upload files, or work online to create tests, depending upon the program. A comprehensive program, the MTX Internet Publishing Project, was developed by Richard Rathe, Director of the Office of Medical Informatics for the College of Medicine at the University of Florida.

Authoring Languages/Programming

Some of the popular authoring languages for education include test development options for stand-alone and Web delivery. Some are comprehensive and some require familiarity with the two most popular programs for tests developed, JavaScript and CGI. The Common Gateway Interface, or CGI, is a standard for communication between Hypertext Markup Language, or HTML, Web documents, and CGI scripts–a gateway between a computer and a script. CGI scripts are programs that communicate with Web documents. After a Web browser requests a CGI script from a Web server, the server sends the CGI script. A test in CGI script has options such as drop-down windows, click buttons, and blanks for typing that are entered and passed back to the server to be stored in a database. Access and rights to use a server are necessary to use CGI.

JavaScript provides the code to the client computer, enabling the client to do the work instead of the server. However, in order for the results to be recorded, it is necessary for the content to be uploaded. There is another step necessary to get the information processed from the server to the examiner. Hazari (n.d.) recommends:

> In general, trainers and instructors should consider client side JavaScript based assessment programs when local data validation, individual browser control (such as hiding browser menus), advanced functionality on client side, and high degree of interactivity are required. For applications where source code needs to be hidden, user navigation closely tracked, server side database updated with user data, use of CGI server based programs would be more appropriate. (¶ 21)

A companion to CGI and JavaScript is Active Server Pages (ASP) developed by Microsoft. The ASP scripts are placed on a server and respond to browsers. ASP technology is used in many business applications and can be adapted to create quizzes.

Commercial, Shareware, and Freeware Software

For persons unfamiliar with scripting language or those unable to obtain support, there are free and inexpensive scripts, public domain software, inexpensive software, shareware, and freeware. In Table 1 are some representative software programs and sources of information about computerized tests and subjects related to assessment. While it is unknown how many programs exist, a major effort was made to find as many as possible. Inclusion of these titles implies no endorsement.

FORMATIVE ASSESSMENT

The use of tests for summative assessment to hold schools accountable is firmly entrenched and seems likely to become more pervasive in the next decade. Members of both major political parties at the national level have advocated high-stakes testing and penalties for schools that do not perform. There is consensus among educators that summative evaluations are unrelated to real performance gains, and some argue that there are many nega-

TABLE 1. Sources of Web-Based Testing Tools

Software Tool and Source	Description
Assessment Systems Corporation http://www.assess.com/softmenu.html	Provides for Adaptive Testing.
CASTLE–Computer Assisted Teaching and Learning http://www.le.ac.uk/castle/	Create online multiple-choice questions
Choices http://computing.netscape.com/computing/download/shareware/main.tmpl	Create multiple-choice quizzes for a computer. Reports a percentage score.
ClozeMaker http://computing.netscape.com/computing/download/shareware/main.tmpl	Develop cloze exercises for computer.
C-Quest http://www.cqtest.com/	Interactive tests on local area networks, PCs, remote PCs, or over the Web.
Create A Quiz http://pc-shareware.com/quiz.htm	Generates on-screen interactive quizzes.
CyberExam http://cyberexam.vlearning.com/	Web environment for interactive tests, assessments, and surveys.
Cyber STAR http://cyberstar.vlearning.com/	Information about which districts, schools, classrooms or students need help on specific learning objectives.
Dazzler Deluxe http://www.intelamedia.com/visitors_index.htm	A codeless authoring tool for creation of complex multimedia programs.
Digital Teacher http://computing.netscape.com/computing/download/shareware/main.tmpl	Create printed or computer-based objective and essay tests.
edutest.com http://www.edutest.com/www/19442/987791679/?cgi-bin=0&sessionID=337c34eb7927eb8eb115b56de02f894c	Online educational assessment, state standards alignment, accountability systems.
Eduware http://www.eduware.com/	Creates exams for any subject or from test banks
Examiner'sPlus http://www.pilotltd.com/	I integrated test preparation tool.
Exammail. http://www.oyston.com/ExamMail/home.html	CGI tool to grade multiple-choice
Hot Potatoes http://web.uvic.ca/hrd/halfbaked/	Freeware suite includes objective and gap-fill exercises for the Web
Interactivetest.com http://www.interactivetest.com/	Multiple-choice test for Web. No programming required.
Learningware.com http://www.learningware.com/	Create quizzes, tests and surveys using software templates.
LXR*TEST http://www.lxrtest.com/html/brochure.htm	Integrated testing program with an online testing option
Martin's JQuiz Generator http://computing.netscape.com/computing/download/shareware/main.tmpl	Create interactive quizzes for web use.
Multiple Choice Javascript	Script for multiple choice questions

TABLE 1 (continued)

Online Quiz and Testing Software http://www.online-testing.net/	Perl and JavaScript software for running quizzes and tests online.
Online Testing http://teach.jsr.cc.va.us/tests/online_testing.htm	Interactive testing that can be taken from any computer connected to the Web.
Pilot Software http://www.pilotltd.com/products.htm.	Test item bank administration, test assessment, scoring and grading system
Proctor http://computing.netscape.com/computing/download/shareware/main.tmpl	This applet displays and grades customized tests over the Internet
Question Mark. http://www.qmark.com/	An authoring, delivery, reporting software to generate quizzes
QUIZ Create 98 http://computing.netscape.com/computing/download/shareware/main.tmpl	Generates online interactive quizzes, exams, surveys, and questionnaires
Quiz Factory http://www.learningware.com/quizfactory/	Test and survey generator
Quiz Master Professional http://shareware.netscape.com/computing/shareware/software_title.tmpl?p=PC&category_id=10&subcategory_id=16&id=42282	Creates graphical quizzes for online or offline testing.
Quiz Mill http://www.onlinearts.net/showroom/index.html#quizmill	Creates online multiple choice, multiple select, and short answer questions.
Quiz Please http://quizplease.com/	Develops multimedia/interactive tests for the Internet and Email-surveys.
QuizIt Online Testing http://users.iconz.co.nz/trout/quizit.htm	Delivers multimedia content, including sounds.
QuizWiz http://www.ccts-ent.com/qwiz/	Produces HTML files and CGI script, which actually handles the evaluation of the quiz.
Quiz Wizard http://www.loomscape.freeuk.com/contact_us.htm	For quizzes or questionnaires developed in HTML.
Quizz http://www.firststep.com.au/software/quizz.html.	Quizz is a Perl script for generating multiple-choice quizzes for Web pages.
Software America, Inc. http://www.softwareamerica.net/	Curriculum and assessment data management software.
Teachertools.com http://www.teachertools.com/	Quick Quiz and Quick Exam test development programs.
Test Generator http://www.testshop.com/home.htm	Creates, administers and distributes computer-based tests.
Test Pro 3.0 http://www.atrixware.com/	Create network tests containing multiple choice, true/false, and/or fill-in.
WebTest http://fpg.uwaterloo.ca/WEBTEST/	Used for interactive testing, tutorial, or survey environment.
Web Quiz Writer http://www.web-quiz.net/	Comprehensive Internet-based testing.
WW Assign http://www.webassign.net/	Database of test questions.

tive impacts. Standardized tests are expensive, depleting state and district budgets. Worse still, some maintain that such tests detract from instruction and cause teachers to "teach to the test" and in some cases to actually teach the test. This concern is expressed by the North Central Regional Laboratory (1995):

> [M]easurement issues become more important as the stakes attached to these assessments increase. The consequences or decisions to be made based on any individual exam determine the degree of technical quality demanded of that exam. If a student is denied a high school diploma or access to an educational opportunity based upon the results of a single assessment strategy, the assessment must meet very stringent technical quality criteria. On the other hand, when the results of a weekly classroom exam are combined with the results of several other assessments to determine a student's grade for the semester, the technical quality of each individual assessment is less of a concern. (¶ 18)

Bloom (1984) long ago advocated the replacement of group instruction with mastery learning or tutorial instruction, because the latter methods are superior in achievement to conventional instruction. Mastery learning results in achievement one standard deviation above a traditional class, and tutorial instruction (one teacher to four or less students) exceeds traditional classes by two standard deviations! Bloom contends that 98% of all children in public schools could achieve at high levels with tutorial instruction, but in large groups frequent assessment is critical to know how to make adaptations for each student, something a teacher cannot do effectively with paper and pencil. The most important component in formative assessment is assuring that students have mastered content before passing to the next level. Frequent evaluation is highly related to achievement gains, because it concentrates both the teacher and the student to mastery of content.

Black and Wiliam (1998) have reiterated the long held premise in education that formative assessment improves learning. They define assessment as "all activities undertaken by teachers–and by their students in assessing themselves–that provide information to be used as feedback to modify teaching and learning activities. Such assessment becomes formative assessment when the evidence is actually used to adapt the teaching to meet student needs" (p. 3). In a review of research about formative assessment, they validate Bloom's contention, finding effect sizes ranging between 0.4 and 0.7, which are larger than those typically found for educational interventions. Extremely impressed, Black and Wiliam observed that such work involves new ways to enhance feedback, requiring significant changes in classroom practice. For assessment to function formatively, results must be used to adjust teaching and learning.

With an item bank, the software can select a set of questions and randomize the order of questions. Bocij and Greasley (1999) conducted a long-term study of 6,000 computer-based formative assessments in three schools, with eight separate courses and more than 2,000 undergraduate students. Their findings are summarized as follows:

1. Pre-test attitudinal measurements suggested that relatively large proportions of students held somewhat neutral opinions toward computer-based assessment.
2. Their opinions changed in favor of computer-based assessment after experience.
3. Students find computer-based tests less threatening than conventional examinations.
4. Students regard computer-based testing to be more impartial and more accurate than conventional tests.
5. Formative computer-based assessments may help to improve the long-term recall of key concepts.
6. No significant differences in performance were recorded between those students with previous experience with information technology and those without.

CONCLUSION

The major obstacle for any teacher is how to conduct frequent formative assessments without taking up valuable class time and spending an inordinate amount of time otherwise marking paper-and-pencil tests or making observations. Due to the influence of constructivism, qualitative research theory, and criticism of tests in general, especially multiple-choice tests, there has been a trend for teachers to use performance-based evaluations with open-ended questions, portfolios of work, demonstrations, samples of writing, and other alternatives. But performance evaluations are more time-consuming than grading tests by hand. In both cases, however, computers can save instructional time and support the interventions identified by Black and Wiliam (1998). With CAT, WBT, or stand-alone applications, teachers can get frequent, immediate results for making adjustments. Portfolio assessments can be maintained electronically and, thereby, engage students in monitoring their own learning while simultaneously using technology skills.

High-stakes testing programs are expanding and should be used with caution. In a review of issues surrounding large-scale testing programs, Klein and Hamilton (1999, ¶ 23) concluded that "despite their variety, none of the large-scale national achievement tests currently in use can be employed to monitor individual student progress or to evaluate the effectiveness of particular schools, districts, or educational programs." Whether a computerized test is comparable to a printed version is irrelevant, if the test is unable to monitor individual student progress. On behalf of the National Academy of Sciences, Heubert and Hauser (1999) made this recommendation to the U.S. Congress:

> Tests should be used for high-stakes decisions about individual mastery only after implementing changes in teaching and curriculum that ensure that students have been taught the knowledge and skills on which they will be tested. Some school systems are already doing this by planning a gap of several years between the introduction of new tests and the attachment of high stakes to individual student performance, during which schools may achieve the necessary alignment among tests, curriculum, and instruction. But others may see attaching high stakes to individual student test scores as a way of leading curricular reform, not recognizing the danger that such uses of tests may lack the "instructional validity" required by law–that is, a close correspondence between test content and instructional content. (¶ 24)

The use of test scores from large-scale program evaluations is questionable because the scores reflect prior experience rather than only the effects of a specific curriculum. Variation among test scores may be explained by factors not associated with school, which is why some students have a greater advantage if they come from more privileged homes. In research projects the investigator attempts to eliminate effects by matching subjects before proceeding with research, but high-stakes testing programs do not consider such factors. To the extent that individual school districts, schools, classrooms, and students differ in terms of experiential and instructional factors, a simple comparison on the basis of test scores is deceiving. The average scores on the Scholastic Aptitude Test (SAT) are higher for children of professionals than children of white-collar workers, which in turn are higher than the children of blue collar workers. High school rank shows no such correlation (Elert, 1992).

Despite the fact that standardized tests do not predict academic success and they are highly correlated with socioeconomic class, school boards, administrators and teachers have no control and little voice in the development, implementation, and use of summative evaluations in high-stakes testing programs. They can, however, use computerized testing and coordinate it with the curriculum for part of the assessment program. The key ingredient for "instructional validity" is use of item banks reflecting what is actually taught in classrooms. Many software programs have their own item banks, it is not typically difficult to import item banks from other sources, and schools can create their own. By aggregating item banks in a continuum of task difficulty according to the school curriculum, formative assessment can be made more meaningful. If the purpose of assessment is understood to be that of assisting students to recognize that they are learning what is intended, providing frequent feedback to students and teachers is an obligation. This represents assessment of the highest validity and computerized testing can help, but this is also the area of least emphasis in school assessment.

REFERENCES

Black, P., & Wiliam, D. (1998). Inside the black box: Raising standards through classroom assessment. *Phi Delta Kappan Online*. Retrieved April 20, 2001 from: *http://pdkintl. org/kappan/kbla9810.htm*

Bloom, B.S. (1984). The search for methods of group instruction as effective as one-to-one tutoring. *Educational Leadership, 41*(8), 4-17.

Bocij, P., & Greasley, A. (1999, July). Can computer-based testing achieve quality and efficiency in assessment? *International Journal of Educational Technology*. Retrieved April 19, 2001, from: *http://www.outreach.uiuc.edu/ijet/v1n1/bocij/index.html*

Brewer, P.W., Dholakia, A., Vouk, M.A., & Bitzer, D.L. (n.d.) *A comparative analysis of Web-based testing and evaluation systems*. Retrieved March 19, 2001, from: *http://renoir. csc.ncsu.edu/MRA/Reports/WebBasedTesting.html*

Bugbee, A. C. (1996). The equivalence of paper-and-pencil and computer-based testing. *Journal of Research on Computing in Education, 28*(3), 282-299.

Bunderson, C. V., Inouye, D. K., & Olsen, J. B. (1989). The four generations of computerized educational measurement. In R.L. Linn (Ed.), *Educational measurement* (3rd ed., pp. 367-407). Washington, DC: American Council on Education.

Cizek, G.J. (1991, April). The effect of altering the position of options in a multiple-choice examination. *Educational and Psychological Measurement, 54*(1), 8-20.

Daiute, C. (1985). *Writing and computers*. Reading, MA: Addison-Wesley.

Dunkel, P.A. (1999). Considerations in developing and using computer-adaptive tests to assess second language proficiency. *Language, Learning & Technology, 2*(2), 77-93.

Elert, G. (1992). *The SAT: Aptitude or demographics?* Retrieved April 19, 2001, from: *http://www.hypertextbook.com/eworld/sat.shtml*

Fair Test: The National Center for Fair & Open Testing. (n.d.) *The testing explosion*. Retrieved April 19, 2001: *http://www.fairtest.org/facts/computer.htm*

Federico, P. (1992). Assessing semantic knowledge using computer-based and paper-based media. *Computers in Human Behavior, 8*, 169-181.

Gibson, E.J., Brewer, P.W., Dholakia, A., Vouk, M.A., & Bitzer, D.L. (N.D.). *A comparative analysis of Web-based testing and evaluation systems*. Retrieved April 19, 2001, from: *http://renoir.csc.ncsu.edu/MRA/Reports/WebBasedTesting.html*

Green, B.F. (1987). Construct validity of computer-based tests. In H. Wainer & H.I. Braun (Eds.), *Test validity* (pp. 77-86). Hillsdale, NJ: Erlbaum.

Green, B.F. (1991). Guidelines for computer testing. In T.B. Gutkin & S.L Wise (Eds.), *The computer and the decision making process* (pp. 245-273). Hillsdale, NJ: Erlbaum.

Haas, C., & Hayes, J. R. (1986). What did I just say? Reading problems in writing with the machine. *Research in the Teaching of English, 20*(1), 22-35.

Hazari, S. *Online testing methods in Web-based courses*. (n.d.) Retrieved April 19, 2001, from: *http://linus.umd.edu/documents/assmnt/onlinetest.htm*

Heubert, J.P., & Hauser, R.M. (1999). *High stakes testing for tracking, promotion, and graduation*. Committee on Appropriate Test Use. Board on Testing and Assessment, Commission on Behavioral and Social Sciences and Education, National Research Council. Washington, D.C.: National Academy Press. Retrieved April 19, 2001, from: *http://stills.nap.edu/readingroom/books/highstakes/*

Honaker, L. M. (1988). The equivalency of computerized and conventional MMPI administration: A critical review. *Clinical Psychology Review, 8*, 561-577.

Klein, S.P., & Hamilton, L. (1999). *Large-scale testing: Current practices and new directions*. Rand: Santa Monica, California. Retrieved April 19, 2001, from: *http://www.rand.org/publications/IP/IP182/*

Legg, S.M., & Buhr, D.C. (1992, Summer). Computerized adaptive testing with different groups. *Educational Measurement: Issues and Practice*, pp. 23-27.

Marsh, G.E. II, McFadden, A.C., & Price, B.J. (1999). An overview of online educational delivery applications. *Online Journal of Distance Education Administration*. Retrieved April 19, 2001, from: *http://www.westga.edu/~distance/marsh23.html*

Mazzeo, J., & Harvey, A. (1988). *The equivalence of scores from automated and conventional educational and psychological tests: A review of the literature* (College Board Report No., 88-8). New York: College Entrance Examination Board.

Mazzeo, J., Druesne, B., Raffeld, P., Checketts, K., & Muhlstein, A. (1991). *Comparability of computer and paper-and-pencil scores for two CLEP general examinations* (College Board Report No. 91-5). New York: College Entrance Examination Board.

Mead, A.D., & Drasgow, F. (1993). Equivalence of computerized and paper-and-pencil cognitive ability tests: A meta-analysis. *Psychological Bulletin, 114*(3), 449-458.

Mourant, R.R, Lakshmanan, R., & Chantadisai, R. (1981). Visual fatigue and cathode ray tube display terminals. *Human Factors, 23*(5), 529-540.

North Central Regional Educational Laboratory (1995). *Critical Issue: Rethinking assessment and its role in supporting educational reform*. Retrieved April 19, 2001, from: *http://www.ncrel.org/sdrs/areas/issues/methods/assment/as700.htm*

Owston, R.D., Wideman, H.H., Pacini, V. & Dodick, D. (1999, April). *The differential effects of computer access level on student achievement in the early school years*. Paper presented at the annual meeting of the American Educational Research Association, Montreal. Retrieved April 19, 2001, from: *http://www.edu.yorku.ca/emate/*

Rudner, L.M. (1998). *An on-line, interactive, computer adaptive testing mini-tutorial.* ERIC Clearinghouse on Assessment and Evaluation. Retrieved April 19, 2001, from: *http://ericae.net/scripts/cat*

Russell, M. (1999). Testing on computers: A follow-up study comparing performance on computer and on paper. *Education Policy Analysis Archives, 7*(20). Retrieved April 19, 2001, from the World Wide Web: *http://epaa.asu.edu/epaa/v7n20/*

Russell, M., & Haney, W. (1997). Testing writing on computers: An experiment comparing student performance on tests conducted via computer and via paper-and-pencil. *Education Policy Analysis Archives.* Retrieved April 19, 2001, from: *http://epaa.asu.edu/epaa/v5n3.html*

Sissel, R. (n.d.). *Computer vs. paper & pencil assessment in ESL.* Retrieved September 21, 2000, from *http://www2.smumn.edu/facpages/~rsissel/resume/cv.html*

Wise, S.L., & Plake, B.S. (1989). Research on the effects of administering tests via computers. *Educational Measurement Issues & Practice, 8*(3), 5-10.

CURRENT TRENDS AND PRACTICES

Carmen L. Gonzales
Laura Sujo de Montes

Effective Practices
in Distance Education

SUMMARY. Distance education is changing the landscape of higher education and many faculty are now developing Web-based courses. This paper describes the lessons learned by the authors' experiences and research and offers a specific set of pedagogical and assessment strategies that they have found to be successful in online settings. The authors have found that classes delivered on the Web provide a viable option for professional development of K-12 teachers, and that the learning that occurs is of equal quality to those university courses taught on campus. Web-based courses offer students an opportunity to take courses anytime, anyplace. *[Article copies available for a fee from The Haworth Document Delivery Service: 1-800-HAWORTH. E-mail address: <getinfo@haworthpressinc.com> Website: <http://www.HaworthPress.com> © 2001 by The Haworth Press, Inc. All rights reserved.]*

CARMEN L. GONZALES is Assistant Professor, RETA, Project Director, New Mexico State University, MSC 3 CUR, P.O. Box 30001, Las Cruces, NM 88003 (E-mail: carmen@nmsu.edu).
LAURA SUJO DE MONTES is Assistant Professor, Northern Arizona University, Center for Excellence in Education, P.O. Box 5774, Flagstaff, AZ 86011-5774 (E-mail: Laura.Sujodemontes@nau.edu).

[Haworth co-indexing entry note]: "Effective Practices in Distance Education." Gonzales, Carmen L., and Laura Sujo de Montes. Co-published simultaneously in *Computers in the Schools* (The Haworth Press, Inc.) Vol. 18, No. 2/3, 2001, pp. 61-77; and: *Evaluation and Assessment in Educational Information Technology* (ed: Leping Liu et al.) The Haworth Press, Inc., 2001, pp. 61-77. Single or multiple copies of this article are available for a fee from The Haworth Document Delivery Service [1-800-HAWORTH, 9:00 a.m. - 5:00 p.m. (EST). E-mail address: getinfo@haworthpressinc.com].

KEYWORDS. Distance education, assessment, online pedagogy, constructivist theory, project-based learning

INTRODUCTION

Technology is changing the landscape of higher education and creating a new set of possibilities for attending college. Many factors, including tradition, funding, credit units, semester schedules, pedagogy and other academic structures, have constrained institutions to geographic boundaries and on-campus classes. However, online education is becoming more readily available at universities and colleges, especially at the graduate level. This is due in part to the presence of mature, motivated students capable of the independent work required for many distance education classes, and faculty familiar with applications to offer the courses (Kearsley, 2000). This paper describes the lessons learned through the authors' experiences and research and offers a specific set of pedagogical and assessment strategies that they have found to be successful.

As the Internet becomes commonplace in activities such as relaxation, shopping, or education, the "school without walls" has slowly emerged and is claiming its niche in the American educational system. In this kind of school, learning takes place anytime and anywhere; resources found at home, museums, libraries, and universities are woven together to connect learners in distinctive new ways to form a community of learners (Spindler, 1995) joined not by geographical location but by common interests. As a consequence, the use of the Internet as a learning space has revolutionized distance education in higher education (Abrahamson, 1998).

Web-based courses offer a new alternative to people who find on-campus settings burdensome or impossible to attend due to work, family commitments, and/or geographic isolation. In order to meet the needs of today's diverse learners, it will be necessary to offer many forms of education such as distance education (Office of Technology Assessment, 1993). The segment of the population that embraces distance education is largely composed of people who need to go back to school either to retrain or to keep abreast with changes in their professions, and classroom teachers are no exception. Because teacher shortages have become severe in certain subjects and geographic areas, "emergency certification" is offered to individuals who enter the teaching profession. As the Elementary and Secondary Education Act calls for fully licensed teachers in the classroom (Wise & Leibbrand, 2000), these new professionals face the challenge of acclimating to a new working environment while fulfilling the educational requirements to keep their jobs. Web-based courses offer them the convenience of a 24-hour classroom where the instructor and/or course materials are available at any time without the constraint of having to travel to a specific location for class meetings.

However, distance education courses, and Web-based courses in particular, are not suitable for everybody. Harris (1994) and Klinger and Connet (1992) described the distance learner as being typically over 26 years of age, highly motivated, self-disciplined, goal oriented, having average or better verbal and quantitative skills, and having relatively easy access to telecommunication facilities. All of these characteristics play an important role in the success or failure of a distance education experience, as will be explained in the following sections.

Online teaching is a relatively new development, but recent research has shown it to have as much rigor and educational merit as is found in face-to-face courses (Odasz, 1994; Sujo de Montes, 1999). It provides opportunities for faculty and students to have ongoing communication to become members of learning communities; to utilize information from voice, text, graphic and television-video sources; to develop technology competencies; and to construct and apply knowledge.

Web tools, combined with telecommunications systems, are becoming a significant delivery method in higher education (de Verneil & Berge, 2000). Successful use of these technologies involves virtual classes that are different from the face-to-face class. Rather than being the "sage on the stage," the instructor becomes the "guide on the side." It requires a shift from a teacher-centered classroom to a student-centered classroom (Rogers, 2000). Because the learner is separated from the instructor, success of the course is dependent on effective organization, clear and meaningful assignments, and the use of assessment and evaluation methods that provide timely feedback on student progress.

Effective assessment and evaluation of Web-based learning environments provide feedback on how learning and teaching are progressing. Formative assessment is a process that guides the performance and learning throughout the course and allows for changes to be made if the course is not proceeding as planned. Summative evaluation reflects the student's final grade and assesses the completed course–both student satisfaction with the class and the instructor (Palloff & Pratt, 1999; Wiggins, 1998).

THEORETICAL FRAMEWORK

As much as research studies suggest that distance education learners' experiences need to be similar to those of local or face-to-face learners' experiences (Simonson, 1997), there is a specific set of pedagogical and assessment issues that need to be addressed when teaching in a Web-based environment. In this paper we will discuss the issues involved in designing and assessing a Web-based course. We will look at the assumptions we make about the learner and the learning process when we identify learning goals, when we design Web-based materials relevant to these goals, and when we select or develop pedagogical approaches to delivery. We will also address the assessment of Web-based content. The most important of those pedagogical issues is the teaching/learning theory used when instruction is delivered over the Web. We believe that the constructivist theory, when linked to project-based learning, offers an excellent pedagogy for successful Web-based learning environments.

Constructivism. Much has been written lately about constructivism, but this approach has existed for several decades and was the prominent perspective among educators in the '30s and '40s (Rice & Wilson, 1999). The renewed interest may be because the information age and new technological capabilities have caused educators to reconceptualize the teaching and learning process and to develop approaches consistent with constructivist theory (Duffy & Jonassen, 1992).

The general tenet of constructivism is that each individual constructs knowledge through interpreting his or her own experiences, and that this construction of knowledge is framed by social interaction. Adams and Burns (1999) offer the following principles of constructivism: (a) learners bring their personal prior knowledge and experiences to the learning situation; (b) learning is internally controlled and mediated; (c) tools, resources, experiences, and contexts help in the construction of knowledge in multiple ways; (d) learning occurs through a process of accommodation and assimilation when old mental models are challenged to create new ones; (e) learning is an active and reflective process; and (f) social interaction provides multiple perspectives to construct knowledge.

In the constructivist view, teachers assume the role of facilitators, of classroom instructional leaders whose job is not to furnish all the answers or to control the content, but to provide a structure that launches student exploration (Adams & Burns, 1999; Perkins, 1999). Constructivism requires teachers to create a meaningful curriculum where students are invited to build on their previous experiences. Because teachers need to design a learning experience that is not only meaningful for students but also challenging, a constructivist classroom is more intellectually demanding from the teacher than regular textbook-based instruction (Brooks & Brooks, 1999).

As learners assume new roles in the teaching/learning interaction, teachers also change from being the "sage on the stage" to a "guide on the side." The goal for teachers in distance education is to develop pedagogically sound courses that model social constructivist learning theory and that are available to learners at times and places convenient to them. In this constructivist environment, students work on complex projects, often in groups, synthesize information to construct their own understandings of a content area, learn skills and concepts, and use them to solve real-world problems. These projects follow from a theory of learning that suggests subject matter becomes meaningful, and therefore understandable, when it is used in context-rich activities (Fosnot, 1996; Norton & Wiburg, 1998). Courses should be designed to emphasize the experiences and sociocultural context of students as well as their own responsibility for learning, for figuring out their own methods of solving problems, and for assessing their own work.

In many cases in distance education courses, students will help determine their own learning goals and will be the source of information about those goals to a greater extent than students in traditional courses (Walhaus, 2000). Because in a constructivist environment students bring their previous knowledge, it is only logical to use the students' daily work, points of view, reactions to readings, interactions with peers, projects, and demonstration of their skills to assess and guide their teaching (Brooks & Brooks, 1999). Trying to capture the students' understanding of the course materials through traditional multiple-choice tests will only ignore the roles that the curriculum, instructional methodology, student motivation, and even the technology interface play on student learning. An excellent way to provide a constructivist environment conducive to authentic assessment is through project-based learning.

Project-based learning. Besides providing a social context for learning, project-based learning can be intrinsically motivating for students because it is born from the students' own interests. When students work in small groups, they feel more willing to share their questions, think out loud, offer their understandings of a concept, and recommend different problem-solving strategies for the group (Crawford & Witte, 1999). In situations like these, students learn how to learn, how to make connections across disciplines and, with the American multicultural classroom, how to make connections across cultural borders. The beauty of project-based learning is that it not only works with K-12 classrooms but with higher education classrooms as well.

The typical graduate distance education course is filled with adults who seek to retrain or sharpen their skills and then apply them to their daily working activities; that is, they come back to school with a purpose in mind. In colleges of education, in-service teachers take online courses while continuing to meet commitments to their jobs, families, and communities. With project-based learning, in-service teachers not only learn new skills but also have the opportunity to experience this kind of learning first hand so they can apply it to their classrooms and make it available for their students (Office of Technology Assessment, 1995). Project-based learning brings social interaction to the classroom through teamwork and collaboration, usually resulting in the creation of a community of learners (Wolk, 1994). In short, this kind of learning becomes just-in-time professional development.

Just-in-time professional development. The U.S. Department of Education (1996, Online) defines professional development as "the rigorous and relevant content, strategies, and organizational supports that ensure the preparation and career-long development of teachers and others whose competence, expectations and actions influence the teaching and learning environment." Distance education courses can offer necessary career-long development and support to in-service teachers.

As teachers in Web-based courses learn through the use of technology, a powerful synergy arises when the technology is used in conjunction with project-based learning. This power resides in the ability to build learning experiences in which students can draw from their previous knowledge, answer their own questions, develop metacognitive skills, build connections with peers and experts, and engage in life-long learning (Rubin, 1996). The inquiry, dialogue, diagnosis, and questioning of assumptions that occur in project-based learning become important for in-service teachers when they use these learning experiences to (a) connect the formal learning setting of the Web-based course to their job setting, (b) acquire new qualifications that enable them to improve their teaching performance, (c) link new knowledge acquired in the course to practical situations in their classroom, and (d) create actual classroom situation improvements (Poell, Van Der Krogt, & Warmerdam, 1998).

In our experience and research, we have found that Web-based courses can become even stronger if there is a face-to-face component (Leach 1996; Sujo de Montes, 1999). This can be done one or two times a semester. This combination of online and face-to-face work helps develop a sense of community among the students.

Electronic communities of learners. Web-based courses are built on the potential of technology to support electronic learning communities (Dede, 1996; Odasz, 1994; Riel & Fulton, 1998). The potential of these communities, when thoughtfully designed, well implemented, and supported, is enormous (Honey, Carrigg, & Hawkins, 1998). Such communities encourage the development of authentic "communities of practice" in which participants can work together at a distance on similar problems while tapping into the vast resources provided by the Internet.

In order to develop a strong learning community, two issues need to be addressed. The first is the need to provide the opportunity for some face-to-face sessions in order to build trust and working relationships among the participants. Research indicates that a combination of face-to-face and distance education is the most effective way of meeting the needs of students (Leach, 1996; Schrum, 1991; Sujo de Montes, 1999).

The second issue involves the actual design and assessment of the Web-based courses. Early distance education courses were often nothing more than lecture notes, tests, and written exercises directly translated into electronic format. More recent course development (Collis & Knezek, 1997; Owston, 1997), as well as our own pilot classes at New Mexico State University (Sujo de Montes & Gonzales, 2000), has taken advantage of the potential that electronic communities provide for collaborative work. Students are asked to become members of smaller groups (three to five people) who work together at a distance discussing readings, developing presentations, and engaging in long-term collaborative projects. Clearly defined learning goals and objectives help to shape and assess the course.

Assessment strategies. A variety of methods should be used to assess student performance and learning. To optimize the assessment potential of a Web-based environment, it is important to articulate the differences between formative and summative evaluation methods. Usage often blurs the distinction between the terms, but for the purposes of this paper, *evaluation* refers to the final grade a student receives, and/or the final evaluation of a course, and is the most often used model at academic institutions. *Assessment,* by contrast, refers to what extent the instructors have successfully facilitated the specific knowledge or skills (learning goals) for the course (Hanna, 1999).

In reflecting on the assessment and evaluation of online courses, Harasim, Hiltz, Teles, and Turoff (1996) state, "In keeping with a learner-centered approach, evaluation and assessment should be part of the learning-teaching process, embedded in class activities and in the interactions between learners and between learners and teachers" (p. 167). This is a description of a formative evaluation process that should be built into the course outline and structure. This form of assessment reflects on both the learner and the teacher. Information gathered from formative evaluation may mean that the instructor will make changes or plan appropriate instruction to reflect the learners' needs (Palloff & Pratt, 1999).

In order to establish a formative process of student assessment, the course designer and/or course instructor must have a set of clearly defined learning goals and outcomes, as well as criteria for evaluating student performance. Formative assessment should closely reflect the goals for the course and focus on outcomes or products of student learning, such as objective assessments and projects/products (Wiggins, 1998). Because the instructor is interested in understanding where the learners have been and where they are going, he/she needs to assess the process as well as the product, through activities such as online journals, bulletin board postings, chat-room logs, self-evaluations, course assignments, rubrics, multimedia presentations, and final class products.

Most academic institutions request the use of an end-of-the-semester course and instructor evaluation. This form of evaluation is summative and generally puts a final numerical value to the course and/or student. Palloff and Pratt (1999) state that, "these evaluation forms rarely address whether or not a class has supported students in achieving their learning objectives" (p. 151). While this form of summative evaluation may not be very useful in determining if the course met the goals set forth at the beginning, it will tell us whether students enjoyed learning using a Web-based delivery method. An instructor also makes a summative evaluation of the student in the form of a final grade. The students' progress as measured by formative assessments throughout the semester should be taken into account in the summative evaluation.

METHODOLOGICAL ISSUES

Over time, we have developed and incorporated a set of features in our Web-based courses that help us provide a climate of cooperation, collaboration, interaction, and support. This has made learning through the Web a more meaningful experience for our students. The courses utilize both asynchronous and synchronous forms of learning. Typically, learning is asynchronous, enabling students to access a broad range of stimulating course resources online anytime, anyplace. Synchronous learning occurs in real time. Both synchronous and asynchronous communication expand options for working in groups and encourage interaction and collaboration among students (Rogers, 2000).

Our courses have incorporated a number of different assessment and evaluation methods, including weekly journals, group work, peer assessment, responses to readings on the bulletin board, online chats, and mid-point and final evaluation surveys. All of this contributed to providing a rigorous online learning experience. In a study conducted by Sujo de Montes (1999) comparing an online course with the same course taught on campus (both taught by the same professor), she found them to be of equal quality. The class products created by face-to-face students were not superior in quality to those created by online students. These results are encouraging in their suggestion that our Web courses are using correct strategies to keep or improve the quality of a course when compared to an on-campus learning experience.

The interface for our courses has been Web Course Tools (WebCT), which is a software program that allows educators, with or without much technical expertise, to create sophisticated Web-based courses using an entirely WWW-based interface (Goldberg, Salari, & Swoboda, 1996). WebCT provides user-friendly access to a password-protected environment that includes bulletin board areas for threaded discussions, course notes and assignments, and real-time chat rooms for group work, and virtual office hours. In addition, it gives instructors access to management tools that allow for administrative course tracking of the students, including the number of logons, online articles read, and postings made. WebCT also has traditional evaluation tools such as quizzes, but these features are not commonly used in a constructivist environment.

Another WebCT feature that fosters communication and interaction, which is integral to the constructivist theory, is the Student Presentation area. In this space, the students, or group of students, can post their projects so they receive feedback from their peers and instructors. Because this WebCT feature requires students to post their work in HTML format, the student presentation area was used as the students became more sophisticated in their technical skills.

The context of Web-based learning offers unique opportunities for assessment and evaluation and creates a learning community that communicates and interacts in new ways. What follows is a recounting of our experiences with Web-based learning and assessment of the process.

Bulletin board. This is a special area where instructors can post messages to discuss readings, ask or answer questions, or socially interact with the rest of the participants in an asynchronous way. The advantage of using a bulletin board is that discussions can be threaded according to the topic, making the electronic conversation more organized as it evolves over time (Kearsley, 2000; Wulf, 1996). Since students are grouped into small teams to work on their projects, they may be assigned a special private bulletin board area where their group can brainstorm about what route to take when creating projects.

One of the benefits of using a bulletin board (and computer-mediated communication in general) for discussion is that interactions are accepted based on the merits of the issue presented and on the task focus rather than on social relationships, ethnicity, ability, or other visual cues that accompany face-to-face interaction (Olaniran, Savage, & Sorenson, 1996). Another benefit of bulletin board discussions is that they make students responsible for initiating communication while encouraging them to clearly articulate their ideas and questions. The necessity of writing in a clear way sharpens the students' critical thinking skills (McComb, 1994). As soon as the students perceive the value of communicating in the bulletin board, the interaction among the students usually grows and is sustained for the duration of the course.

The bulletin board area gives the instructor a very important tool for assessing the students' knowledge and understanding of the course content. In the duration of a Web-based course, the bulletin board becomes a much-visited area. Each week, questions are posed for the course and students respond to them. Because all messages remain on the system, it is easy to review the quantity and quality of the posts, as well as what each person has contributed to the discussion. In this way, the bulletin board interaction becomes an integral part of student assessment. At any time during the course, the instructor can make adjustments to the content to further explain something that is not clear, or to move ahead (Kearsley, 2000; Palloff & Pratt, 1999).

Virtual office hours using chat rooms. Synchronous communication in a chat room, also called real-time conferencing, simulates the interaction that may take place in a face-to-face classroom with the advantage that learners can interact from anywhere with an Internet connection (Kearsley, 2000; Owston, 1997). Because the interaction is in real time, it is spontaneous and dynamic. When real-time conferencing is used as part of a course, the instructor generally defines the topic of discussion beforehand and moderates the chat session (or designates someone to serve in that role).

As part of our interactive learning environment, virtual office hours were made available to students once a week in a chat room. On a pre-established day of the week and time, students and instructors met in the main chat room to clarify questions about assignments and technology problems. Because some of the students' questions about how to troubleshoot a certain task using a piece of software were too specific for the interaction in the main room, the graduate assistant or the instructor would move to another chat room where the question could be answered without interfering with the rest of the interaction among the participants. In this way, interaction and attention were more personalized and tailored to the needs of each student. However, interacting in a chat room is not always an easy task. The discussion in a chat session is often difficult to follow because there are likely to be several conversations taking place at the same time among different participants. It is desirable to have a moderator, often times the instructor, who keeps people focused on a topic(s) and balances the degree of participation by individuals. All in all, virtual office hours played a major role in creating a classroom-like atmosphere for distance learners (Sujo de Montes, 1999).

The chat room sessions can be useful in assessing the needs of the students on a weekly basis. The transcripts from each chat session can be reviewed and analyzed by the instructor(s). Although the information may be less organized than the bulletin board discussion areas, it is easy to determine the understanding, or lack of understanding, of the content and to make adjustments as required.

Weekly electronic journals. Electronic journals provide an environment for students to write, react, respond and reflect about class issues (Bennett, 1999). In our experiences with Web-based courses, weekly electronic journals were used for two main reasons. First, they provided a tool to open the dialogue between the students and the instructor. Second, they were used as a way of "keeping in touch" with the online students to know how the class was progressing for them. Modra (1989) writes that journals are important because through them students become teachers and teachers become students. Writing journals are crucial in extending the capacities of both instructor and students to learn, analyze, and critique their daily reality in order to reflect upon, understand, and transform it. Through weekly journals, the students were able to vent any frustrations and accomplishments with the class projects and with group work.

Journals were an excellent assessment tool because they gave us a window into the students' personal experiences of being distance learners and provided us with immediate feedback of the course materials. Since online distance learning in higher education is such a new forum, there are no set rules about what type of assignments are effective. Through journals, the instructors gauged the responses to the assignments and learned if they were clearly explained and if the time line to complete them was appropriate. From our experience with online journals, we learned that the way a student feels about the course is as important as what he or she learns (Sujo de Montes & Gonzales, 2000). In a face-to-face class, students may experience frustration with their group members, or they may have a personality conflict with the instructor. Students usually experience a range of feelings while being part of a face-to-face class; most are apparent through talking or body language and cues. On the other hand, in a Web-based course, body language is removed from the interaction, and expressing a feeling requires a carefully considered statement to avoid misunderstandings. Thus it is understandable that dealing with personal feelings in a Web-based course is as important as dealing with the course content.

For a distance educator, it is imperative to provide and promote opportunities for interaction with the students so that they feel there is actually "somebody at the other end of the line." McHenry and Bozik (1995) have pointed out that students' perceptions of the class are influenced by the class interaction. In other studies, Bloom (cited in McHenry & Bozik, 1995) found that interaction greatly influenced students' cognitive learning, interest in the subject, and confidence in their own capabilities. Journals are an important piece in keeping the student-instructor interaction flowing in a Web-based course. Although journals are not graded or corrected, they do require a response. Timely responses to journals are important to foster interaction.

Schedule of activities. In a Web-based course, the virtual classroom is always open, facilitating self-paced and self-directed learning (Harasim, 1990). The asynchronous nature of Web-based learning provides the user with control over the time of interaction and the time available to read or reread a message and formulate a comment. However, this self-paced learning does not come without disadvantages. For a distance-learning student, it is easy to procrastinate or to incorrectly distribute the course tasks over the period of a semester, leading to rushing and frustration at the end of the course session. To help students organize and pace their Web-based learning experience, a schedule of activities is provided at the beginning of the semester. In this schedule, all the assignments, resources, projects, and due dates are listed and distributed along the semester, helping students organize and plan their work. Also, a weekly message is sent out by the instructor delineating assignments for the week, so that the students are receiving multiple scaffolds.

The schedule of activities is not only important to help students organize their work but also to build in assessment as an integral part of each assignment. In the schedule of activities, we include links to different forms of assessment used to evaluate the class projects. For instance, links to sites that have rubrics, or a site with an instructor-created rubric for the assignment, are provided for students as part of the assigned task. By placing these links in the schedule of activities, students are reminded of the criteria that will be used to assess their products. Students also use these instruments to provide constructive feedback to their peers' assignments.

In addition, the schedule of activities provides a link to the course evaluation form. At the end of the course, students are asked to evaluate the course online. Our Web courses are evaluated using an interactive Web-based form that allows students to use a Likert scale to evaluate their online experience. A text box is also provided for students to input comments about what they liked, disliked, or thought needed improvement. The course evaluation form does not ask for a student identifier so comments received are anonymous, giving students freedom to express their honest opinions.

CONCLUSION

Web-based instruction is becoming an important component of higher education. However, the impact these environments have in the teaching-learning dyad is still unclear. Due to the newness of this medium of delivery, pedagogy and assessment methods that work in this environment are just being developed and tested (Oren, Nachmias, Mioduser, & Lahav, 2000). We have presented several pedagogical and assessment features that we believe need to be considered when teaching on the Web. We discussed pedagogical approaches such as constructivism and project-based learning. We believe a learner-centered approach is of utmost importance in a Web-delivered course. Constructivist pedagogy can bring the student into the learning experience as an active partner, making it more meaningful and rewarding. The use of project-based collaborative learning in Web-based graduate education courses may easily become just-in-time professional development for in-service teachers when they are able to ask and investigate questions that are relevant to their daily teaching practice.

In order to create a rewarding online learning experience, formative assessment and summative evaluation need to be combined with an effective learner-centered pedagogy. When Web-based course instructors set clearly defined learning goals and expected outcomes, develop criteria for evaluating the student's performance, and use multiple methods of assessing learning and teaching, they promote an environment that is conducive to learning and reflection. By providing activities that build interaction among students and between students and instructors, a dynamic electronic community of learners can be produced. The purpose of this interaction needs to be twofold: (a) to provide the learner with tools to learn, communicate, and feel ownership of the educational experience; and (b) to provide the instructor with another channel to assess the students' progress and understanding of the course materials. These types of learning communities do not form on their own. They take social engineering, and students and instructors must play active roles in building them (Riel, 1999).

Finally, course organization strategies, such as the schedule of activities and weekly messages, have proven to be valuable tools not only in helping the students develop a sense of accomplishment while self-pacing their learning experiences, but also by providing tools to assess their progress and sending a clear message that assessment is, and must be, an integral part of any learning experience. A primary role of the online instructor is to facilitate student learning by providing a set of scaffolds to give structure to Web-delivered courses. The role of the student is to utilize this structure to organize him/herself in a productive way in this electronic environment. Ongoing communication and interaction in an online experience is imperative so that instructors can assess student understanding of course materials, provide students with feedback about their course progress, and receive timely comments to modify the course lessons and assignments.

We have found several themes that shape Web-based education. These are often interrelated and overlapping and include collaboration, student-centeredness, community, exploration, shared knowledge, and authenticity (Kearsley, 2000). These elements may exist in classrooms, but taken together, they define a new way of learning and teaching that is fundamentally different from the way we currently teach and learn in brick-and-mortar schools. Distance education has often been perceived as occurring in an impersonal, mechanistic context. Through our experiences, we have learned that with the utilization of specific pedagogical approaches, an online distance learning experience can be very personal and nurturing and can provide students with as much stimulation and interaction as a traditional on-campus classroom.

REFERENCES

Abrahamson, C. E. (1998). Issues in interactive communication in distance education. *College Student Journal, 32*(1), 33-43.

Adams, S., & Burns, M. (1999). *Connecting student learning & technology.* Austin, TX: Southwest Educational Development Laboratory.

Bennett, L. (1999). In response . . . Designing an online journal. *T.H.E. Journal, 26*(7), 52-56.

Brooks, M. G., & Brooks, J. G. (1999). The courage to be constructivist. *Educational Leadership, 57*(3), 18-24.

Collis, B., & Knezek, G. (1997). From research into practice: Telecommunications in educational settings. In B. Collis & G. Knezek (Eds.), *Teaching and learning in the digital age: Research into practice with telecommunications in educational settings* (pp. 1-8). Denton, TX & Eugene, OR: TCET and ISTE (co-publishers).

Crawford, M., & Witte, M. (1999). Strategies for mathematics: Teaching in context. *Educational Leadership, 57*(3), 34-38.

Dede, C. (1996, April). The transformation of distance education to distributed learning. *Learning and Leading in Educational Technology, 23*(7), 25-30.

de Verneil, M., & Berge, Z.L. (2000, Spring/Summer). Going online: Guidelines for faculty in higher education. *Educational Technology Review, 13*, 13-18.

Duffy, T.M., & Jonassen, D.H. (1992). *Constructivism and the technology of instruction: A conversation.* Hillsdale, NJ: Erlbaum.

Fosnot, C.T. (1996). *Constructivism: Theory, perspectives, and practice.* New York: Teachers College Press, Columbia University.

Goldberg, M. W., Salari, S., & Swoboda, P. (1996). World Wide Web course tool: An environment for building WWW-based courses. *Computer Networks and ISDN Systems*, 28. [Online]. Available: *http://homebrew.cs.ubc.ca/webct/papers/p29/index.html*

Hanna, D.E. (1999). *Higher education in an era of digital competition: Choices and challenges.* Madison, WI: Atwood.

Harasim, L. M. (1990). Online education: An environment for collaboration and intellectual amplification. In L. M. Harasim (Ed.), *Online education: Perspectives on a new environment* (pp. 39-64). New York: Praeger.

Harasim, L.M., Hiltz, S.R., Teles, L., & Turoff, M. (1996). *Learning networks.* Cambridge, MA: MIT Press.

Harris, J. B. (1994). Telecommunications training by immersion: University courses online. *Machine-Mediated Learning, 4*(2&3), 177-185.

Honey, M., Carrigg F., & Hawkins, J. (1998). Union City online: Architecture for networking and reform. In C. Dede (Ed.), *Learning with technology: The 1998 Yearbook of the Association for Supervision and Curriculum Development* (ASCD). Alexandria, VA: ASCD.

Kearsley, G. (2000). *Online education: Learning and teaching in cyberspace.* Belmont, CA: Wadsworth/Thomson Learning.

Klinger, T. H., & Connet, M.R. (1992). Designing distance learning courses for critical thinking. *T H E Journal, 20*(3), 87-90.

Leach, J. (1996). Teacher education–Online! *Educational Leadership, 54*(3), 68-71.

McComb, M. (1994). Benefits of computer-mediated communication in college courses. *Communication Education*, *43*, 159-169.

McHenry, L., & Bozik, M. (1995). Communicating at a distance: A study of interaction in a distance education classroom. *Communication Education*, *44*, 362-371.

Modra, H. (1989). Using journals to encourage critical thinking at a distance. In T. Evans & D. Nation (Eds.), *Critical reflections on distance education. Deakin studies in education series: 2* (pp. 123-146). Philadelphia, PA: Falmer Press.

Norton, P., & Wiburg, K. (1998). *Teaching with technology*. New York: Harcourt Brace.

Odasz, F. (1994, January). Online teaching: A significant new pedagogy, the community as a K-100 university. *Journal for the U.S. Distance Learning Association*, *8*(1), 1-4.

Office of Technology Assessment. (1993). *Adult literacy and new technologies: Tools for a lifetime*. Washington, DC: U.S. Government Printing Office.

Office of Technology Assessment. (1995, April). *Teachers and technology: Making the connection* (OTA-EHR-616). Washington, DC: U.S. Government Printing Office.

Olaniran, B. A., Savage, G. T., & Sorenson, R. L. (1996). Experimental and experiential approaches to teaching face-to-face and computer-mediated group discussion. *Communication Education*, *45*, 244-259.

Oren, A., Nachmias, R, Mioduser, D., & Lahav, O. (2000). Learnet–A model for virtual learning communities on the World Wide Web. *International Journal of Educational Telecommunications 6*(3), 201-213.

Owston, R. D. (1997). The World Wide Web: A technology to enhance teaching and learning? *Educational Researcher*, *26*(2), 27-33.

Palloff, R.M., & Pratt, K. (1999). *Building learning communities in cyberspace: Effective strategies for the online classroom*. San Francisco, CA: Jossey-Bass.

Perkins, D. (1999). The many faces of constructivism. *Educational Leadership*, *57*(3), 6-11.

Poell, R. F., Van Der Krogt, F. J, & Warmerdam, J. H. M. (1998). Project-based learning in professional organizations. *Adult Education Quarterly*, *49*(1), 28-43.

Rice, M. L., & Wilson, E. K. (1999). How technology aids constructivism in the social studies classroom. *Social Studies*, *90*(1), 28-34.

Riel, M. (1999). The Internet: A land to settle rather than an ocean to surf and a new "place" for school reform through community development. Global Schoolhouse: Lightspan Partnership, Inc. [Online]. Available: *http://gsh.lightspan.com/teach/articles/netasplace.html*

Riel, M., & Fulton, K. (1998, April). *Technology in the classroom: Tools for doing things differently or doing different things*. Paper presented at the annual meeting of the American Educational Research Association, San Diego, CA.

Rogers, D. L. (2000, Spring-Summer). A paradigm shift: Technology integration for higher education in the new millennium. *Educational Technology Review*, *13*, 19-27.

Rubin, A. (1996). Educational technology: Support for inquiry-based learning. *TERC research monograph* (pp. 34-71). Cambridge, MA: TERC [Online]. Available: *http://*

ra.terc.edu/alliance/TEMPLATE/alliance_resources/reform/tech-infusion/ed_tech/ed_tech_frame.html

Schrum, L. (1991). Information technologies in our schools: Telecommunications enhancements for preservice and in-service teacher education. *The Writing Notebook. 8*(1), 1-19.

Simonson, M. R. (1997). Distance education: Does anyone really want to learn at a distance? *Contemporary Education, 68,* 104-107.

Spindler, M. (1995). Shaping a community of learners. *T.H.E Journal, 23*(2), 6.

Sujo de Montes, L. (1999). *The use of Internet-based university courses as a tool for professional development of K-12 teachers.* Unpublished doctoral dissertation. Las Cruces, NM: New Mexico State University.

Sujo de Montes, L., & Gonzales, C. (2000, February 10-13). More than having a connection: Qualitative factors that affect learning in a Web-based university course. In D.A. Willis, J.D. Price, & J. Willis. (Eds.), *Proceedings of the Society for Information Technology and Teacher Education, 11th International Conference.* (pp. 177-182). San Diego, CA: Association for the Advancement of Computing in Education.

U.S. Department of Education. (1996). The mission and principles of professional development. *Goals 2000.* [Online]. Available: *http://www.ed.gov/G2K/bridge.html*

Walhaus, R.A. (2000). E-learning: From institutions to providers, from students to learners. In R.N. Katz, & D.G. Oblinger (Eds.), *The "E" is for everything: E-commerce, E-business, and E-learning in the future of higher education* (pp. 21-52). San Francisco, CA: Jossey-Bass.

Wiggins, G. (1998). *Educative assessment: Designing assessments to inform and improve student performance.* San Francisco, CA: Jossey-Bass.

Wise, A. E., & Leibbrand, J. A. (2000). Standards and teacher quality: Entering the new millennium. *Phi Delta Kappan, 81*(8), 612-621.

Wolk, S. (1994). Project-based learning: Pursuits with a purpose. *Educational Leadership, 52*(3), 42-46.

Wulf, K. (1996). Training via the Internet: Where are we? *Training and Development, 50*(5), 50-55.

Leping Liu
D. LaMont Johnson

Assessing Student Learning in Instructional Technology: Dimensions of a Learning Model

SUMMARY. A study of methods to assess student learning in instructional technology courses was conducted using an IT learning model that consists of four dimensions. Static assessment and dynamic assessment methods were employed to assess student (a) attitudes toward technology, (b) learning and use of technology, (c) technology integration, and (d) self-mastering and teaching technology. *[Article copies available for a fee from The Haworth Document Delivery Service: 1-800-HAWORTH. E-mail address: <getinfo@haworthpressinc.com> Website: <http://www.HaworthPress.com> © 2001 by The Haworth Press, Inc. All rights reserved.]*

KEYWORDS. IT learning model, static assessment, dynamic assessment, qualitative and quantitative data, attitudes, technology integration, computer technology

LEPING LIU is Assistant Professor, Department of Reading, Special Education and Instructional Technology, College of Education, Towson University, Towson, MD 21252 (E-mail: lliu@towson.edu).
D. LAMONT JOHNSON is Professor, Department of Counseling and Educational Psychology, University of Nevada, Reno, NV 89557 (E-mail: ljohnson@unr.edu).

[Haworth co-indexing entry note]: "Assessing Student Learning in Instructional Technology: Dimensions of a Learning Model." Liu, Leping, and D. LaMont Johnson. Co-published simultaneously in *Computers in the Schools* (The Haworth Press, Inc.) Vol. 18, No. 2/3, 2001, pp. 79-95; and: *Evaluation and Assessment in Educational Information Technology* (ed: Leping Liu et al.) The Haworth Press, Inc., 2001, pp. 79-95. Single or multiple copies of this article are available for a fee from The Haworth Document Delivery Service [1-800-HAWORTH, 9:00 a.m. - 5:00 p.m. (EST). E-mail address: getinfo@haworthpressinc.com].

© 2001 by The Haworth Press, Inc. All rights reserved.
79

Those who teach instructional technology (IT) courses quickly come to realize the importance of assessment to explore appropriate ways to improve student learning through the use of technology (Bonewell, 1997; Brown, 1996; Grin & van de Graaf, 1996; Hargreaves, 1997; Ivers & Barron, 1998; McMillan, 2001; Tanner, 2001). Generally, some of the major issues related to this process include defining goals, selecting or designing valid and reliable instruments, and choosing appropriate methods for data collection (Huba & Freed, 2000). Since instructional technology courses tend to differ rather markedly in content and method of delivery from more traditional education courses, assessment methods specifically tailored to these courses are vital (Hartmann & Lakatos, 1998; Huba & Freed, 2000; Ward & Murray-Ward, 1999; Worthen, White, Fan, & Sudweeks, 1999; Ysseldyde, 1998). While some literature exists in this area, a systematic method for assessing student learning of IT is needed.

The model we have developed is based on simple learning principles: establishing learning objectives, collecting data based on the learning experience, and evaluating the data with an eye toward improving learning (Healey & Matthews, 1996; Keystone, 1998; Kumar & Bristor, 1999; Lejk & Wyvill, 1997; Liu & Cheeks, 2001; Marzano, Pickering, & McTighe, 1993; Schot, 1992; Williams & Brown, 1990).

Over time, we developed an IT course assessment model derived from an earlier learning model introduced by the Association for Supervision and Curriculum Development (ASCD) (Marzano, Pickering, Arredondo, Blackburn, Brandt, & Moffet, 1992). In this paper we first summarize that model and discuss general methods for applying it. Since both static and dynamic assessment procedures are involved in using the model, an explanation of these two procedures is presented. In the final section of the paper, we present practical examples of ways to apply our model by relating it to specific courses we have taught and evaluated over time.

DIMENSIONS OF THE INSTRUCTIONAL TECHNOLOGY LEARNING MODEL

In developing a learning model that applies to instructional technology courses, we searched some well-developed existing models and found that the ASCD learning model could be employed as a framework. The ASCD model describes five dimensions of learning (Marzano, Pickering, & McTighe, 1993, pp. 1-5):

- Dimension 1: Positive attitudes and perceptions about learning
- Dimension 2: Acquiring and integrating knowledge
- Dimension 3: Extending and refining knowledge
- Dimension 4: Using knowledge meaningfully
- Dimension 5: Productive habits of mind

Marzano, Pickering, and McTighe (1993) viewed this model as a general learning framework that applies to most discipline areas, including math, language arts, science, and social science. We began by assuming that the ASCD model also matched IT learning. Through the process of testing this assumption, we modified the ASCD model to more closely fit IT learning. A brief explanation of our modifications follows.

Dimension 1 (positive attitudes and perceptions about learning) has been shown to be important in IT learning. Research suggests that student attitudes toward learning and using technologies significantly influence student learning achievements: The more positive the students' attitudes are, the higher are their computer learning achievement scores. Our own research suggests further that certain critical attitude variables strongly influence positive attitudes and perceptions about learning. These attitude variables include motivation, enjoyment, anxiety, and sense of importance (Liu & Fernandez, 1988; Liu & Johnson, 1998). Therefore, we modified dimension 1 and called it *positive attitudes toward technology*.

Dimension 2 (acquiring and integrating knowledge) implies a phase of learning where learners acquire new knowledge. In IT learning, this phase usually includes acquiring new concepts and mastering new technologies, such as basic computing skills, educational software, multimedia authoring tools, and Web applications. Therefore, we modified this dimension and called it *using technology*.

Dimension 3 (extending and refining knowledge) and Dimension 4 (using knowledge meaningfully) suggest higher level learning such as comparing, classifying, making inductions/deductions, abstracting, decision-making, investigating, and solving problems (Marzano, Pickering, & McTighe, 1993). In IT learning at this level, students learn to use technologies as tools to improve classroom teaching and learning through integration of IT into the curriculum. Here, IT learning involves extending and refining knowledge and technology skills. In this phase, IT learning becomes heavily influenced by instructional design, such as the design of computer-based instruction, Web-based instruction, comprehensive courseware, or any technology-based classroom instruction.

Therefore, for our third dimension, we combined the two ASCD model dimensions into one, which we called *integrating technology*.

Dimension 5 (productive habits of mind) represents some of the most important aspects of learning. It addresses mental development and the acquisition of mental habits such as being clear and seeking clarity, being aware of one's own thinking, being open-minded and ready to try new and different things, and being able to learn on one's own (Marzano, Pickering, & McTighe, 1993). These aspects of mental development are also important in IT learning. Through most IT courses, students develop the ability to learn new technologies on their own and then teach others to use them. We modified the last dimension of IT learning and called it *self-mastering and teaching technology*.

The derivation of our IT model from the ASCD learning model, which forms the framework within which we perform assessments of IT learning, is summarized in Table 1.

STATIC ASSESSMENT VERSUS DYNAMIC ASSESSMENT

To appreciate our IT model, it is important to understand the difference between static and dynamic assessment.

In traditional assessment, one test is usually used to measure what the student knows or can do at a given point in time. This reveals little of the student's progress during the semester or over time. This is called *static assessment* (Bunderson, Inouye, & Olsen, 1989) and has two important characteristics: (a) it specifies a point and reflects the student's standing at that point, and (b) it usually employs the same assessment procedures and instruments for all students, very often ignoring individual circumstances for fear they will influence test performance.

However, when we consider learning about technology and learning to use technology in terms of a process (Liu & Cheeks, 2001; Liu & Johnson, 1998), we want to view students' learning as a modifiable sequence that can be tuned when changes occur in either the students or the environment. In other words, we want to monitor the learning curve to know when and where the students make progress or have specific needs. Assessment that monitors a learning process and records data over time is called *dynamic assessment* (Bunderson, Inouye, & Olsen, 1989).

The static assessment data plot in Figure 1 shows that there are two assessment measures conducted during the learning period, one at the beginning, and a second at the end of the learning period. The end result

TABLE 1. ASCD Learning Model and IT Learning Model

	ASCD Learning Model	IT Learning Model
Dimensions	1. Positive attitudes and perceptions about learning	1. Positive attitude toward technology
	2. Acquiring and integrating knowledge	2. Using technology
	3. Extending and refining knowledge	3. Integrating technology
	4. Using knowledge meaningfully	4. Self-mastering and teaching technology
	5. Productive habits of mind	

shows that students made progress during the semester. In the dynamic assessment data plot, assessment measures were conducted throughout the learning period, and we can tell specifically that rapid progress was made in week 5 (or after the fifth unit). Assuming that the two data plots in Figure 1 represent the same learning unit and the same students, it is easy to see how much more information relating to student learning is available when dynamic assessment is used.

In performing assessment in each dimension of the IT model we made use of both static and dynamic assessment procedures. As we will illustrate in the following sections, the selection of which assessment procedure to use depends on the assessment goals, instructional goals, and characteristics of technologies being learned.

DIMENSION 1:
POSITIVE ATTITUDES TOWARD TECHNOLOGY

A student's attitude toward learning and using technologies is a significant factor that influences his or her learning (Liu & Fernandez, 1998; Liu & Johnson, 1998). Four critical attitude variables that have been identified from our previous research are (a) enjoyment–the degree to which students enjoy learning and working with a computer (Cooper & Stone, 1996); (b) motivation–the degree of willingness of students to learn and use the computer (Kellenberger, 1996); (c) importance–the extent to which students see learning and using the computer as functional (Pelton & Pelton, 1996); and (d) computer anxiety–the degree of fear that students feel while learning and using a computer (King & Bond, 1996).

FIGURE 1. Static Assessment vs. Dynamic Assessment

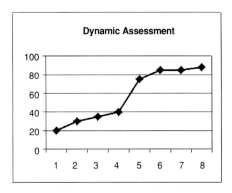

In Dimension 1, we assessed these four attitude variables in an IT course, with a questionnaire consisting of 24 statements designed to measure the extent to which students feel positive about learning and using technology based on the four attitude variables just described (Liu & Johnson, 1998). The purpose of the attitude assessment was to learn how students felt about computer technologies so that we could help them establish more positive attitudes through their learning. To assess students' attitudes *before* their learning, the best time to collect data is at the beginning of the semester. Therefore, we used static measurement, collecting data at the beginning and the end of the semester. The first set of data was used as a reference to determine students' individual special needs. We used a second set of data to measure how their attitudes influenced their achievement.

Attitude data were collected over three semesters from 609 students taking a computer literacy class. Using the data collected, we conducted a multiple regression analysis. The four attitude variables were used as predictor-variables, and students' computer achievement scores were used as the response variable. The results showed that (a) there was a linear relationship between the four attitude variables and computer achievement (see Table 2) and (b) the four predictor-variables were significant to the linear model, indicating that the more positive the student's attitudes were toward computer technology, the higher was their learning achievement (see Table 3). The coefficient of multiple determination, $R^2 = 0.7750$, indicated that approximately 77% of the variation of the response variable (computer achievement) could be accounted for by this linear model.

These results are consistent with research findings and again show the importance of knowing something about students' attitudes when trying to improve their learning.

DIMENSION 2: USING TECHNOLOGY

To assess learning about and using new technologies, we first needed to identify the learning outcomes–what to assess. In our IT courses, the basic requirements for learning a new technology are:

1. Knowing what it can do and how it works
2. Being familiar with its basic functions
3. Using it to create simple applications
4. Finding technical-support resources

Our purpose for assessing this dimension was to determine whether students could use the technology (meet requirements 1 and 2), and

TABLE 2. Model Trends–Attitude Assessment

Regression	Degrees of Freedom	Type I Sum of Squares	R-Square	F-Ratio	Prob > F
Linear	4	39283	0.7750	502.8	0.0000*
Quadratic	4	104.293378	0.0021	1.335	0.2557
Crossproduct	6	283.412223	0.0056	2.418	0.0857
Total Regression	14	39671	0.7827	145.1	0.0000

TABLE 3. Parameter Estimates–Attitude Assessment

Parameter Variable	DF	Standard Estimate	T for H0: Error	Parameter = 0	Prob > |T|
Intercept	1	28.195436	1.72707288	16.326	0.0001*
Enjoyment	1	0.779569	0.08125853	9.594	0.0001*
Motivation	1	0.562532	0.07734021	7.273	0.0001*
Important	1	0.224335	0.06580099	3.409	0.0007*
Free from Anxiety	1	0.985993	0.04856144	20.304	0.0001*

whether they were ready to create more advanced applications with it and learn more advanced functions about it on their own (meet requirements 3 and 4); that is, to be ready to advance to the next dimension of IT learning.

In the IT course we are using here as an example, students' learning outcomes are mostly based on *how* they learned. The measurable outcomes are quiz scores and tasks completed. In this course, we created instructional modules to assist students in learning a new program (Liu, 2001). The modules included three sections:

1. Detailed step-by-step instructions that enable students to use the program to complete a simple task;
2. An assignment to create another self-designed simple application; and
3. A 10-question quiz to assess basic knowledge and skills. A score over 80% is required to pass the quiz. Students can take the quiz three times with different questions generated by the testing system.

To complete a module, students complete two tasks (one following the instruction; a second created on their own) and pass the quiz with a score over 80%. In this IT course, students needed to complete 10 to 12 such modules.

We used dynamic measurements to assess students' learning in this dimension. Quantitative and qualitative data were collected during the entire learning period. The quiz scores served as the quantitative data that were recorded into our course management system after students completed each module. The qualitative data, a technology portfolio, consisted of all the tasks in the modules. The technology portfolio could be presented as (a) hard copy printouts, (b) electronic copy–files saved on a disk, or (c) online portfolio–all tasks converted into an HTML version and put on the Web. These two sets of data, quiz score and technology portfolios, clearly provide good measures of student learning progress.

Had we only looked at student final scores on each quiz, the curve would be flat because we required a score of over 80% to pass. Therefore, a better understanding of each student's learning curve, or learning progress, might be obtained from looking at the times that each student took each quiz. Figure 2 shows the results of such analysis for three students.

We can tell that student A had difficulty with the first six quizzes. Then, starting from quiz seven, student A passed each quiz on the first try. Student B had less difficulty. Starting with quiz 4, student B only needed to take each quiz one time to pass it. Student C experienced difficulty passing the quizzes all the way through and was only able to pass a quiz with one try on the final module. Although all three students passed all the quizzes, we can see that student C might require some extra help and encouragement in getting through the course.

DIMENSION 3: INTEGRATING TECHNOLOGY

The general goal of technology integration is to use technology as a tool to improve teaching/learning (Johnson & Liu, 2000). Technology integration occurs when we design lesson segments, lesson units, and entire courses. In most of our intermediate and advanced IT courses, technology integration is a major component. To illustrate how outcomes can be measured through a series of tasks, we will illustrate by using an IT course "Computer Based Instruction (CBI)" designed as an introduction to using multimedia-authoring tools (*ToolBook* or *Director*). In this course, students were required to design a lesson segment to teach one topic of interest. The lesson segment had to include a self-developed CBI program created with the authoring tool. To assist students in better understanding the term *integration*, we designed a series of tasks that students had to complete as part of the CBI project:

FIGURE 2. Assessing the Learning of New Technologies

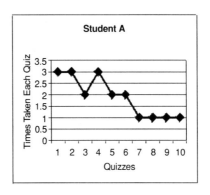

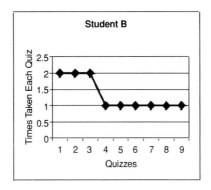

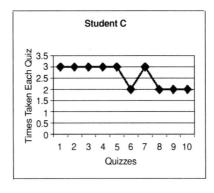

1. A research paper on CBI background defining the major issues in this field
2. CBI planning:
   a. Select topic
   b. Analyze audience
   c. State goals and objectives
   d. Collect and outline content information
   e. Make CBI theoretical decisions
   f. Develop a task checklist
   g. Develop CBI evaluation criteria
3. CBI design:
   a. Use CBI structured modeling
   b. Develop storyboards
4. CBI program implementation
5. Group evaluation and revision of the program

For each task we provided students with a worksheet to guide them, as well as assessment standards for each task (Liu, 2000b).

A dynamic assessment method was used, and task performance data were collected after each single task. Corrections and improvements were made after each task to ensure a well-developed CBI integration project. The following are two examples of how the dynamic assessment results helped to improve students' CBI design in "structured modeling" and "storyboarding."

Assessing CBI Structured Modeling Methods

In CBI design, structured modeling is used to provide a verbal model or graphical overview of the entire system. Structured modeling is implemented with modeling tools such as Data Flow Diagram (DFD), Data Dictionary, Entity Relationship Diagram (ERG), State Transition Diagram (STG), Structure Chart, Structured Program Flowchart, and Process Specification Tools (Burch, 1992).

Students in the course used one of three modeling methods: (a) freestyle method–they did some thinking about the program they would develop and made a mental outline that could be changed or adjusted at anytime; (b) outline method–they made an outline on paper of the main structure of the program; and (c) structured modeling–they used a concept mapping software package, *Inspiration,* to create a detailed structure flowchart.

Based on their chosen model, students next designed the draft version of their instructional program. The navigation link-design score of the program was used as the assessment score for the task of structured modeling.

We compared scores for the three modeling method groups. A descriptive analysis showed that the means of the three groups were free style group (group A) = 9.93; outline method group (group B) = 22.36; structured modeling (group C) = 36.70. These results, as outlined in Figure 3, showed the structured modeling method to be the best for CBI program navigation design. Therefore, we suggest the use of this method to all students.

Later, an experimental study was conducted (Liu, 1999) using 45 subjects. The results suggested the same pattern with significant differences among the three groups ($F_{2,42} = 55.34$, $p < 0.0001$). These results indicated that the treatments–the three modeling methods–did make a difference in the response variable of the navigation link designs. Results also showed that (a) significant differences were found between the free-style group and the outline group ($F_{1,28} = 22.81$, $p < 0.0001$); (b) significant differences were found between the outline group and the structured modeling group ($F_{1,28} = 32.84$, $p < 0.0001$); and (c) significant differences were found between the free-style group and the structured modeling group ($F_{1,28} = 110.38$, $p < 0.0001$).

Assessing CBI Storyboarding Methods

Another example of dynamic measurement was the assessment of CBI storyboarding. Storyboards contain all the information that will be placed on the screens (in the screen templates) when students are planning instructional programs. Also information is entered into the storyboard that will assist the programmer and production specialists in developing the media components of the instructional program. In short, storyboards serve as the blueprint for the instructional program. A detailed storyboard contains all the descriptive information required to produce the text, graphics, animations, audio, and video. The links for each button or interaction are also specified.

In our CBI course, students used three types of storyboarding methods: (a) index card–one card is one screen–all the elements designed for that screen are written on a 5-by-7 index card; (b) paper form–similar to index card except for size of the paper–all elements are listed and space is left for detailed explanation; (c) PowerPoint slide–one slide is one

FIGURE 3. Assessing CBI Modeling Methods

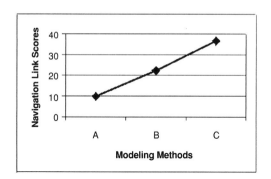

screen–and contains the same components as index cards or paper formats, as well as graphics, color, and so on.

We scored student draft versions of CBI programs according to four quality items: screen displays, interactions, orientation, and navigation; we then compared the three groups' scores and found differences as shown in Figure 4. As is clearly demonstrated in Figure 4, the PowerPoint slide method was the best storyboarding method of the three. Therefore, we suggested its use to all students.

Later, an experimental study was conducted (Liu, 2000a) using 87 subjects, where the differences were significant among the quality scores of CBI programs created with the three different storyboarding methods ($F = 452.72$). The results suggested the same pattern as shown in Figure 4: Scores for the group using the PowerPoint method were significantly higher than those groups using the paper format ($t = 25.70$, $p < 0.0001$), and index card format ($t = 26.41$, $p < 0.0001$).

Similarly, we assessed each of the CBI tasks and provided students suggestions to improve their designs. The quantitative data for this assessment consisted of the scores on each step of the CBI program design using a set of multimedia application evaluation forms (Ivers & Barron, 1998). Qualitative data for this assessment consisted of a design portfolio that contained the research paper, all the planning worksheets (including worksheets for topic selection, audience analysis, statement of goals and objectives, content outline and information collection, CBI theoretical decision making, and CBI evaluation criteria), designing worksheets (including structure modeling flowcharts and all storyboards), and an electronic copy of the final program. From the two sets

FIGURE 4. Assessing CBI Storyboarding Methods

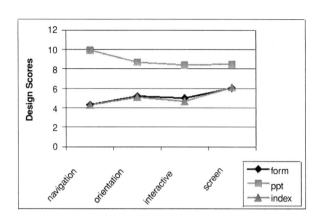

of data, we were able to evaluate the progress students made during the semester.

DIMENSION 4: SELF-MASTERING
AND TEACHING TECHNOLOGY

The last dimension of IT learning, self-mastering and teaching technology, implies that students should be able to learn and master technologies on their own. At this level, we assessed a small number of students who took independent studies and learned new technologies (e.g., some new programs) on their own. The basic requirements were to (a) learn how to use the program, (b) design an integration project or a real-life project using the program, and (c) develop instructional modules to teach the program.

Results of student projects, including an electronic copy of the program with appropriate documentation and the instructional modules, were collected as qualitative data. We used a program evaluation criteria worksheet (Liu, 2000) to check the quality of each project. We did not use quantitative scores for this kind of self-learning. We conducted a one-point static assessment for these independent studies.

Another aspect of assessing this level of learning would be a follow-up dynamic assessment process conducted after graduation to evaluate the lifelong learning progress to determine how students develop and enhance their ability to learn and use new technologies in the world of employment. This, however, is beyond the scope of our current study.

SUMMARY

In this paper, we presented some examples of assessing student IT learning. The assessment was performed under an IT learning model as summarized in Table 4.

The results of our study suggest that both static and dynamic measurement methods are appropriate for IT learning assessment, and that both quantitative and qualitative data are critical to show different facets of student learning. The IT learning model makes it easier to identify *what to assess* and to determine appropriate assessment methods. The results also suggest that students can learn more effectively if assessment is performed appropriately.

TABLE 4. IT Learning Assessment Methods

IT Learning Model	Static Assessment	Dynamic Assessment	Quantitative Data	Qualitative Data
1. Positive attitudes toward technology	√		√	
2. Using technology		√	√	√
3. Integrating technology		√	√	√
4. Self-mastering and teaching technology	√	√		√

REFERENCES

Bonewell, C. C. (1997). Using active learning as assessment in the postsecondary classroom. *Clearing House, 71*(2), 73-78.
Brown, E. (1996). Outcome: First target of technology assessment. *Physician Executive, 22*(3), 34-36.
Bunderson, C. V., Inouye, D. K., & Olsen, J. B. (1989). The four generations of computerized educational measurement. In R. L. Linn (Ed.), *Educational measurement* (3rd ed., pp. 367-407). New York: Macmillan.
Burch, J. G. (1992). Systems analysis, design, and implementation. Boston, MA: Boyd & Fraser.
Cooper, J., & Stone, J. (1996). Gender, computer-assisted learning, and anxiety: With a little help from a friend. *Journal of Educational Computing Research, 15*(1), 67-91.
Grin, J., & van de Graaf, H. (1996). Technology assessment as learning. *Science, Technology & Human Values, 21*(1), 72-101.
Hargreaves, D. J. (1997). Student learning and assessment are inextricably linked. *European Journal of Engineering Education, 22*(4), 401-410.
Hartmann, G. C., & Lakatos, A. I. (1998). Assessing technology risk: A case study. *Research Technology Management, 41*(2), 32-40.
Healey, M., & Matthews, H. (1996). Learning in small groups in university geography courses: Designing a core module around group projects. *Journal of Geography in Higher Education, 20*(2), 167-171.
Huba, M. E., & Freed, J. E. (2000). *Learner-centered assessment on college campuses.* Boston: Allyn & Bacon.
Ivers, K. S., & Barron, A. E. (1998). *Multimedia projects in education: Designing, producing, and assessing.* Englewood, CO: Libraries Unlimited.
Johnson, D. L., & Liu, L. (2000). First step toward a statistically generated information technology integration model. *Computers in the Schools, 16*(2), 3-12.
Kellenberger, D. W. (1996). Preservice teachers' perceived computer self-efficacy based on achievement and value beliefs within a motivational framework. *Journal of Research on Computing in Education, 29*(2), 124-140.
Keystone, D. (1998). Assessment of technology. *Primary Education, 4*(4), 8-14.
King, J., & Bond, T. (1996). A Rasch analysis of a measure of computer anxiety. *Journal of Educational Computing Research, 14*(1), 49-65.
Kumar, D., & Bristor, V. J. (1999). Integrating science and language arts through technology-based macrocontexts. *Educational Review, 51*(1), 41-54.
Lejk, M., & Wyvill, M. (1997). Group learning and group assessment on undergraduate computing courses in higher education in the UK: Results of a survey. *Assessment and Evaluation in Higher Education, 22*(1), 81-92.
Liu, L. (1999). Different approaches of system-analysis in multimedia courseware design. In D. A. Willis, J. D. Price, & J. Willis (Eds.), *Technology and teacher education annual 1999* (pp. 830-835). Charlottesville, VA: Association for the Advancement of Computing in Education.
Liu, L. (2000a). Different storyboarding methods in multimedia courseware design. In D. A. Willis, J. D. Price, & J. Willis (Eds.), *Technology and teacher education annual 2000* (pp. 784-790). Charlottesville, VA: Association for the Advancement of Computing in Education.

Liu, L. (2000b). *Theory and design of computer-based instruction* (custom course packets). Towson, MD: Towson University.

Liu, L. (2001). *Educational computing.* Towson, MD: Towson University.

Liu, L., & Cheeks, C. (2001). Assessing technology-based use of information. In D. A. Willis, J. Price, & J. Willis (Eds.) *Technology and teacher education annual 2001* (pp. 2374-2376). Charlottesville, VA: Association for the Advancement of Computing in Education.

Liu, L., & Fernandez, G. (1998, October 14-17). *Multiple regression and model selection on developing a computer achievement model.* Paper presented at WUSS (Western Users of SAS Software) conference, Oakland, CA.

Liu, L., & Johnson, D. L. (1998). A computer achievement model: Computer attitude and computer achievement. *Computers in the Schools, 14*(3/4), 33-54.

Marzano, R. J., Pickering, D. J., Arredondo, D. E., Blackburn, G. J., Brandt, R. S., & Moffet, C. A. (1992). *Dimensions of learning: Teachers manual (teacher's manual).* Alexandria, VA: Association for Supervision and Curriculum Development.

Marzano, R. J., Pickering, D. J., & McTighe, J. (1993). *Assessing student outcomes: Performance assessment using dimensions of learning model.* Alexandria, VA: Association for Supervision and Curriculum Development.

McMillan, J. H. (2001). Classroom assessment: Principles and practices for effective instruction. Needham Heights, MA: Allyn & Bacon.

Pelton, L., & Pelton, T. W. (1996). Building attitudes: How a technology courses affects preservice teachers' attitudes about technology. In B. Robin, J. D. Price, J. Willis, & D. A. Willis (Eds.), *Technology and teacher education Annual, 1996* (pp. 167-172). Charlottesville, VA: Association for the Advancement of Computing in Education.

Schot, J. W. (1992). Constructive technology assessment and technology dynamics: The case of clean technologies. *Science, Technology & Human Values, 17*(1), 36-57.

Tanner, D. A. (2001). *Assessing academic achievement.* Needham Heights, MA: Allyn & Bacon.

Ward, A. W., Murray-Ward, M. (1999). *Assessment in the classroom.* Albany, NY: Wadsworth.

Williams, C. J., & Brown, S. W. (1990). A review of the research issues in the use of computer-related technologies for instruction: What do we know. *International Journal of Instructional Media, 17*(3), 213-227.

Worthen, B. R., White, K. R., Fan, X., & Sudweeks, R. R. (1999). *Measurement and assessment in schools.* New Yor: Longman.

Ysseldyde, S. (1998). *Assessment* (7th Ed.). Boston, MA: Houghton Mifflin.

Walter F. Heinecke
Natalie B. Milman
Lisa A. Washington
Laura Blasi

New Directions in the Evaluation of the Effectiveness of Educational Technology

SUMMARY. Drawing from work by Shadish, Cook, and Leviton (1991) on social program evaluation, the authors discuss recent changes in evaluation theory and practices, and they connect these changes to technology and student learning. Concluding with a list of recommendations for evaluating the effectiveness of technology in teaching and learning, the authors challenge the purposes of education and prevalent goals for eval-

WALTER F. HEINECKE is Assistant Professor, EDLF Curry School, University of Virginia, Ruffner Hall, 405 Emmet St. S., Charlottesville, VA 22903-2495 (E-mail: heinecke@virginia.edu).
NATALIE B. MILMAN is Assistant Professor, Department of Teacher Preparation & Special Education, Graduate School of Education & Human Development, The George Washington University, Washington, D.C. 20052 (E-mail: nmilman@gwu.edu).
LISA A. WASHINGTON is Research Associate, Rockman Et Al, 605 Market Street, Ste. 305 San Francisco, CA 94105 (E-mail: lisa@rockman.com).
LAURA BLASI is a doctoral student, EDLF Curry School, University of Virginia, Ruffner Hall, 405 Emmet St. S., Charlottesville, VA 22903-2495 (E-mail: lnb8b@virginia.edu).

A version of this paper was originally prepared for National Conference on the Evaluation of Educational Technology, sponsored by the U.S. Department of Education, Office of Educational Technology, held July 12-13, 1999.

[Haworth co-indexing entry note]: "New Directions in the Evaluation of the Effectiveness of Educational Technology." Heinecke, Walter F. et al. Co-published simultaneously in *Computers in the Schools* (The Haworth Press, Inc.) Vol. 18, No. 2/3, 2001, pp. 97-110; and: *Evaluation and Assessment in Educational Information Technology* (ed: Leping Liu et al.) The Haworth Press, Inc., 2001, pp. 97-110. Single or multiple copies of this article are available for a fee from The Haworth Document Delivery Service [1-800-HAWORTH, 9:00 a.m. - 5:00 p.m. (EST). E-mail address: getinfo@haworthpressinc.com].

97

uation. After questioning how technology can impact student learning, they call for new and expanded definitions of student learning outcomes. Recommendations include redefining technology as a process rather than as a product, conducting implementation evaluations prior to outcome evaluations; reducing the reliance on standardized test scores as the primary outcome measure; and adopting multifaceted evaluation approaches (including case studies). *[Article copies available for a fee from The Haworth Document Delivery Service: 1-800-HAWORTH. E-mail address: <getinfo@haworthpressinc.com> Website: <http://www.HaworthPress.com> © 2001 by The Haworth Press, Inc. All rights reserved.]*

KEYWORDS. Assessment, evaluation, technology, learning, social program evaluation, state-of-the-art, diffusion of innovations

INTRODUCTION

In this article we discuss recent changes in evaluation theory and practices, and connect these changes to technology and student learning. It is evident that there are multiple definitions of *evaluation, technology,* and *student learning.* These multiple definitions must be engaged prior to substantive debate over the course of future directions. We highlight what we believe are several promising practices and conclude with a list of recommendations for evaluating the effectiveness of technology in teaching and learning.

RECENT CHANGES IN EVALUATION PRACTICES

We should say at the outset that *evaluation* means many things to many people. According to Glass and Ellett (1980), "evaluation–more than any science–is what people say it is, and people currently are saying it is many different things" (Shadish, Cook & Leviton, 1991, p. 30). In a recent examination of evaluation practice, we are encouraged to question the purpose and conduct of evaluations. Shadish, Cook, and Leviton (1991) recommend that, in any evaluation endeavor, we ask fundamental questions about five key issues:

1. *Social programming*: What are the important problems this program could address? Can the program be improved? Is it worth improv-

ing? If not, do new programs need to be created? Shadish, Cook, and Leviton (1991) discuss social program evaluation in depth–in terms of its history, tasks, and theory. For the purposes of evaluating technology and student learning we need to ask: What is the role of evaluation towards furthering the goals of social programs?

In order to maximize helpful change in the public interest, we can ask: Is it more effective to modify the philosophy or composition of whole programs? Or, should we improve existing programs incrementally– perhaps by modifying regulations and practices, or by influencing decisions to phase out local programs?

Within social programming, we can then question the role of the evaluator. Should the evaluator identify and work with change agents, or merely produce and explain evaluation results without forming alliances with change agents? Should evaluators try to change present programs or test ideas for future programs? Under what circumstances should the evaluator refuse to evaluate because the relevant problem is not very important or the program is not likely to ameliorate the problem?

2. *Knowledge use*: How can I assure my results get used quickly to help this program? Do I want to do so? If not, can my evaluation be useful in other ways? Should conceptual or instrumental use have priority? Should the evaluator identify and attend to intended users of evaluations? If so, which users? What increases the likelihood of use, especially for instrumental versus conceptual use?

3. *Valuing*: Is this a good program? By which notion of "good"? What justifies the conclusion? By whose criteria of merit should we judge a social program? Should prescriptive ethical theories play a significant role in selecting criteria of merit? Should programs be compared to each other or to absolute standards of performance? Should results be synthesized into a single value judgment?

4. *Knowledge construction*: How do I know all this? What counts as a confident answer? What causes that confidence? How complex and knowable is the world, especially the social world? What are the consequences of oversimplifying complexity?

Does any epistemological or ontological paradigm deserve widespread support? What priority should be given to different kinds of knowledge, and why? What methods should evaluators use? What are the key parameters influencing that choice?

5. *Evaluation practice*: Given limited skills, time, and resources, and given the seemingly unlimited possibilities, how can I narrow my options to do a feasible evaluation? What is my role–educator, method-

ological expert, judge of the program–worth? What questions should I ask, and what methods should I use? Whose values should be represented in the evaluation? What should the role of the evaluator be? Which questions should the evaluator ask? What should the evaluator do to facilitate use? What are the important contingencies in evaluation practice that guide these choices?

Experts on program evaluation (House, 1993; Schorr, 1997; Shadish, Cook, & Leviton, 1991) indicate that program evaluation has undergone a major transformation in the last three decades. It has changed from

> monolithic to pluralist conceptions, to multiple methods, multiple measures, multiple criteria, multiple perspectives, multiple audiences, and even multiple interests. Methodologically, evaluation moved from primary emphasis on quantitative methods, in which the standardized achievement test employed in a randomized experimental control group design was mostly highly regarded, to a more permissive atmosphere in which qualitative research methods were acceptable. (House, 1993, p. 3)

The most fundamental shift has been away from a blind faith in the science of evaluation and experimental research methods based on standardized test scores. These changes in the practice of evaluation have significant implications for questions about the future of the evaluation of technology and student learning outcomes.

HOW DOES TECHNOLOGY IMPACT STUDENT LEARNING?

The primary question to which we turn is: How does technology impact student learning? We don't, however, make implementation decisions based on this question. What do we know about this relationship using data and evaluation tools currently available? What could we learn in the future about technology and student learning assuming the application of new evaluation tools and strategies? The answer to the first question is straightforward: The relationship depends on how you define student learning and how you define technology.

If one defines student learning as the retention of basic skills and content information as reflected on norm-referenced and criterion-referenced standardized tests, then, evidence suggests, there is a positive relationship between certain types of technology and test results. For instance, it is well established that if a teacher uses computer-assisted instruction (CAI) or computer-based learning (CBL) approaches, where the computer is used to manage the "drill-and-skill" approach to teaching and learning, students will show gains on standardized test scores. This view of technology reduces the equation to only a student, a computer, and a test. It ignores the effects of schools, teachers, family, and community life on the learning process. Even though we cannot control for these variables, we must not discount them.

If, on the other hand, one views the goal of education as the production of students who can engage in critical, higher order, problem-based inquiry, then entirely different uses of technology emerge. For instance, the World Wide Web can be used as a source of information from which students can draw to solve real-world problems. As they can apply technology knowledge and skills to real-world problems, we can evaluate these outcomes–but this evaluation is not as simple as the standardized testing route. Standardized tests are an efficient means for measuring certain types of learning outcomes, but we must ask ourselves: Are these the outcomes we value? To a certain extent, we are living out the consequences of decisions influenced by previous evaluation methods. Shaped by prior approaches to evaluation, these conditions constrain our thinking about the purpose and effectiveness of technology in education.

Policymakers, evaluators, and practitioners may have very different answers to fundamental questions about the effectiveness of educational technology. Everyone is asking for results of the investment of technology in education. Perhaps the primary difficulty in coming up with new ways of evaluating or assessing the impact of educational technology is that there is little consensus about its purpose (Trotter, 1998). Policymakers often work from a cost-benefit model with increases in norm-referenced and criterion-referenced test scores viewed as the primary benefits. This model appears to be at odds with the view held by teachers or by the public that educational technology benefits include preparing students for the workforce, increasing student interest in learning, increasing student access to information, and transforming learning into an active experience, all rated above technology's impact on basic skills by parents in a 1998 public opinion survey sponsored by the Milken Exchange (Trotter, 1998).

The question really should not be, Does educational technology work? Rather, When does it work and under what conditions (Hasselbring cited in Viadera, 1997)? In practice, student achievement outcomes are mediated by the processes of teacher integration of technology into instruction. Technology can be used to improve basic skills through the automated practice of "drill and skill." Technology can also be used to facilitate changes in teacher practices that promote students' critical, analytic, higher order thinking skills as well as their real-world problem-solving abilities. The ability of teachers to foster such changes depends significantly on training that shows them how to integrate technology into content specific instructional methods. This has been shown through programs such as the Adventures of Jasper Woodbury conducted at Vanderbuilt University, the National Geographic Society's Kid's Network, and work done at the University of Massachusetts, MIT, and TERC with Simcalc.

QUESTIONING THE PURPOSES OF EDUCATION

Any innovation in our system of education, including technology, raises persistent questions about the purposes of education (Nickerson, 1988).

1. Is it to provide training in fundamental and basic skills?
2. Is it to prepare students for the work force?
3. Is it to produce citizens for an effective democracy?
4. Is it to produce an equitable society?
5. Is it to produce life-long learners?
6. Is it to prepare students with critical thinking skills for a complex new world?

According to educational researcher Larry Cuban, unless educational policymakers can agree and clarify the goals for using technology, it makes little sense to try and evaluate it (Trotter, 1998).

This need for clarity raises questions about assessment and evaluation of educational technology. Do traditional, standardized assessments measure the benefits that students receive from educational technology? In the evaluation of social programs in general, the profession of evaluation has moved away from standardized test scores as a meaningful measure of the impact of programs. Evaluation theorists like Mackie and Cronbach (House, 1993) have argued that there are too many critical relationships occurring in social phenomenon to be adequately captured by the traditional experimental design. "Social programs are far more complex composites, themselves produced by many factors that interact with one another to produce quite variable outcomes. Determining contingent relations between the program and its outcomes is not as simple as the regulatory theory posits" (House, 1993, pp. 135-136). Besides improvements in retention of rote facts, technology can improve student attitudes toward the learning process. Perhaps we should be assessing actual, authentic tasks produced through the processes of student interaction and collaboration. Perhaps we should be developing technologically based performance assessments to measure the impact of technology on student learning.

We have been fairly successful in determining the impact of technology on basic information retention and procedural knowledge. However, we have been less than successful in evaluating the impact of educational technology on higher order or metacognitive thinking skills.

NEEDED:
NEW AND EXPANDED DEFINITIONS
OF STUDENT LEARNING OUTCOMES

Needed more than anything else is a new set of learning outcomes for students. New learning outcomes must clearly focus on the demands of the new world environment. We need students who can think critically, solve real-world problems using technology, take charge of their life-long learning process, work collaboratively, and participate as citizens in a democracy. Experts in the area of technology and education such as Jan Hawkins (1996) and Henry Jay Becker (1992) have provided ideas that could be developed into criteria for new ways of thinking about technology, teaching, and learning. These new learning outcomes could be translated into learning benchmarks, and new types of assessment and methods for measuring outcomes could be developed to measure these benchmarks.

What we are looking for is a transition from "isolated skills practice" toward integrating technologies as tools throughout the disciplines. Jan Hawkins (1996) was not alone when she argued that, in order to realize high standards, education needs to move beyond traditional strategies of whole group instruction and passive absorption of facts by students. New more effective methods are based on engaging students in complex and meaningful problem-solving tasks. Technologies need to be used to bring vast information resources into the classrooms. We need a transition from inadequate support and training of teachers to support for all teachers to learn how to use technologies effectively in everyday teaching (Hawkins, 1996).

According to Becker (1992), in an ideal setting, teachers use a variety of computer software, often working collaboratively to address curricular goals. "Students exploit intellectual tools for writing, analyzing data, and solving problems, and they become more comfortable and confident about using computers" (Becker, 1992, p. 1). At the school, exemplary teachers use computers in lab settings as well as classroom settings for consequential activities to accomplish authentic tasks, rather than busywork such as worksheets, homework assignments, quizzes, or tests. Means and Olson (1994) outline a set of criteria for successful technology integration projects including an authentic challenging task, a project where all students practice advanced skills, and a project where work takes place in heterogeneous, collaborative groups. In this scenario the teacher acts as coach and provides guidance, as work occurs over extended blocks of time.

EVALUATING FOR NEW VISIONS OF TECHNOLOGY TEACHING AND LEARNING

It is clear that teaching and learning processes are embedded within complex systems. The challenge is to develop evaluation models that reflect this complexity. Just as technology has caused us to reevaluate the nature of knowledge and instruction, it prompts us to reevaluate the forms of evaluation that are brought to bear when examining educational technology. According to Schorr (1997) we need a new approach to the evaluation of complex social programs, one that is theory-based, aiming to investigate the project participant's theory of the program; one that emphasizes shared rather than adversarial interests between evaluators and program participants. According to Schorr, this new approach could employ multiple methods designs and aim to produce knowledge that is both rigorous and relevant to decision-makers. In order to accomplish these tasks, it will be necessary to design evaluations of technology in K-12 settings based on the experiences of evaluators, the experiences of program developers, the "state of the art" in the field of technology and in theories of learning.

Several studies and reports have done an exemplary job at pointing us in promising directions for future evaluations of the effectiveness of educational technology. Bodilly and Mitchell (1997), for instance, have prepared an evaluation sourcebook for "Evaluating Challenge Grants for Technology in Education," published by the RAND Corporation. Bodilly and Mitchell acknowledge that the outcomes sought in technology infusion projects are complex and are "not entirely captured by traditional educational measures" (p. xiv). They seek better learning outcomes "on a complex variety of dimensions rather than improvements in traditional test scores" (p. xiv) but they point out that some stakeholders may be interested in test scores as measures of student learning. Bodilly and Mitchell indicate that performance outcomes are the results of complex causes–technology may be only one of many input variables causing changes. A project's implementation and outcomes are heavily influenced by its context. While goals of various educational technology projects are part of that context, the conditions of each project are specific to its situation and may not be captured by a uniform evaluation design. They assert that multiple evaluation designs are required.

In terms of outcome goals, Bodilly and Mitchell (1997) propose a wide variety of possibilities beyond traditional test scores, including "short term changes in student outcomes, like disciplinary referrals or homework assignments completed," or longer term indicators such as "changes in test scores or student performances," "increased college going rates," "increases in job offers to students" (pp. 14-15). Other outcomes are defined as "higher order thinking skills, more sophisticated communication skills, research skills, and social skills" (p. 23). More sophisticated outcome measures must be located or developed by evaluators in order to gauge new effects of technology on learning.

According to Bodilly and Mitchell (1997), other outcome measures might be found in participants' (teachers and students) perceptions about the implementation, quality and benefits of the program. These might reflect student engagement levels as well as satisfaction levels. Other interim performance indicators might include the effect of the program on community and family participation or involvement, and student and teacher retention. Declines in disciplinary referrals and special education placements may also serve as outcome measures. The federal government, state departments of education, school districts, or schools might develop criteria for standards of good practice indicators and associate learning outcome benchmarks.

Other indicators of student outcomes such as "higher order thinking skills" and "ability to apply knowledge in meaningful ways" might be measured "by performance assessments, portfolios, learning records, and exhibitions" (Bodilly & Mitchell, p. 39). Norm-referenced and criterion-referenced assessments can also supplement these alternative outcomes (Bodilly & Mitchell, 1997). School districts are encouraged to use multiple and varied measures of outcomes. Student performance indicators such as attendance, reductions in dropout rates, successful transitions to work and to post-secondary institutions should be considered (Bodilly & Mitchell, 1997). Baseline data should be established at the beginning of the project. Bodily and Mitchell (1997) also propose that a list of common indicators across projects be used as a tool for summative program evaluation.

Bodilly and Mitchell refer to work on the evaluation of technology in educational reform conducted by Herman (1995) and Means (1995). They conclude that broad-based technological reforms, those that attempt multiple changes in a school besides the insertion of a single computer-based course, such as an attempt to create a constructivist curriculum across all grade levels supported by computer technology are more difficult to measure in terms of outcomes. Bodilly and Mitchell (1997) state that "efforts to trace the effects of these projects must take into account measuring effects in dynamic situations where many variables cannot be controlled and where interventions and outcomes have not been well defined for measurement" (p. 16). They also assert that "the complex environments in which technology projects are embedded make inference of causal relations between project activities and outcomes tenuous" (p. 20).

Implementation analysis becomes important under these conditions (Bodilly & Mitchell, 1997). With all of these complexities, the effects of technology on student outcomes may not be measured in short-term evaluations. Evaluation must take into account the different phases of a school's integration of technology, including purchasing and installing hardware and software, teacher training, and integrating technology into the curriculum and instruction. According to Bodily and Mitchell (1997), evaluation designs must therefore be longitudinal in design and account for changes in the target population. "Tracking comparison groups not exposed to technology or using national surveys to assess the likely level of background effects" will often be necessary (Bodilly & Mitchell, 1997, p. 25).

Researchers conducted a two-year evaluation of the Boulder Valley Internet Project (Sherry, Lawyer-Brook, & Black, 1997). The project employed a variety of evaluation methods and developed a theoretical tool, The Integrated Technology Adoption Diffusion Model, to guide the evaluation. According to this model evaluations should include the contexts within which technological innovations occur. This includes looking at technological factors, individual factors, organizational factors, and teaching and learning issues. Evaluation designs must be flexible enough to attend to the varying degrees of adaptation occurring with different content areas. Evaluations must include implementation assessments, formative assessments, as well as standard summative and outcome assessments. Evaluations must include the quality of training programs offering teachers the opportunity to learn new technologies within relevant, subject-specific contexts. Sherry, Lawyer-Brook and Black (1997) proposed three questions be posed about evaluating educational technology:

1. How can or will teachers use technology to attain their instructional objectives?
2. How can or will technology fit in with teachers' current teaching styles?
3. What value can technology add to the teaching and learning process? (p. 231).

We would add: How does the technology allow the teacher to teach content in new ways?

RECOMMENDATIONS

We need to take a formative approach to the evaluation of technology, because of the rate of change in technologies. Technology changes quickly while teachers are often asked to keep up and integrate new ideas at the same pace. The definition of the innovation within education is thus constantly at issue. We must spend time documenting the program, and its context, both of which may be changing over time (Bodilly & Mitchell, 1997; Schorr, 1997).

In order to get at the complexities of these processes, multiple measures (quantitative and qualitative) should be used. These should include traditional experimental and quasi-experimental designs as well as qualitative and mixed-methods designs and school include such methods as paper surveys, e-mail/Web-based surveys, informal and in-depth interviews, focus group interviews, classroom observations, document analysis, and case studies (Sherry, Lawyer-Brook, & Black, 1997).

Evaluation design should incorporate longitudinal studies of cohorts of students over several years. In addition, evaluation designs should rely less on participants' self-reported attitudes and more on observations of participants' actions within learning contexts. We need to be in classrooms to observe how teachers are incorporating technology into their instruction and what effect this is having on student learning processes. We would recommend further efforts such as those by Milken and Elliot Soloway (Trotter, 1998), to improve the format for research designs to allow for comparisons across sites.

Future evaluations should not focus on simple outcomes measures such as posttests but should also focus on complex metrics describing the learning process, such as cognitive modeling (Merrill, 1995). Research and evaluation need to demonstrate the potential of educational technology, but in a way that attends to the layers of complexity that surround the processes. We need to include a wide variety of experts and stakeholders, while we also:

1. Conduct implementation evaluations prior to outcomes evaluations, spending time necessary to determine whether an innovation has been adopted or fully implemented before trying to determine its effectiveness (Bodilly & Mitchell, 1997; Hall & Hord, 2001).
2. Focus on description of the program, treatment, or technological innovation, while developing stronger descriptions of how the technological innovation is configured (Bodilly & Mitchell, 1997; Schorr, 1997).
3. Recognize the complexity of educational technology; define technology as an innovative process linking teaching and learning outcomes rather than a product defined as improvements on standardized test scores produced from an educational black box.
4. Reduce the reliance on standardized test scores as the primary evaluation outcome, while replacing dogmatic applications of experimental designs with designs that allow us to view the complexity of technology-based reforms of teaching and learning from multiple perspectives (Bodilly & Mitchell, 1997; Schorr, 1997).
5. Adopt multifaceted approaches to evaluation that include case studies and theoretical modeling, which includes individual, organizational, technological, and teaching/learning aspects of adoption and diffusion of innovations. This means using participant observation as a form of data collection. This type of data collection is not inexpensive but provides evidence beyond self-reported data or gross outcome measures like standardized test scores (Schorr, 1997; Sherry, Lawyer-Brook, & Black, 1997).

CONCLUSION

In conclusion there are two points to be emphasized. First, evaluators of educational technology need to keep their eye on the ball. What is it we are evaluating. It is certainly not only the technology itself, but rather some interaction of technology, context, teaching, content and learning. The digital divide while extremely important aspect of any technology evaluation, may not be the only divide we are facing as evaluators. In the field of educational reform there may be a pedagogical divide between those focused on facts and skills and those focused on higher order, problem-based learning as desired outcomes. How is technology being used to foster learning content in ways previously unavailable? Content itself must be broadened to include not just facts and skills but processes such as "conducting history" (Milman & Heinecke, 2000). We must be ready to evaluate for unanticipated learning outcomes generated in the process of technology integrations. The focus on content should be central.

Second and related, evaluators of educational technology need to take into account the larger contextual issues at play in any education reform effort. We must frame our evaluations to examine the political, normative and technical aspects of technological innovations in education (Oakes, Quartz, Gong, Guiton, & Lipton, 1993). Problems of gauging the impact of technology on learning are not solely technical but are moral and political as well. We offer these recommendations toward evaluating new visions of technology for teaching and learning. In order to reach for this vision, we need to consider recent changes in evaluation practices while questioning the purposes of education. Technology may enable us to teach and learn in entirely new ways. With new and expanded definitions of student learning outcomes, we may be able to evaluate the effectiveness of technology in education in the next century.

REFERENCES

Becker, H.J. (1992). *How our best computer-using teachers differ from other teachers: Implications for realizing the potential of computers in schools.* Unpublished manuscript. Department of Education, University of California, Irvine.

Bodilly, S., & Mitchell, K.J. (1997). *Evaluating challenge grants for technology in education: A sourcebook.* Santa Monica, CA: Rand.

Hall, G.E., & Hord, S.M. (2001). *Implementing change: Patterns, principles, and pot-holes*. Boston: Allyn & Bacon.

Hawkins, J. (1996). *Technology in education: Transitions*. Paper presented at the National Education Summit, Pallisades Executive Conference Center, Pallisades, NY.

Herman, J.L. (1995). Evaluating the effects of technology in school reform. In B. Means (Ed.), *Technology and education reform: The reality behind the promise* (pp. 133-167). San Francisco: Jossey-Bass.

House, E. (1993). *Professional evaluation: Social impact and political consequences*. Newbury Park, CA: Sage.

Means, B. (1995). Introduction: Using technology to advance educational goals. In B. Means (Ed.), *Technology and educational reform: The reality behind the promise* (pp. 1-21). San Francisco: Jossey-Bass.

Means, B., & Olson, K. (1994). The link between technology and authentic learning. *Educational Leadership, 7(1), 15-18.*

Merrill, D. (1995). *Evaluation of educational technology: What do we know, and what can we know*. Santa Monica, CA: Rand Corp.

Milman, N., & Heinecke, W. (2000). Innovative integration of technology in an undergraduate history course. *Theory and Research, 28*(4), 546-565.

Nickerson, R.S. (1988). Technology in education: Possible influences on context, purposes, content, and methods. In R.S. Nickerson & P.P. Zodhiates (Eds.), *Technology in education: Looking toward 2020* (pp. 285-317). Hillsdale, NJ: Lawrence Erlbaum.

Oakes, J., Quartz, K.H., Gong, J., Guiton, G., & Lipton, M. (1993). Creating middle schools: Technical, normative, and political considerations. *The Elementary School Journal, 95*(5), 461-480.

Schorr, L. B. (1997). *Common purpose: Strengthening families and neighborhoods to rebuild America*. New York: Anchor Books.

Shadish, W.R., Cook, T.D., & Leviton, L.C. (1991). *Foundations of program evaluation*. Newbury Park, CA: Sage.

Sherry, L., Lawyer-Brook, D., & Black, L. (1997). Evaluation of the Boulder Valley Internet Project: A theory-based approach to evaluation design. *Journal of Interactive Learning Research, 8*(2), 199-233.

Trotter, A. (1998). A question of effectiveness, *Education Week*. Retrieved August 1, 2001, from the World Wide Web: *http://www.edweek.org/sreports/tc98/intro/in-n.htm*

Viadera, D. (1997). A tool for learning: *Technology counts, Education Week*. Retrieved August 1, 2001, from the World Wide Web: *http://www.edweek.org/sreports/tc/class/cl-n.htm*

Jarkko Alajääski
Jyrki Suomala

Another Perspective
on Assessing the Significance
of Information Technology
in Education

SUMMARY. The significance of information technology in education is usually assessed or evaluated on terms of some measures of effectiveness. In different school settings the effectiveness is operationalized in different ways, and in the literature various methods of determining the effectiveness have been discussed (e.g., Secretary's Conference on Educational Technology 1999). In this article, models for assessing the significance of information technology in education based on the teachers' subjective perspective are introduced. Theoretical backgrounds of the models are based on methods developed in information management science to assess the impact of information technology (IT) in industry and business. The first model is comprised of categorizing the rationales for using IT in education, the second model assesses the strategic impact of existing IT applications on one hand and of future IT applications on the other on education, and the third model assesses the roles of applications of IT in teaching. Also, the empirical findings of a small scale test of the

JARKKO ALAJÄÄSKI is Senior Lecturer, Mathematics Education, University of Turku, Department of Teacher Education in Rauma, P.O. Box 175, FIN-2610 Rauma, Finland (E-mail: jarkala@utu.fi).
JYRKI SUOMALA is Lecturer, Research Methods, Laurea Plytechnic, Espoo-Institute, Leppävaara, Vanha maantie 9, FIN-02600, Finland (E-mail: jyrki.suomala@laurea.fi).

[Haworth co-indexing entry note]: "Another Perspective on Assessing the Significance of Information Technology in Education." Alajääski, Jarkko, and Jyrki Suomala. Co-published simultaneously in *Computers in the Schools* (The Haworth Press, Inc.) Vol. 18, No. 2/3, 2001, pp. 111-125; and: *Evaluation and Assessment in Educational Information Technology* (ed: Leping Liu et al.) The Haworth Press, Inc., 2001, pp. 111-125. Single or multiple copies of this article are available for a fee from The Haworth Document Delivery Service [1-800-HAWORTH, 9:00 a.m. - 5:00 p.m. (EST). E-mail address: getinfo@haworthpressinc.com].

two latter models in the Teacher Training School in Rauma (TTSR), a primary school in Finland with about 260 pupils and 19 teachers, are introduced. *[Article copies available for a fee from The Haworth Document Delivery Service: 1-800-HAWORTH. E-mail address: <getinfo@haworthpressinc.com> Website: <http://www.HaworthPress.com> © 2001 by The Haworth Press, Inc. All rights reserved.]*

KEYWORDS. IT, information technology, educational technology, education, Finland, information management, teaching, technology effectiveness

The national information strategy of the Ministry of Education in Finland echoes the corresponding strategies in many other countries in taking the information society as an important starting point in preparing the curricula for schools. According to the strategy, the task of the school is to give every girl and boy basic skills of knowledge acquisition, maintenance, and communication needed in an information society. Teachers need not only know how to manage and communicate information in their own field(s), but they also have to be able to teach methods of obtaining and using information to enable learners to work independently. They should also have the ability to use the necessary media for open and flexible learning and be able to modify and develop material in ways that make it usable in school settings (Finnish Ministry of Education, 1995, pp. 39-41).

The Finnish school system echoes the systems of many other countries in making considerable investments in information technology (IT) to be used in education. The school is maintained by the society and is free of charge for the pupils. The school need not be profitable in the sense of normal cost-benefit calculations, but some kind of economical housekeeping must be targeted in its work. This presupposes appropriate measures to be developed and used to assess the significance of IT in education (Alajääski, 2000; Alajääski & Multisilta, 2000).

Usually the assessment of the significance of an exploited technology is done in terms of effectiveness which involves the outcomes of the use of the technology to be weighted or measured against the objectives set for the technology. In different school settings, the effectiveness is operationalized in different ways. In the 1999 Secretary's Conference on Educational Technology various methods of determining the effectiveness were discussed. A need for broadening current practices for assessing the impact of technology on education was proposed, and the role of teachers was seen to be crucial in the process. Instead of, or in addition to, standardized tests, the schools are looking for new methods of assessment (Heinecke et al., 1999; McNabb, Hawkes, & Rouk, 1999; Shakeshaft, 1999). In education, the role of teachers' conceptions of learning in general, and, especially their conceptions of the significance of IT, has been regarded as essential in the assessment process (Bruner, 1996; Li, 1999; Zhihui, 1996).

In this article, models of assessing the significance of IT in education based on the teachers' subjective perspectives are introduced. In the models, the focus is on the impact of IT rather than on its effectiveness. Theoretical backgrounds of the models are based on methods developed in information management science to assess the impact of IT in industrial and business organizations. It is assumed that teachers are able to evaluate the impact of information technology in schools. The first model includes categorizing the rationales for using IT in education, and the other two models assess the strategic impact of existing applications and of future applications of IT on education on one hand and assess the roles of IT applications in teaching on the other.

In this article, empirical findings of small-scale tests of the two latter models in the Teacher Training School in Rauma (TTSR), a primary school with about 260 pupils and 19 teachers, are introduced. The tests are a cohort study about the significance of using IT in education in a modern IT-based learning and teaching environment.

EFFECTIVENESS VERSUS IMPACT

Theoretically

In analyzing of the significance of IT in education, at least two different approaches may be taken: (a) defining the effectiveness of IT as a learning or other relevant outcome (significance by effectiveness), and (b) defining the impact of IT in education as subjectively experienced (significance by impact).

The significance by impact is the focus of this article. No exact relationship between the outcomes and the objectives is measured, but the significance of IT is based on the teachers' subjective experience relevant to the changes and/or effects caused by IT in teaching and/or learning. The impact measures the educational, economic, social, and cultural effects of the development of the information society on one hand and the application of IT and networking on the other. A variety of groups of participants (teachers, pupils, parents, etc.) may serve as the actual assessors. In this article, the teachers are regarded as the experts in the assessment process. McNabb et al. (1999, Online) consider critical issues in evaluating the effectiveness of technology and state that teachers "are the first to recognize increases in students' self-esteem and confidence" and "enhanced content area understanding" (p. 11). They see also that "some of the best results in evaluating technology come from schools recognizing and harnessing the expertise teachers have in identifying technology-induced learning outcomes" (p. 12). Because, the teachers' conceptions about the significance or usefulness of IT in education appear to affect their teaching behaviors, evaluating the significance of IT in education by the teachers' subjective experiences is important (Zhihui, 1996).

Operationally

There are many ways to operationalize the significance of IT impact in education. The teachers see educational technology benefits as including preparing students for jobs, increasing student interest in learning, increasing student access to information, and making learning an active experience. At a more grassroots level, when learning is defined as the retention of basic skills and content information, the students will show gains on standardized test scores. Outcomes must focus on the demands of the new world environment. We need students who can think critically, solve real-world problems using technology, take charge of their life-long learning process, work collaboratively, and participate as citizens in a democracy.

Heinecke et al. (1999) refer to Bodily and Mitchell (1997) in saying that in terms of outcome goals, for instance, "short term changes in student outcomes like disciplinary referrals, homework assignments completed or longer term indicators such as changes in test scores or student performances, increased college going rates, and increases in job offers to students" are sought. Outcome measures may be defined also as "higher order thinking skills, more sophisticated communication skills, research skills, and social skills" and they "might be found in participants' (teachers and students) perceptions about the implementation, quality and benefits" of the education. And: "performance indicators might include the effect of the education on community and family participation or involvement, and student and teacher retention. Declines in disciplinary referrals and special education placements may also serve as outcome measures" (Heinecke et al., 1999, Online).

Earl's Model for Categorizing the Rationales for IT

Earl (1990) introduced a theoretical model for classifying the rationales of using IT. Alajääski (1996) modified the model to be used in connection with using IT in teaching. There are three categories of rationales in the model, the first two of which (A and B) are based on technological imperative, and the third one (C), which is based on organizational imperative. In Figure 1 the modified model for teaching and learning is presented.

In category A, alongside acquisitions of IT, learning benefits are expected to occur, or even all the problems in the school are expected to be solved without any further developments in teaching practices. It often happens that the acquired equipment is left alone in the backroom to get dusty and out of date. In category B, teaching is adjusted to the needs of acquired IT and, at the same time, learning benefits are expected to follow. Typically then, keyboard skills, and the operation of various software programs are taught. The system designers' aims and information processing needs serve as starting points, and the organization must reconcile itself to the demands of IT. In category C, the aims and settings of the school are the starting points of the process in which IT is acquired in the school. Maintaining the learning benefits is attempted by invest-

FIGURE 1. Putting IT in Its Place in Education

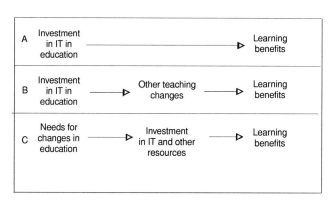

(Alajääski, 1996, 2000)

ing in various appropriate facilities including IT. The school's future visions and problem areas in teaching have to be investigated first. Subsequently, the use of IT can be regarded as one option among others. The purposes, settings, and IT together will determine the use of IT (Alajääski, 1996, 2000).

Earl's model (Earl, 1989,1990) was developed for industrial and business purposes. Earl realized that the promises of IT have too often turned out to be highly exaggerated. When promises and, accordingly, expectations have been strong (e.g., competitive advantages, economical savings, rationalizing the routines) and yet there have often been disappointments, frustration has resulted. Decision-makers have begun to doubt the possibilities offered by IT in industry and business, and, therefore, it has become more difficult to obtain financing (Clark & Salomon, 1983; Earl, 1989, 1990). There are clues that the same might be happening in schools (Ekholm, 2000).

ASSESSING THE IMPACT OF IT IN EDUCATION

In industrial and business organizations assessing the impact of IT is regarded as essential because that assessment (a) increases understanding of using IT, (b) determines the significance of IT to the organization, and (c) analyzes the best way to manage IT (Earl, 1989). The same rationales also apply to assessing the impact of using IT in education.

The IT Strategic Grid

Earl (1989) refers to a method introduced by McFarlan, McKenney, and Pyburn (1983), in which subjective assessments of the strategic impact of existing and future IT applications serve as a basis for classifying organizations into an IT strategic grid. The significance of both current and future applications are assessed in a low/high scale by answering two questions: What is the strategic impact of existing applications? What is the strategic impact of future applications? Therefore, organizations fall into an IT strategic grid with four possible categories, for which McFarlan uses the following metaphors: support, factory, turnaround, and strategic. As examples of typical industrial/business organizations in the different categories, Earl (1989) gives the following: a cement company (support), a steelworks (factory), a retailer (turnaround), and a credit card company (strategic). However, as Earl (1989) stated, the organization's position in the IT-strategic grid is dynamic, and the analysis should be renewed periodically.

Alajääski (2000) used McFarlan's model to assess (a) the strategic impact of existing IT applications in teaching and (b) the strategic impact of future IT applications in teaching. The response scale is in both dimensions (existing and future): 1 = very low, 2 = low, 3 = medium, 4 = high, 5 = very high (Alajääski, 2000; Alajääski & Multisilta, 2000). Because of the analysis, a school falls into one of four categories of the IT strategic grid (Figure 2).

In support schools, the strategic impact of existing and future applications is regarded as low. In factory schools, the strategic impact of existing applications is high but that of future applications is low. The school is in a state of equilibrium, and it is believed to carry on with its teaching unchanged so that no new applications are needed. In turnaround schools, the strategic impact of existing applications is low but the expectations set on future applications are high. The schools in this category have moved or are moving to a new IT atmosphere. In strategic schools, the strategic impacts of both existing and future applications are assessed to be high. The schools in this category are constantly watching and predicting the future, and they have a novelty-seeking and creative IT atmosphere (Earl, 1989; Ruohonen, 1988). Also, a school's position in the IT strategic grid of teaching is dynamic. Therefore, the school's position may change both within a category and from one category to another. Thus, the analysis must be renewed periodically. The

FIGURE 2. The IT Strategic Grid of School Teaching

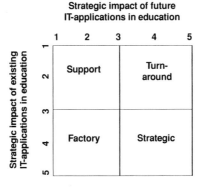

(Alajääski, 1996, 2000)

analysis may be executed by school subjects (native language, mathematics, history, etc.) and/or by IT's application fields (word processing, spreadsheet, World Wide Web).

The d^4 Schemas and d^4 Profiles

Another method for assessing the impact of using IT in an organization, the d^4–method, is based on classifying the organization subjectively into one of four optional categories, depending upon the role of IT applications in the organization:

1. IT is the means of delivering goods and services (delivery).
2. Business strategies increasingly depend on IT for their implementation (dependent).
3. IT potentially provides new strategic opportunities, but is not necessary (drive).
4. IT has no strategic impact (delayed) (Earl, 1989).

Alajääski (2000) used this analysis for education as follows: aptness-of-description assessments are made for all four categories by responding to the question, How well do you agree with the following statements describing the role of IT in teaching in your school?

1. IT is the means of teaching (delivery, d^1)
2. Teaching increasingly depends on IT (dependent, d^2)
3. IT provides new alternatives for teaching (drive, d^3)
4. IT has no strategic impact on teaching (delayed, d^4)

The response scale is 1 to 5 (totally disagree, disagree, neutral, agree, totally agree).

The d^4 schema of the school is defined by an ordered list of the categories according to the descending order of the aptness-of-description assessment means/medians (e.g., $d^1d^2d^3d^4$). The d^4 schema describes the type of school in respect to the significance of IT in teaching. In the d^4 schema of schools with a low significance of IT in teaching (type LIT school), the categories d^3 and d^4 are ahead of the categories d^1 and d^2 (e.g., $d^3d^4d^2d^1$), and in the schema of the schools with a higher significance of IT in teaching (type HIT school), d^1 and d^2 are ahead of d^3 and d^4 (e.g., $d^1d^2d^3d^4$). There are, of course, mixed types, as well. When the scales on both axes are interpreted as interval scales, the regression can be specified.

The d^4 profile of a school is defined by a line diagram sketched by the aptness-of-description assessment means and/or medians for the categories $d1$, $d2$, $d3$, and $d4$. The analysis may be executed also by school subjects (native language, mathematics, etc.) and/or by IT's application fields (word processing, spreadsheets, etc.). Figure 3 is a sample d^4 profile with a d^4 regression line.

The sample d^4 profile in Figure 3 is $d3d4d2d1$ and the regression line increases from left to right. Thus, the profile is from a LIT-type school. In HIT-type schools respectively, the regression line decreases.

The d^4 schema and d^4 profile of a school are dynamic. Therefore, the development of a school's IT plan can be followed by defining the d^4 schema and d^4 profile of the school periodically.

THE DEVELOPMENT OF THE IMPACT OF COMPUTER TEACHING IN A MODERN IT-BASED TEACHING ENVIRONMENT

Alajääski (2000) used the IT strategic grid and the d^4 schemas and d^4 profiles to study the significance (by impact) of IT in a school in which a major change of the teaching/learning environment was completed from a traditional to a modern one with lots of information and communication technology.

The Research Problem

The research problem was the following: What is the significance of using different IT applications in education in a school with a modern IT-based teaching environment as assessed by the teachers?

METHOD

Two of the models introduced were tested in small scale in the Teacher Training School in Rauma (TTSR, University of Turku, Department of Education), a primary school with about 260 pupils in grades one through six, and 19 teachers. The pretest was executed in February 1997. In July 1997 the school received a new school building with a modern IT-rich teaching environment. The posttest was executed in March 1999.

FIGURE 3. A Sample d⁴ Profile with the Regression Line

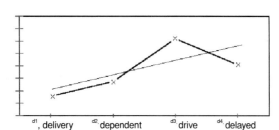

$$^{d1},\text{ delivery} \quad ^{d2}\text{ dependent} \quad ^{d3}\text{ drive} \quad ^{d4}\text{ delayed}$$

The development of the significance of the IT applications in education is measured by the IT strategic grid and the d^4 method.

RESULTS

The development of the positions of different application fields in the school's IT strategic grid. In Figure 4 the positions by application field of TTSR in the IT strategic grid are shown for 1997 and 1999.

In both tests, e-mail, World Wide Web, and word processing are in the strategic category. From the pretest to the posttest, the only significant category shifts were for games (from support to turnaround), graphics (from strategic to turnaround), spreadsheets (from turnaround to support), and databases (from turnaround to support). The mean for the first two category shifts increased relationally in impact, while the mean for the latter two shifts decreased correspondingly. In whole, the roles of the application programs, especially spreadsheets and databases, remained marginal in the school researched. The role did not become stronger even after moving into an IT-rich teaching environment. Explanations for this may be twofold: On the one hand, the teachers may not have experienced any need for using the application programs, especially spreadsheets and databases, while the more "modern" and perhaps more entertaining applications of e-mail, Internet, and games may have been considered more important. This being the case, the possibility for serious work with IT in schools would be exceeded and overtaken by the more entertaining aspects of IT and the students would not see the point of IT. On the other hand, the knowledge and mastery of the marginally used application programs may have been too narrow and

FIGURE 4. Positions of Different Application Fields in the TTSR School's IT Strategic Grid

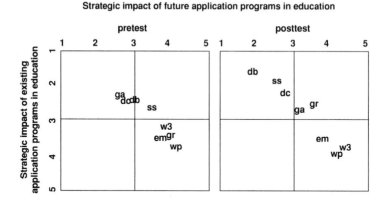

Strategic impact of future application programs in education

db = databases, dc = data communication, em = e-mail, ga = games, gr = graphics, ss = spreadsheets, w3 = World Wide Web, wp = word processing
(Alajääski & Vasama, 2000)

thus the capabilities of these programs were not understood by the primary school teachers (Dybdahl, Sutinen, & Tarhio, 1998).

There is a need for extensive training for both pre-service and in-service teachers. This should be taken into consideration in preparing information strategies for the primary schools. However, in the information strategy of the Ministry of Education for 2000-2004 (Information Strategy of Education and Research, 1999), the role of application programs is not very promising. In the strategy, three levels of skills are to be taught to teachers: (a) basic skills necessary for all teachers; (b) information and communication technology skills to be taught to 50% of the teachers; and (c) specific skills, which should be mastered by 10% of the teachers. At the first level, from the application programs, only word processing is included. At the second level, a general introduction to the spreadsheets and databases is included. At the third level, introduction to programming is also included (Alajääski & Vasama, 2000).

We believe that it is important for students to learn IT applications. A good option for doing so in primary schools would be by exploiting the application programs discussed. Also by the pedagogical considerations, the application programs are of great value (Makrakis, 1988; Meisalo & Tella, 1987).

The development of the d^4 schemas and d^4 profiles. The role of applications (existing and future) is described by the d^4 profiles. In Figures 5 and 6 the d^4 profiles of TTSR in pre- and posttest are shown.

The means and medians of the assessments are higher for future applications than for existing applications for delivery and dependent roles. For drive and delayed roles the assessments are higher for existing applications than for future applications. In the pretest, the regression coefficients are 0.55 (existing applications) and −0.08 (future applications). Similarly, in the posttest, the coefficients are 0.70 (existing applications) and 0.13 (future applications).

For existing applications, the d^4 schema of TTSR is d4d3d2d1 both in the pre- and posttest (Figure 4). Therefore, for existing applications both in the pre- and posttest, TTSR is a type LIT school. For future applications, the d^4 schema of TTSR is d3d2d1d4 in the pretest and d3d2d4d1 (or d3d2d1d4) in the posttest (Figure 5). For future applications then, both in the pre- and posttest, the type of TTSR is mixed, with a minor shift toward the type LIT from the pretest to the posttest.

CONCLUSION

Empirically, results showed no major significance for using IT in teaching in the TTSR, despite using a modern IT-rich teaching environment. This reiterates the importance of learning methods for using technology rather than learning the sophisticated capabilities of the technology itself (Leidner & Järvenpää, 1993). High investments for IT

FIGURE 5. Median and Mean d^4 Profiles for Existing Applications in TTSR

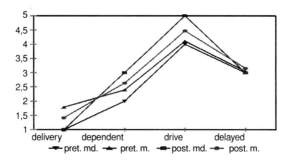

pret. = pretest, post. = posttest
(Alajääski, 2000)

FIGURE 6. Median and Mean d⁴ Profiles for Future Applications in TTSR

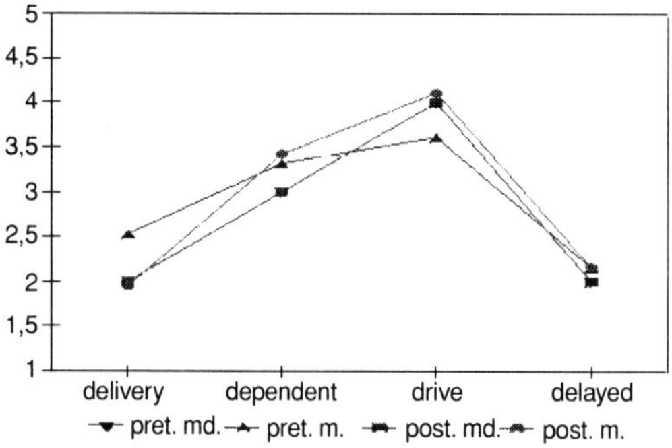

delivery   dependent   drive   delayed

▼ pret. md. ▲ pret. m. ➤ post. md. ✳ post. m.

pret. = pretest, post. = posttest
(Alajääski, 2000)

do not automatically increase the significance of IT in teaching. More research is needed to find appropriate ways to use the acquired machinery.

DISCUSSION

The main purpose of the study was to try to clarify the possibility for
assessing the significance of IT in primary school education using modifications of assessment methods used previously in information management science. Because the Finnish state and municipal authorities
are investing much in computers in the schools, it is important to know
how significant the teachers are experiencing the effects of these investments in their teaching. The developed models seem to work satisfacto-
rily. However, additional research is needed concerning the usability of
the models at different levels (primary, secondary, etc.) of education.

REFERENCES

Alajääski, J. (1996). Myths behind the computer teaching. In T. Laes (Ed.), *Images of academic teacher education* (Publication B:53, pp. 196-225). Rauma, Finland: University of Turku, Department of Teacher Education.
Alajääski, J. (2000). *The development of the mastery of computer teaching: Related topics and the impact of computer teaching in an IT-based teaching environment as*

assessed by the teachers in the teacher training school in Rauma (Publication No. 287). Tampere, Finland: Tampere University of Technology. (In Finnish, with English summary).

Alajääski, J., & Multisilta, J. (2000). Theoretical models for evaluating the significance of information technology in schools. In D. A. Willis, J. D. Price, & J. Willis (Eds.), *Proceedings of SITE 2000 Conference: 11th international conference of the Society for Information Technology & Teacher Education* (pp. 2402-2407), February 8-12, 2000. Charlottesville, VA: Association for the Advancement of Computing in Education (AACE).

Alajääski, J., & Vasama, J. (2000, August 12-15). Doing IT in primary education. In L. Svensson, U. Snis, C. Sorensen, H. Fägerlind, T. Lindroth, M. Magnusson, & C. Österlund (Eds.), *Proceedings of IRIS23 conference* (pp. 751-760). Uddevalla, Sweden: Laboratorium for Interaction Technology, University of Trollhättan. [Online]. Available: <http://iris23.htu.se/proceedings>.

Bodily, S., & Mitchell, K. (1997). *Evaluating challenge grants for technology in education: A sourcebook.* Santa Monica, CA: Rand.

Bruner, J. (1996). *Culture and education.* Cambridge, MA: Harvard University Press.

Clark, R. E., & Salomon, G. (1983). Media in teaching. In M. E. Wittrock (Ed.), *Handbook of research on teaching* (3rd ed., pp. 464-478). New York: Macmillan.

Dybdahl, A., Sutinen, E., & Tarhio, J. (1998, May 11-12). Excel as a teaching tool. In J. Multisilta & J. Niemi (Eds.), *Proceedings of LeTTeT and MaTILDA '98 joint conference* (pp. 35-40). Pori, Finland: Tampere University of Technology, Department of Information Technology, Pori School of Technology and Economics.

Earl, M. J. (1989). *Management strategies for information technology.* New York: Prentice Hall.

Earl, M. J. (1990). *Putting IT in its place: A polemic for the nineties* (Oxford Institute of Information Management, Research, and Discussion Papers, RPD90/2). Oxford, England: Templeton College, University of Oxford.

Ekholm, E. (2000, September 21). Tutkimus Ruotsissa: *Tietokoneopetus laimenemassa kouluissa.* (Research in Sweden: Computer teaching is weakening in the schools.) *ITviikko* (The Finnish weekly magazine ITweek), p. 11.

Finnish Ministry of Education, (1995). *Training and research in the information society: A national strategy (knowledge strategy of education and research).* Helsinki: The State Printing Press. Helsinki: Art-Print Painotalo. [Online]. Available: <http://www.minedu.fi/infostrategy.html>.

Finnish Ministry of Education (1999). *Information strategy of education and research.* [Online]. Available: <http://www.minedu.fi/toim/koul_tutk_tietostrat/> (In Finnish).

Heinecke, W. F., Blasi, L., Milman, N., & Washington, L. (1999, July 12-13). New directions in the evaluation of the effectiveness of educational technology. The Secretary's Conference on Educational Technology 1999. Washington, D.C. [Online]. Available: <http://www.ed.gov/Technology/TechConf/1999/whitepapers/paper8.html>.

Leidner, D. E., & Järvenpää, S. (1993). The information age confronts education: Case studies on electronic classrooms. *Information Systems Research, 4*(1), 24-54.

Li, Q. (1999). Teachers' belief and gender differences in mathematics: A review. *Educational Research, 41*(1), 63-76.

Makrakis, V. (1988). *Computers in school education. The cases of Sweden and Greece* (Studies in Comparative and International Education, No. 11). Stockholm, Sweden: Institute of International Education, University of Stockholm.

McFarlan, F. W., McKenney, J. L., & Pyburn, P. (1983, January-February). The information archipelago–Plotting a course, *Harvard Business Review*, p. 11.

McNabb, M., Hawkes, M., & Rouk, U. (1999, July 12-13). *The summary of the conference: Critical issues in evaluating the effectiveness of technology.* The Secretary's Conference on Educational Technology 1999. Washington, D.C. [Online]. Available: <http://www.ed.gov/Technology/TechConf/1999/confsum.pdf>.

Meisalo, V., & Tella, S. (1987). *Information technology in the teacher's world. Basics of using IT in teaching and didactics.* Helsinki, Finland: Otava (In Finnish).

Ruohonen, M. (1988). Education for information management. In T. Leino (Ed.), *Controlled information technology: A cornerstone of success.* Turku, Finland: The Club for Business Management Science (In Finnish).

Secretary's Conference on Educational Technology. (1999, July 12-13). *Evaluating the effectiveness of technology.* Washington, D.C. [Online]. Available: <http://www.ed.gov/Technology/TechConf/1999>.

Shakeshaft, C. (1999, July 12-13). Measurement issues with instructional and home learning technologies. The Secretary's Conference on Educational Technology 1999. Washington, D.C. [Online]. Available: <http://www.ed.gov/Technology/TechConf/1999/whitepapers/paper9.html>.

Zhihui, F. (1996). A review of research on teacher beliefs and practices. *Educational Research, 38*(1), 47-65.

Jessica Kahn
Robert Pred

Evaluation of a Faculty Development Model for Technology Use in Higher Education for Late Adopters

SUMMARY. The design, implementation, and evaluation of the second phase in a two-year faculty development initiative by the Southeastern Pennsylvania Consortium on Higher Education (SEPCHE) is presented. The initiative addressed instruction of SEPCHE faculty in the use of technology in college teaching. Six workshops were conducted for faculty in specific disciplines to create working relationships among SEPCHE faculty, establish faculty as mutually supportive resources, to decrease attitudinal and behavioral barriers toward adoption of new technology by "late adopters," and to improve teaching effectiveness through the application of new technology. Faculty from SEPCHE, rather than outside consultants, served as expert presenters. Workshops included mastery of software and adaptation for specific disciplines, Internet search strate-

JESSICA KAHN is Associate Professor, Department of Technology and Education, Chestnut Hill College, 9601 Germantown Avenue, Philadelphia, PA 19118 (E-mail: jkahn@chc.edu).
ROBERT PRED is Assistant Professor, Department of Technology and Education, Chestnut Hill College, 9601 Germantown Avenue, Philadelphia, PA 19118 (E-mail: robpred@chc.edu).
The research was sponsored in part by a grant obtained by the Southeastern Pennsylvania Consortium for Higher Education (SEPCHE) from the Barra Foundation.

[Haworth co-indexing entry note]: "Evaluation of a Faculty Development Model for Technology Use in Higher Education for Late Adopters." Kahn, Jessica, and Robert Pred. Co-published simultaneously in *Computers in the Schools* (The Haworth Press, Inc.) Vol. 18, No. 4, 2001, pp. 127-150; and: *Evaluation and Assessment in Educational Information Technology* (ed: Leping Liu et al.) The Haworth Press, Inc., 2001, pp. 127-150. Single or multiple copies of this article are available for a fee from The Haworth Document Delivery Service [1-800-HAWORTH, 9:00 a.m. - 5:00 p.m. (EST). E-mail address: getinfo@haworthpressinc.com].

127

gies and usable sites, Web site design, and electronically mediated course delivery. Faculty indicated satisfaction with the workshops in exit interviews, and attitudinal and usage changes are documented by evaluation four months later. *[Article copies available for a fee from The Haworth Document Delivery Service: 1-800-HAWORTH. E-mail address: <getinfo@haworthpressinc.com> Website: <http://www.HaworthPress.com> © 2001 by The Haworth Press, Inc. All rights reserved.]*

KEYWORDS. Assessment, computer-technology, faculty development, higher education, internet information, measurement instruments, technology use

This paper reports the design, implementation, and evaluation of the second phase of a two-year faculty development initiative undertaken by the Southeastern Pennsylvania Consortium on Higher Education (SEPCHE). SEPCHE consists of eight small, liberal arts colleges located in and around the Philadelphia area. The initiative addressed the need for faculty development about using technology in college teaching. A needs assessment survey of the eight college faculties revealed that most faculty were using technology applications to do their own work, but had little knowledge or expertise about technology use in their college courses. Faculty members reported that use of the Internet, both as a delivery system and also for content-specific resources, was an area with which they were largely unfamiliar. Based upon the findings of the needs assessment, the SEPCHE faculty development committee obtained funding from a private foundation to fund a pair of simultaneous two-day workshops for faculty in the use of technology in their specific academic disciplines. These workshops were designed to meet the needs identified in the needs assessment study; namely, the use of Internet and software resources in college teaching.

OVERVIEW OF FACULTY DEVELOPMENT INITIATIVE

The first faculty development workshops for SEPCHE took place in January 1999, and the evaluation of these pilot workshops has been reported elsewhere (Kahn & Pred, 2000a). These workshops, conducted for education faculty and for science faculty, were conducted separately at two SEPCHE institutions. The focus of this report is a more ambitious second round of six faculty development workshops, conducted in January 2000. These were held simultaneously at six separate SEPCHE college locations for the following disciplines: (a) language and literature; (b) nursing and allied health sciences; (c) business, mathematics, and economics; (d) philosophy, history, and theology; (e) psychology and sociology; and (f) art and art history. Each workshop was organized by a member of the SEPCHE faculty development committee, under the direction of the project coordinator. The goals and objectives of the faculty development workshops included the following: (a) to create working relationships among SEPCHE faculty, (b) to establish faculty as mutually supportive resources, (c) to decrease attitudinal and behavioral barriers toward adoption of new technology, and (d) to help faculty improve their college teaching by effectively applying new technology.

The structure of the workshops was derived in part from research on faculty development in the use of technology in education. In reviewing the literature on faculty development, a number of recommendations were identified: that faculty development should be conducted in a relaxed, comfortable, and individualized environment (Utay & Utay, 1998); that time be provided for teachers to discuss and consider what they have learned (Utay & Utay, 1998); and that training be practical and applicable to the instructors' and participants' respective academic disciplines (Noon, 1998). The workshops took place during two full days of winter break, with the hope that faculty would be better able to concentrate.

Research demonstrates that faculty-to-faculty mentoring can serve as a valuable tool in technology education (Kress & Hafner, 1996). Therefore, the two-day workshops were structured to include opportunities for collaboration among participants in related academic disciplines from the eight participating colleges (e.g., all the foreign language professors participated in a workshop on one campus, while all the allied health and nursing professors participated in a workshop at another location). Participating faculty were therefore able to share common concerns and vocabulary, and be more likely to participate in the transfer of ideas because of shared backgrounds (Rogers, 1995; Valente, 1996).

Using Rogers' (1995) theory of diffusion of innovations, the SEPCHE faculty targeted for participation could be described as "late adopters." Late adopters may interact with their peers about technology, but rarely are found in leadership positions with respect to technological innovation. Individuals who are late adopters of new technology are somewhat more skeptical of the benefits of new technology relative to early adopters. Late adopters approach innovation cautiously, and may not adopt new technologies until they have already been adopted by the majority. According to Jacobsen (1997), late adopters will not adopt while they feel uncertain and will wait until they feel safe. Workshop experiences were designed that directly related to subject matter, since it was anticipated that these participants would value practicality (Littlejohn & Sclater, 1998). Following the recommendations of Jacobsen (1997) about encouraging early adopters to share their expertise, and the strategies suggested by Brace and Roberts (1996) for faculty development, we chose as presenters volunteers from among the SEPCHE faculty, those who could demonstrate their technology usages for their peers. In this manner, the workshops were designed to address best practices in faculty development, tailored specifically for each respective academic discipline. For those planning to conduct future workshops, a detailed timeline for the project and explanations of the decision-making process that informed it are available from the authors (Kahn & Pred, 2000b).

A DESCRIPTION OF THE FACULTY DEVELOPMENT WORKSHOPS IN TECHNOLOGY

The challenges for the committee organizing the project included, making the connection between how to operate the technology and what to do with it in a course, addressing groups of faculty with widely varying levels of technological expertise, and creating opportunities for collaboration and discussion. In most workshops these challenges were successfully met simultaneously. There was straightforward instruction in how to use particular pieces of software, coupled with demonstrations of the software's value in a particular course. Where expertise varied, faculty members explored the use of technology at the level where they were comfortable. For example, the more technologically competent pursued the construction of distance courses, or the creation of WebQuests, while the less adventurous or experienced examined Web sites and considered how they might use those resources in their courses. The two days were divided into large group presentations, and small group work and discussion time, thus enabling collaboration and exchange of information at several levels.

The faculty facilitators provided technological support and information, circulating through the lab and assisting during hands-on sessions. It had been their responsibility to identify workshop presenters and design the agenda for the workshops. Additional faculty members were recruited to demonstrate some technology usage with which they were familiar. Each workshop focused on demonstrating uses of technology in the teaching of the specific content area. But even though the disciplines were varied, some commonalities existed among workshop topic choices.

Workshops included: (a) mastery of software application features and adaptation for specific disciplines, (b) Internet search strategies and usable sites, (c) Web site design, and (d) electronically mediated course delivery. Specific applications (e.g., PowerPoint, PhotoShop, Excel, SPSS) were taught in several of the workshops, each in terms of its usefulness for teaching the content area. Faculty members appreciated the opportunities for experiential learning with regard to software applications and the adaptation of each software application to their respective disciplines. Unlike other how-to sessions previously attended by these faculty members, these sessions made direct connections between the operation and management of the software and its instructional value. The use of search engines and the identification of Web sites for use in scholarship activity and instruction of college courses were also addressed in most of the workshops. Lists of sites for specific disciplines were distributed, and faculty members considered how they might incorporate them into their courses.

The creation of Web pages in HTML as well as with authoring tools was presented in several workshops. Faculty members learned how to create their own Web pages where they could list "hot links" to content area Web sites for their students. A number of participants reportedly became particularly interested in becoming more familiar with methods for creating distance components of college courses, or entire courses online. The use of Web-based course tools (e.g., Blackboard.com and e-College) was explored in several of the workshops. Demonstrations of coursework were delivered over the Web, either as part of a course, or as an entire course, and many took the opportunity to begin to create electronically mediated courses.

All presentations were made by faculty members from the participating colleges, rather than by outside experts or professional consultants. Many of the SEPCHE experts could be considered "early adopters" (Rogers, 1995) who were self-taught in the area of technological expertise they were presenting. Unlike professional consultants, these technology users had credibility because they were faculty members who were knowledgeable both about the content area being presented and the demands of college teaching, and who worked within familiar, shared time constraints and equipment limitations. It was anticipated that this familiarity would help to create a relaxed, informal atmosphere in the workshops.

Although the workshops were developed separately and differed substantially by discipline, the workshop days were structured similarly. Here are excerpts from sample agendas for two academic disciplines, Technology in Art Education, and Nursing and Allied Health:

> *Technology in Art Education:* Demonstration of a personal Web site that promotes the artist's work and links to specific gallery Web sites. Explanation of the Yahoo search engine to enhance courses, by linking students to specific museums and galleries. Demonstration of Adobe Photoshop to generate and manipulate graphics on screen for use on course Web sites and also in art instruction. Presentation of HTML language and Web site design. Introduction to ClarisWorks HomePage Web site design. Hands-on Web site design.

> *Nursing and Allied Health:* Demonstration of PowerPoint and its use in the Health Information Management Curriculum and a hands-on session on PowerPoint. Presentation on the use of Excel in the Nursing Curriculum with a sample problem. Presentations on "The Use of the Internet for Patient Information" and "The Use of the Internet for Student/Faculty Research," accompanied by instruction in the use of search engines. Presentation on the National Scalable Cluster Project. Introduction to e-College and Blackboard.com.

From these sample agendas, the following commonalities can be identified: (a) the mastery of the features of an application and its adaptation for specific disciplines, (b) search strategies on the Internet and identification of usable sites, (c) Web site design, and (d) electronically mediated course delivery.

METHOD

Assessing the Impact/Effectiveness of the Faculty Development Model

The evaluation phase was designed to ascertain participants' perceived value of the workshops, including the collaborative format, and the use of in-house faculty experts as workshop facilitators. The format for the assessment closely followed that used in evaluating the two pilot workshops conducted the previous year (Kahn & Pred, 2000a). The assessment included both qualitative and quantitative evaluations. For each workshop, one participant was designated to collect qualitative data, including both behavioral observations and comments. At the end of each day, an evaluation instrument was administered to all participants (reproduced in Appendix A).

Another goal of the evaluation was to ascertain whether faculty members integrated technology into their courses as a result of the workshops. A follow-up evaluation was conducted via e-mail to all participants several months after the workshops. In the follow-up survey, the results of which are presented in a following section, participants were queried about their experiences to establish the longer term behavioral and attitudinal impact of the workshops.

Development of Evaluation Instrument

An earlier version of the evaluation instrument had been used in the two SEPCHE pilot faculty development workshops, one for science faculty and the other for education faculty (Kahn & Pred, 2000a). The original instrument consisted of 10 statements designed to assess the workshop participants' perceived benefits of the technology workshops. The participants were asked to express their level of agreement with each statement using a five-point, Likert-type response scale, in which 5 equals Strongly Agree and 1 equals Strongly Disagree. A separate evaluation form was designed for each day of the workshop. The first seven questions were identical on both forms, while items 8 through 10 were modified slightly for the second day. The instrument was administered at the beginning and at the conclusion of the workshop to assess the possible attitudinal and/or cognitive impact of the workshops on participants. The evaluation primarily addressed two issues: (a) whether the participants' level of comfort with new technology/software had been increased by the workshop experience and (b) the degree of likelihood that participants would apply what they learned about technology/software in their college classrooms after their participation.

The current version of the evaluation instrument has been modified slightly, to divide item six into two parts and is reproduced in its entirety in Appendix A. To illustrate item content of the evaluation instrument, participants were queried about the quality of instruction (e.g., "The instructors demonstrated a comprehensive knowledge of the workshop material" and "The material was covered at just the right pace"), and the perceived benefits of the workshop (e.g., "My knowledge level of the potential uses of this technology/software increased as a result of to-day's session."). They were also queried about their level of comfort with the new technology (e.g., "As a result of today's session, my comfort level with the use of this technology/software has increased."). Following administration of the instrument, reliability analyses were conducted, the results of which follow.

Administration of the Evaluation Instrument

Although each workshop was geared toward a specific discipline, such as social sciences, the overall evaluation plan was not to evaluate workshop outcomes by discipline. As the intent of the initiative was to conduct successful workshops in all subject areas, and since responses across workshop populations were remarkably similar, all scores were analyzed in aggregate. Evaluation forms were distributed by a desig-nated group evaluator, a person other than the workshop facilitator, to reduce the possibility of social desirability response set and demand characteristic effects. Another method used to reduce social desirability set was to assure participants that their individual responses would be confidential and that workshop facilitators would receive only aggre-gate, rather than individual, feedback.

RESULTS

Assessment of Evaluation Instrument Reliability

In order to measure the potential impact (i.e., attitudinal/behavioral change) resulting from the workshop experience, the evaluation in-strument must first be shown to be reliable. An acceptable level of reli-ability for survey research is generally considered to be above .70. Instruments used in clinical psychology require reliability levels of ap-proximately .85 or higher; whereas in experimental research, satisfac-tory levels of reliability can be lower (Rosenthal & Rosnow, 1991). To enhance reliability, responses to items one through seven were summed to form a composite scale measure (excluding item Q6a, new for 2000 workshops). Using SPSS for Windows (Release 10.0.5, 1999) reliability coefficients were computed using a measure of internal-consistency reliability, conventionally known as Cronbach's alpha coefficient (Rosenthal & Rosnow, 1991).

The seven-item scale for day one was found to have a Cronbach *alpha* coefficient of .82 ($n = 103$), while for day two it was found to have an *alpha* of .86 ($n = 101$). Sample sizes for each analysis varied due to the deletion of cases with missing values. The results suggest that the evaluation instruments have a high reliability. Therefore, it was concluded that the mean composite scores from day one could then be compared in valid fashion with the mean composite scores from day two. Details of the inferential statistical analyses follow, along with a discussion of the descriptive statistical findings.

Quantitative Analyses

Sample: Facilities for the six workshops were designed to accommodate approximately 150 participants (twenty-five at each workshop), consisting of college faculty from the eight participating SEPCHE institutions. Some participants were able to attend only one of the two workshop days, while others were able to stay for only partial sessions. As a result, the number of participants who completed days one and two of the workshop, and who returned pre- and post-measure evaluation forms for both workshops was lowered to 114. The actual usable sample size was further reduced, due to the presence of incomplete (e.g., skipped or omitted) survey items, to a range from 93 to 98. While there are methodological options for how missing values can be statistically managed to minimize loss of data, we selected a more conservative approach by not replacing missing values with overall mean item scores which tends to inflate the sample size. Therefore, any case with missing values on a given item was eliminated from statistical analysis.

Appendix B presents descriptive statistics aggregated across the workshops, item by item, for each day. It is clear from the findings that the workshops were positively received. The mean evaluation score was 4 or higher (5 = most favorable rating), indicating agreement or strong agreement with positive statements about the workshops. For 13 of the 20 statements (i.e., 10 per day over two days) about the quality of the workshops, the median score was 5 (i.e., Strongly Agree), which suggests highly favorable evaluations of the workshops. Descriptive statistics for individual items follow.

Computing Composite Scale Total Scores (Items One to Seven)

As described above, evaluation items Q1 through Q7 were repeated on days one and two to assess possible changes in respondents' perceptions. As can be seen in Appendix B, the mean ratings for all seven items viewed individually (Q1 through Q7) increased on the second day, showing a consistent upward trend. This supports the interpretation that knowledge level, comfort level, and perceived benefits all increased as a result of participation in the two-day workshops. While there may be some minor fluctuations in average ratings among the eight participating colleges, when combined there is a statistically significant increase in the average ratings from day one to day two. However, a comparison of outcomes based on single items can be strengthened (i.e., statistically more powerful and reliable), by constructing a composite score. Therefore, to increase the reliability of assessment, the seven items were summed to compute separate scale scores for both days, with unit weighting.

Assessing Short-Term Impact of Workshops

The mean composite scores for each workshop day were compared using a repeated measures design using the t-test for dependent samples. This test is appropriate for the present research design that consisted of the administration of pre- and post-measure tests separated by an intervention (i.e., the faculty development workshops in technology). The t-test for dependent samples is generally considered to be statistically more powerful than the t-test for independent samples (Kirk, 1995). The observed increase in composite scale scores from day one (mean = 30.55) to day two (mean = 31.72) was found to be statistically significant (t-test for paired sample means = 1.77, $df = 92$, $p < .05$, 1-tailed p-value = .0405).

The statistically significant comparison between pre- and post-evaluation measures suggests that the increases can be attributed to the successful components of the workshops. The change in mean composite scale totals suggests that over the course of the two-day workshops, participants reportedly experienced statistically significant increases in: (a) overall comfort level with software technology, (b) overall knowledge level for utilizing software/technology, and (c) perceived benefits of incorporating technology in their classrooms. Responses to several specific statements from the evaluation instrument are reported in detail below, as they are indicative of the success of the project. Descriptive statistics for both individual items and the composite scale total are shown in Appendix B.

"The instructors demonstrated a comprehensive knowledge of the workshop material" (Q3): Over 90% of respondents agreed (ratings 4 and 5 combined) with this statement on both day one (93%; mean = 4.55) and day two (95%; mean = 4.61). This finding is particularly interesting, in light of the fact that "experts" were recruited from among the SEPCHE college faculty, rather than hiring outside consultants. Participants' impressions of their workshop instructors' knowledge levels actually increased slightly over the two days (day one, 64% strongly agreed; day two, 70% strongly agreed).

"The material was covered at just the right pace" (Q4): Ratings suggest that participants' comfort level with the pacing of the workshops also increased by the conclusion of the workshops (day one, 46%; day two, 56%). The reason for the increase seems to be that the workshops provided ample hands-on time and support to faculty.

"My knowledge level of the potential uses of this technology/software increased as a result of today's session" (Q5): On day one, 49% strongly agreed that their knowledge increased; whereas, after day two, 57% strongly agreed that their knowledge level had increased. The upward trend in scores for this item supports the overall conclusion that participants perceived an increase in their own knowledge level.

"Before today's session, my comfort level with the use of this technology/software was somewhat low" (Q6a): The numbers of participants agreeing with this statement decreased from 23% on day one, to 19% after day two.

"As a result of today's session, my comfort level with the use of this technology/software has increased" (Q6b): Item Q6b extracts information similar to that obtained in Q6a, but from another perspective. Phrased in the "affirmative," Q6b queries whether participants perceived an *increase* in their own comfort level. Note that in contrast, Q6a queries whether their comfort level is *somewhat low*. After day one, 76% agreed that their comfort levels had increased. After day two, 88% agreed that their comfort level had increased. In other words, while participants indicated low levels of comfort with technology before the workshops (see responses to Q6a), they described their level of comfort with technology as having increased as a result of the workshop (see Q6b). This perception of comfort is critically important, because it suggests that faculty may continue to be independent learners about technology, enthused and receptive, rather than uncomfortable and dismissive.

"I clearly see some benefits to incorporating aspects of this technology in my courses" (Q7): At the conclusion of day one, 57% strongly agreed to clearly seeing benefits to incorporating aspects of the technology in their courses. This suggests that while those who "volunteered" to participate may already have been predisposed toward using technology, those attending were impressed with the material presented and its potential value for the classroom. At the conclusion of day two, an even greater number, 62%, strongly agreed that they could clearly see the benefits of this technology.

Analysis of Non-Repeated Items Excluded from Composite Measure

While the first seven questions, which addressed the participants' level of comfort with technology and their appraisal of the workshops, were administered on both days one and two, the remaining three questions were unique for each day, and therefore omitted from the composite scale measure. These items queried participants about their future plans to use technology in their courses.

"Working in groups to learn new software with professors from other institutions was valuable" (Q9; day two): The social aspect of working with one's peers in a supportive environment was highly valued by participants. Eighty-seven percent (87%) agreed that the collaborative nature of this experience contributed to the perceived value of the two-day workshops. (See the qualitative analysis section for specific comments on this topic).

"I clearly see benefits to incorporating the use of the World Wide Web in developing my courses" (Q10; day one): Almost all of the participants agreed (88%) to clearly seeing benefits of incorporating the WWW in the development of their courses. The meaning of this item differed for individual participants. Some respondents were possibly describing the value of content-specific Web sites as instructional resources (e.g., foreign language sites or virtual museum tours), while others were possibly describing the value of the Internet as a mode of delivery for a distance component of a college course, using course development tools such as Blackboard.com or e-College.com. One of the strengths of these workshops was the fact that both of these avenues for technology use were demonstrated by presenters and explored by participants. This conclusion was reached as a result of the qualitative comments received immediately following the workshops, as well as in the follow-up e-mail surveys, conducted four months later, in which participants indicated the variety of ways in which they were currently using

the World Wide Web. In the following section of the report, the qualitative findings regarding the evaluation of the workshops are addressed.

Qualitative Analysis:
Written Comments Obtained from Survey Instrument

The majority of respondents were reportedly pleased with their experience, indicating the workshops were enjoyable and informative. It has been argued elsewhere (Utay & Utay, 1998) that "teachers must receive training and support in a comfortable, fun, individualized environment. Teachers need time to think about, discuss, experiment with, and integrate what they learn" (p. 17). This seems to be the experience of workshop participants, illustrated by the following comments:

> I found today's workshop to be very informative. Lots of great tools, wonderful explanations of current technological methods.

> The whole workshop was a privileged situation to learn. I did not know anything about online courses before. It would be wonderful to repeat the experience.

Their comments also indicate that they understood the connections between information about technology and use in their courses.

Opportunity for collaboration. Participants also lauded the opportunity for collaboration with faculty members from other colleges in their disciplines. One of the goals of the workshop was to create collaborative relationships among faculty from the eight colleges, especially where similar courses were being taught. It is clear that, for many participants, this was a worthwhile goal, and they reportedly felt this goal was achieved.

> Very worthwhile opportunity to network with others in my own and related disciplines!

> This was a terrific idea–the SEPCHE faculty need to do more together. The sharing of ideas was a very valuable piece of the workshop.

Unlike the present workshops, which involved active learning, some faculty development programs primarily involve passive learning methods, consisting of listening to "expert" presenters (outside consultants). It is likely that the present faculty development model using active learning and collaborative exercises is a far more memorable format for participants. This is a hypothesis that could be empirically evaluated in future investigations. It is worth noting that participants saw the collaborative element of the present workshops as a valuable new experience, indeed a "precedent" in the words of one participant, suggesting that faculty would welcome additional opportunities for development.

Levels of expertise. It could be the case that participants who arrived with lower comfort levels with technology prior to the workshop may have been overwhelmed by the ambitious agenda. However, such faculty are representative of those who would truly appreciate more opportunities for an active learning experience with opportunities to practice their new skills. The following comments suggest that some faculty would be receptive to being tracked or monitored in terms of their progress with the incorporation of technology in the classroom:

> There is a lot of material provided, and it will require quite a lot of assimilation. An opportunity to practice and then evaluate the workshop might actually be more valuable.

> Excellent and useful. We will need to continue the instruction on an individual basis.

A few participants noted that they wished the groups had been divided into "beginner" versus "advanced" sections. This feedback came from a few who reportedly were at the bottom as well as the top end of the learning curve. These reactions suggest that opportunities to participate in additional faculty development workshops would likely be well received, particularly if given a choice as to the specific skill level of the workshop. A few respondents noted that they would like to have had more opportunity to practice and would appreciate additional meetings to continue development of their new skills. Only one respondent reportedly found the workshop uninteresting and unhelpful. Other participants commented that they learned valuable information but perhaps would not be able to use it immediately, due to the lack of facilities on their home campuses. In summary, participants clearly reported that they found the workshops useful, the presenters highly competent, and the opportunity for collaboration valuable.

Follow-Up Evaluation Using an Electronic Mail (E-mail) Survey

Rationale: There are limitations to an evaluation restricted to measuring the impact immediately following the conclusion of the workshop. The predictive validity of responses to queries regarding the likelihood of future technology use is somewhat limited. Asking respondents to estimate the likelihood of usage, immediately following the conclusion of a relatively brief, two-day workshop does not allow the respondent to process and synthesize all of the new information. The assessment of likelihood of use immediately following training may be somewhat diagnostic, but we recognize the inherent limitations of immediate usage decisions. Therefore, participants were contacted several months following the conclusion of the workshops to assess the longer term attitudinal and behavioral impact of the technology workshops on instructional practices.

Procedure: A total of 100 participants, who had given previous permission to be contacted for a follow-up survey, were contacted via e-mail and asked the following questions: (a) What are you doing with technology in your courses now? (b) In what Web activities are you engaged? (c) What software are you using? (d) In which courses are you using technology? (e) What are your future plans for technology use? (f) Are your plans a result of the workshop? (g) Would you attend another workshop? (h) If "yes," what would you like to see in future workshops? Of the 100 e-mail surveys forwarded, 29 responses were received, representing a return rate of 29%. Non-responders were then sent a reminder message via e-mail three weeks later and an additional 21 responses were returned, for a final return rate of 50%, a very strong survey response.

The following qualitative findings must be viewed in light of how those who replied to the e-mail follow-up may differ from non-respondents, because the sample may not be representative of the entire workshop population. It may be safer to suggest that the compliant sample would be comprised, for the most part, of those who were enthusiastic about the benefits received from the workshops. Of the 50 people who responded to this survey, 46 indicated that they were presently utilizing technology in their classrooms and indicated future plans to do more. The small remaining minority cited the lack of sufficient computing equipment and software for their lack of technology usage and identified activities that they were planning to do. Respondents reported being engaged in: (a) conducting courses partially or completely online, (b) incorporating Web pages and e-mail into courses, (c) using Web resources for research and lesson planning, and, (d) using specific software packages, such as PowerPoint or Photoshop, WebQuests, graphing calculators, videotapes, digital cameras, and image scanning.

All but one respondent indicated a willingness to come to another workshop, and most had specific suggestions for topics for future workshops. The respondents' willingness to learn more and ability to identify future topics of interest can be viewed as further evidence of the success of these workshops. Based on the results of the follow-up survey, participating faculty are apparently thinking about technology and are curious to learn more.

Comments in the e-mail survey identified the perceived value of the workshops. Faculty members told us that the workshops (a) provided them with useful information in well organized and competently presented formats, (b) provided support for activities they were already considering or had begun to do, and (c) gave them insight into the educational worth of particular activities. Some specific comments in each of these areas follow. On the informative nature of the workshops, faculty told us that what they learned at the workshops was useful and valuable.

> The workshop provided me with excellent additional resources and background knowledge that enhanced my use of technology.

> The workshop helped pull digital information together.

> We recently provided an overview of search engines and conducting research over the Web. This was a direct result of the workshop provided by SEPCHE. I also used this same information for students in my cohort classes, who are required to do a mini-literature search. This also was a result of the information provided at the workshop.

The follow-up survey also queried participants about the motivational factors underlying their current use of technology. In answer to the question "Is this [the faculty member's technology usage] a result of the workshop?" it was clear that faculty were encouraged to move forward in integrating technology in their courses as a result of having participated in the workshops. Participants also commented on the incentive provided by the workshops:

> I was better informed about the nature of on-line classes because of the workshop–I might not have accepted the opportunity this

early [to develop an online course] if I was not exposed to the information presented.

[The workshop] definitely jumpstarted what I knew I was planning to begin doing at some time . . . but the workshop really got me to see that I knew more already than I was giving myself credit for, and at the same time how much I still needed to learn.

Participation in this workshop gave many people specific examples of ways in which they might improve their courses with technology. Many of the SEPCHE faculty reportedly did not know what was available, and had not considered the educational possibilities for various forms of technology integration. As a result of the workshops, they reported that they had gained insight into the educational possibilities of appropriate technology:

The workshop helped raise my awareness to the potential of technology in the classroom.

The workshop reaffirmed for me the need to integrate technology into my courses.

The e-mail survey was conducted to assess the depth of implementation of the technology activities. These activities provide evidence that faculty members actively and independently sought new ways to improve their college teaching with electronically mediated communication, Web resources, and various software packages.

DISCUSSION

The workshops were designed to introduce technology to as many members of the eight college faculties as possible and to create collaborative relationships among faculty around the issue of technology use in higher education. Late adopters may have very good reasons for not using technology such as unavailability of computers and Internet access, lack of knowledge about worthwhile technology uses, and/or lack of time and instructional support. By working in the computer labs of the eight colleges with their own software and equipment, participants became aware of the available resources. By organizing these faculties in their academic disciplines, connections between the technology and the content areas were easily made. By using faculty members as presenters, networks of technical support across campuses were created. By holding workshops over a two-day period during winter break, a learning opportunity that was both convenient and relevant was provided. The immediate feedback, as well as the April/May e-mail survey, indicates that these design factors were important contributions to the success of the workshops.

These workshops have assisted late adopters to become engaged in using technology in their courses. Because technology changes and develops and pedagogical uses of technology undergo transformations at seemingly breathless speed, instruction in one use of technology is insufficient to insure continued use of all technology. What is needed is a sense of the possible values of technology and encouragement to explore technology integration in various disciplines. Late adopters who become interested and enthusiastic about technology will (as the April/May e-mail survey suggests) think about further uses of technology and be open to suggestions and to further faculty development initiatives. This openness is, in part, a result of the workshop design: a relaxed atmosphere, a variety of topics, connection to academic disciplines, and opportunity for collaboration and discussion.

REFERENCES

Brace, S., & Roberts, G. (1996). *Supporting faculty's development and use of instructional technology.* (ERIC Document Reproduction Service No. ED 400 814)

Jacobsen, M. (1997). *Bridging the gap between early adopters' and mainstream faculty's use of instructional technology.* (ERIC Document Reproduction Service No. ED 423 785)

Kahn, J., & Pred, R. (2000a, February). *Technology use in higher education: A faculty development model.* Paper presented at the annual meeting of the Society for Information Technology and Teacher Education. San Diego, CA. Charlottesville, VA: Association for the Advancement of Computing in Education.

Kahn, J., & Pred, R. (2000b). *Technology use in higher education: A faculty development model* (Coordinator's manual). Unpublished manuscript. Philadelphia, PA: Chestnut Hill College.

Kirk, R. (1995). *Experimental design: Procedures for the behavioral sciences (3rd ed.).* Pacific Grove, CA: Brooks/Cole.

Kress, M., & Hafner, A. (1996). *Process and facilities as critical success factors in training and supporting faculty to use multimedia/computer technologies.* (ERIC Document Reproduction Service No. ED 405 824)

Littlejohn, A., & Sclater, N. (1998). *Overcoming conceptual barriers to the use of Internet technology in university education.* (ERIC Document Reproduction Service No. ED 427 717)

Noon, S. (1998). Four stages of technology adoption, part two: Training the 'software technician' to use technology in the classroom. *Classroom Connect, 5*(3), 11.

Rogers, E. (1995). *Diffusion of innovations (4th ed.)*. New York: Free Press.

Rosenthal, R., & Rosnow, R. (1991). *Essentials of behavioral research: Methods and data analysis* (2nd ed.). New York, New York: McGraw-Hill.

Utay, C., & Utay, J. (1998). Four steps to enhanced technology staff development: The tag team. *Connections, 14*(2), 16-17.

Valente, T. (1996). Social network thresholds in the diffusion of innovations. *Social Networks, 18*(1), 69-89.

APPENDIX A-1

SEPCHE Faculty Development Workshop

Technology Workshop Evaluation Form for "First Day" Activities on Wednesday, January 5, 2000

Your evaluation of today's activities will be helpful in the planning of future faculty development programs. Please take a few moments to complete the following questions. All responses will be kept confidential. Please circle the appropriate number to the right of each statement.

		Disagree Strongly		Neither Agree nor Disagree		Agree Strongly
1)	Overall, today's sessions were well planned and organized.	1	2	3	4	5
2)	Today's activities were clearly explained.	1	2	3	4	5
3)	The instructors demonstrated a comprehensive knowledge of the workshop material.	1	2	3	4	5
4)	The material was covered at just the right pace.	1	2	3	4	5
5)	My knowledge level of the potential uses of this technology increased due to today's session.	1	2	3	4	5
6a)	BEFORE today's session, my comfort level with the use of this technology/software was somewhat low.	1	2	3	4	5
6b)	AS A RESULT OF today's session, my comfort level with the use of this technology/software has increased.	1	2	3	4	5
7)	I clearly see some benefits to incorporating aspects of this technology in my courses.	1	2	3	4	5
8)	I would feel comfortable trying to incorporate aspects of this technology in my courses.	1	2	3	4	5
9)	I plan to incorporate some aspects of this technology in my courses.	1	2	3	4	5
10)	I clearly see benefits to incorporating the use of the World Wide Web in developing my courses.	1	2	3	4	5

11)   Courses in which I might use this technology include: *(#11 continues from previous columns:)*
(please provide titles rather than course numbers)

11a)   11e)

11b)   11f)

11c)   11g)

11d)   11h)

Thank you for your assistance with this survey. Would you be willing to answer a brief follow-up survey?
No _____   Yes _____ [If Yes, please provide the following:]

Name _____   Phone _____   E-mail_____

Please provide additional comments about this workshop on the back of this form.

APPENDIX A -2

SEPCHE Faculty Development Workshop

Technology Workshop Evaluation Form for "Second Day" Activities on Thursday, January 6, 2000

Your evaluation of today's activities will be helpful in the planning of future faculty development programs. Please take a few moments to complete the following questions. All responses will be kept confidential. Please circle the appropriate number to the right of each statement.

		Disagree Strongly		Neither Agree nor Disagree		Agree Strongly
1)	Overall, today's sessions were well planned and organized.	1	2	3	4	5
2)	Today's activities were clearly explained.	1	2	3	4	5
3)	The instructors demonstrated a comprehensive knowledge of the workshop material.	1	2	3	4	5
4)	The material was covered at just the right pace.	1	2	3	4	5
5)	My knowledge level of the potential uses of this software increased due to today's session.	1	2	3	4	5
6a)	BEFORE the two workshops, my comfort level with the use of this technology/software was somewhat low.	1	2	3	4	5
6b)	AS A RESULT OF the two workshops, my comfort level with the use of this technology/software has increased.	1	2	3	4	5
7)	I clearly see some benefits to incorporating aspects of this software in my courses.	1	2	3	4	5
8)	I was introduced to software that I feel can be useful in my courses.	1	2	3	4	5
9)	Working in groups to learn new software with professors from other institutions was valuable.	1	2	3	4	5
10)	I was able to design some valuable activities for my course(s) using the software.	1	2	3	4	5

11) The software I am most likely to use includes: *(please provide specific software names)*

12) Courses in which I might use this software include: *(please provide titles rather than course numbers)*

11a)

11b)

11c)

11d)

12a)

12b)

12c)

12d)

Thank you for your assistance with this survey. Would you be willing to answer a brief follow-up survey?
No _____   Yes _____ [If Yes, please provide the following:]

Name _____   Phone _____   E-mail_____

Please provide additional comments about this workshop on the back of this form.

APPENDIX B

Descriptive Statistics for Survey Instrument Administered January, 2000

Items 1 through 7 were asked on Day 1 and Day 2, and are reported together to facilitate comparison across days (based on 1 to 5 point scale; Strongly Agree = 5; Strongly Disagree = 1):

Q1 Overall, today's sessions were well planned and organized.

Workshop Session	Strongly Agree		Neither Agree nor Disagree		Strongly Disagree	Item Statistics	
						MEAN	MEDIAN
Day 1 (Jan. 5)	51.9%	37.7%	6.6%	3.8%	0.0%	4.38	5.00
Day 2 (Jan. 6)	62.5%	29.8%	3.8%	1.9%	1.9%	4.49	5.00

Q2 Today's activities were clearly explained.

Workshop Session	Strongly Agree		Neither Agree nor Disagree		Strongly Disagree	Item Statistics	
						MEAN	MEDIAN
Day 1 (Jan. 5)	61.9%	29.5%	6.7%	1.9%	0.0%	4.51	5.00
Day 2 (Jan. 6)	64.5%	26.9%	4.8%	2.9%	1.0%	4.99	5.00

Q3 The instructors demonstrated a comprehensive knowledge of the workshop material.

Workshop Session	Strongly Agree		Neither Agree nor Disagree		Strongly Disagree	Item Statistics	
						MEAN	MEDIAN
Day 1 (Jan. 5)	63.9%	28.7%	5.6%	1.9%	0.0%	4.55	5.00
Day 2 (Jan. 6)	69.9%	25.2%	1.9%	1.9%	1.0%	4.61	5.00

Q4 The material was covered at just the right pace.

Workshop Session	Strongly Agree		Neither Agree nor Disagree		Strongly Disagree	Item Statistics	
						MEAN	MEDIAN
Day 1 (Jan. 5)	46.3%	31.5%	11.1%	10.2%	0.9%	4.12	5.00
Day 2 (Jan. 6)	55.9%	26.5%	9.8%	4.9%	2.9%	4.27	5.00

Q5 My knowledge level of the potential uses of this technology/software increased as a result of today's session.

Workshop Session	Strongly Agree		Neither Agree nor Disagree		Strongly Disagree	Item Statistics	
						MEAN	MEDIAN
Day 1 (Jan. 5)	48.6%	43.0%	4.7%	2.8%	0.9%	4.36	4.00
Day 2 (Jan. 6)	57.3%	33.0%	5.8%	1.9%	1.9%	4.42	5.00

Q6a Before today's session, my comfort level with the use of this technology/software was somewhat low.**

Workshop Session	Strongly Agree		Neither Agree nor Disagree		Strongly Disagree	Item Statistics	
						MEAN	MEDIAN
Day 1 (Jan. 5)	23.1%	22.2%	25.0%	22.2%	7.4%	3.31	3.00
Day 2 (Jan. 6)	19.2%	26.0%	28.8%	19.2%	6.7%	3.32	3.00

Q6b As a result of today's session, my comfort level with the use of this technology/software has increased.

Workshop Session	Strongly Agree		Neither Agree nor Disagree		Strongly Disagree	Item Statistics	
						MEAN	MEDIAN
Day 1 (Jan. 5)	35.2%	40.7%	17.6%	4.6%	1.9%	4.03	4.00
Day 2 (Jan. 6)	42.3%	45.2%	8.7%	2.9%	1.0%	4.25	4.00

Q7 I clearly see some benefits to incorporating aspects of this technology/software in my courses.

Workshop Session	Strongly Agree		Neither Agree nor Disagree		Strongly Disagree	Item Statistics	
						MEAN	MEDIAN
Day 1 (Jan. 5)	56.5%	37.0%	6.5%	0.0%	0.0%	4.50	5.00
Day 2 (Jan. 6)	62.1%	29.1%	6.8%	1.9%	0.0%	4.51	5.00

Aggregated Scores for the summation of Items 1 through 7:

	Mean	N	Std. Dev.	Std. Error
Day 1 Total	30.55	93	3.78	0.39
Day 2 Total	31.72	93	6.61	0.69
Mean Difference	1.17	93	6.40	0.66

** p < .01, t paired samples test = −2.825, df = 97, 1-tailed sig. (.003)
Analysis includes only respondents who completed evaluations for both Days 1 and 2. Adjusted means for listwise deletion for Day 1 = 4.04 (n = 98) and Day 2 = 4.28 (n = 98).

Note: p < .05, t paired samples test = 1.77, df = 92, one-tailed p value = .0405. Includes only respondents who competed evaluations for both Days 1 and 2 using listwise deletion of respondents. Unadjusted means for Day1 = 30.50 (n = 103) and Day 2 = 31.79 (n = 101).

Items 8 through 10 differed on Days 1 and 2 to address differences in workshop content, and are reported separately below:

Items Assessed Only on First Day of Workshop (January 5):

Q8 I would feel comfortable trying to incorporate aspects of this technology in my courses.

Workshop Session	Strongly Agree		Neither Agree nor Disagree		Strongly Disagree	Item Statistics	
						MEAN	MEDIAN
Day 1 (Jan. 5)	39.3%	38.3%	17.8%	3.7%	0.9%	4.11	4.00

Q9 I plan to incorporate some aspects of this technology in my courses.

Workshop Session	Strongly Agree		Neither Agree nor Disagree		Strongly Disagree	Item Statistics	
						MEAN	MEDIAN
Day 1 (Jan. 5)	49.1%	31.5%	14.8%	4.6%	0.0%	4.25	4.00

Q10 I clearly see benefits to incorporating the use of the World Wide Web in developing my courses.

Workshop Session	Strongly Agree		Neither Agree nor Disagree		Strongly Disagree	Item Statistics	
						MEAN	MEDIAN
Day 1 (Jan. 5)	56.3%	32.0%	9.7%	1.0%	1.0%	4.42	5.00

<u>Item Assessed Only on Second Day of Workshop (January 6):</u>

Q8 I was introduced to Web sites/software that I feel can be useful in my courses.

Workshop Session	Strongly Agree		Neither Agree nor Disagree		Strongly Disagree	Item Statistics	
						MEAN	MEDIAN
Day 2 (Jan. 6)	56.3%	32.0%	8.7%	2.9%	0.0%	4.12	5.00

Q9 Working in groups to learn new software with professors from other institutions was valuable.

Workshop Session	Strongly Agree		Neither Agree nor Disagree		Strongly Disagree	Item Statistics	
						MEAN	MEDIAN
Day 2 (Jan. 6)	59.0%	28.0%	11.0%	2.0%	0.0%	4.44	5.00

Q10 I was able to design some valuable activities for my course(s) using the software.

Workshop Session	Strongly Agree		Neither Agree nor Disagree		Strongly Disagree	Item Statistics	
						MEAN	MEDIAN
Day 2 (Jan. 6)	19.1%	36.2 %	33.0%	8.5%	3.2%	3.60	4.00

Moses Peart
Caryl J. Sheffield

Technology Training for Teacher Education in Jamaica: A Case for Needs Assessment

SUMMARY. The major challenges facing education systems in the information age include issues of how to prepare for and capitalize on the technological revolution and how to integrate computer technology into the curriculum. Jamaica, like most developing countries, is taking on these challenges with perhaps as much focus and increased importance as any developed country such as the United States. This paper explores the approach taken, particularly with teacher educators in Jamaican colleges, to begin the process by an assessment of the computer-related professional development needs of the college faculty. The paper makes recommendations for developing a technology training program based on the needs assessment. Underlying these issues is the necessity for a national policy to coordinate the country's efforts to integrate information technology into teacher education. Additional recommendations intended to provide guidance for the formulation of such an integrated policy development and implementation framework are offered. *[Article copies available for a fee from The Haworth Document Delivery Service:*

MOSES PEART is Lecturer/Researcher, Instructional Systems, Institute of Education, University of the West Indies, Kingston 7 Jamaica (E-mail: peartm@netcomm-jm.com).
CARYL J. SHEFFIELD is Professor, Elementary/Early Childhood Education Department, California University, 250 University Avenue, California, PA 15419 (E-mail: Sheffield@cup.edu).

[Haworth co-indexing entry note]: "Technology Training for Teacher Education in Jamaica: A Case for Needs Assessment." Peart, Moses, and Caryl J. Sheffield. Co-published simultaneously in *Computers in the Schools* (The Haworth Press, Inc.) Vol. 18, No. 4, 2001, pp. 151-164; and: *Evaluation and Assessment in Educational Information Technology* (ed: Leping Liu et al.) The Haworth Press, Inc., 2001, pp. 151-164. Single or multiple copies of this article are available for a fee from The Haworth Document Delivery Service [1-800-HAWORTH, 9:00 a.m. - 5:00 p.m. (EST). E-mail address: getinfo@haworthpressinc.com].

151

1-800-HAWORTH. E-mail address: <getinfo@haworthpressinc.com> Website: <http://www.HaworthPress.com> © 2001 by The Haworth Press, Inc. All rights reserved.]

KEYWORDS. Faculty development, teacher education, technology integration, instructional technology, computer literacy, developing countries, Jamaica, needs assessment, professional development, teachers colleges

One of the many challenges facing the education system at all levels in Jamaica is how to capitalize on the technological revolution that is currently sweeping the planet. From elementary schools to advanced degree programs, educators are seeking ways to integrate computer technology into the curriculum. This is especially true for the teachers' colleges.

While technology integration in education is of concern to most countries, in developing countries like Jamaica, it takes on increased importance. The constant and rapid innovation in information technology, particularly in telecommunications and computer hardware and software, further challenges Caribbean countries that are already straining to provide technological resources to their higher education institutions (Educational Change, 1999). To make matters worse, teachers colleges in developing countries lack state-of-the-art educational technology (Osin, 1998). In addition to hardware and software limitations, the training of teachers has not kept pace with the introduction of the technology. As of 1997, only 3.7% of new teachers in Jamaica have had any training in the use of computers in education (Peart, 1998). A comprehensive professional development program for teacher educators is a necessity for systematically addressing these issues, providing them with the knowledge they need to effectively use information technology in pre-service teacher education.

This paper explores the approach undertaken by educators in Jamaica to address these challenges. It focuses particular attention on the process of assessing the computer-related professional development needs of the faculty of the teachers colleges in Jamaica. It also makes recommendations for training based on the needs assessment. Underlying these issues is the necessity for a national policy to coordinate the country's efforts to integrate information technology into teacher education. Additional recommendations intended to provide guidance for the formulation of such an integrated policy development and implementation framework are offered.

RATIONALE

In Jamaica, several agencies are pooling their resources to assist in advancing the use of information technology in the teachers colleges. The Joint Board of Teacher Education (JBTE), a regional body established by the Ministries of Education in the Caribbean countries of Belize, Bahamas, and Jamaica, is charged with the responsibility of executing the teacher education program in these countries. The JBTE is responsible for the curriculum, professional development, and certification processes to ensure that the best available knowledge, skills, and creative input are brought to bear upon teacher preparation programs. Established in 1965, the JBTE serves 12 colleges involved in the training of teachers, with 10 located in Jamaica.

The JBTE has recently embarked on an intensive process of review and redesign of the teacher education programs in the colleges. Apart from the need for such periodic updating of programs, this recent effort has been clearly driven by new challenges associated with the rapid introduction of computers in education. Seeking a systematic instructional design approach to developing a comprehensive instructional technology training program, JBTE conducted a needs assessment, to provide useful information regarding the previous training, comfort level, and interests of the teachers college faculty, and to make recommendations regarding training topics, program design, and delivery strategies.

DATA COLLECTION

Data for the needs assessment were collected from three sources: interviews, a review of instructional technology courses, and a questionnaire. Interviews with selected faculty and administrators provided general information regarding the current technology skill levels of most faculty. Interviewees were asked to respond to several questions regarding the level of instructional technology use by faculty and to project use of technology in the future. Three course syllabi, *Technology in Education, Information Technology,* and *Computer Studies,* were analyzed to develop an understanding of the current use of instructional technology in the classroom/laboratory and the skills of the teachers responsible for those courses.

The questionnaire (Appendix A) was the most comprehensive source of information. This instrument contained items that assessed both cognitive and affective factors important to providing faculty development in computer literacy and to understanding the role of instructional technology in learning environments (Ganske & Hamamota, 1984; Sheffield, 1995). Content items were based on the International Society for Technology in Education (ISTE) performance standards for all teachers (International Society for Technology in Education, 2000). For the purpose of the needs assessment, analysis was limited to items related to computer technology from specific sections of the survey.

Information from *Section I* (Biographic Data) is used to develop group and individual profiles of the target population. These will facilitate decisions regarding the likely characteristics of potential participants (e.g., teaching areas) in the proposed training program.

Information from *Section II* (Information Technology Skills Inventory) is used to generate a general picture of the types and distribution of entry level skills of the target participants. This inventory not only provides indicators of training needs, but also highlights existing strengths that can be creatively used in the training delivery. Using a Likert-type scale, respondents were asked to indicate their level of training in specific information technology categories, from no formal training to training that resulted in the awarding of a certificate or degree.

Information from *Section III* (Comfort Level and Confidence) provides a general indication of the affective issues that may constrain faculty willingness to make greater use of new information technologies. This information is useful for structuring training program delivery and identifying support materials that can most effectively move the target group through the successive stages of the technology skills development. Respondents indicated their comfort level using a three-choice Likert scale: not comfortable, fairly comfortable, and very comfortable.

Information from *Section VII* (Opinions on Needs and Interests) consists of open-ended responses to several questions. Content analysis of the items in this section can reveal attitudes that should be addressed and possible strategies to enhance the effectiveness of the program. This section is also a critical source for indicators of some of the contextual realities to be faced by the training program. The following open-ended questions were analyzed:

1. How important is training in technology to you?
2. What specific computer software or application tool(s) are you most interested in?
3. Give examples of some attributes or features you expect a course in technology to have.

DATA ANALYSIS

Frequency distributions were generated for each survey response. Visual examination of the data in graph form was sufficient to identify the areas of low skill or comfort level. As a result, additional statistical analyses were not required for the purposes of the needs assessment. The determination of priority training needs was based on items that had relatively high proportions of responses indicating lack of skill. Finally, content analysis of the open-ended responses supplemented the statistical tabulations.

As Table 1 indicates, faculty at 12 tertiary institutions (10 teachers colleges and 2 universities) that provide teacher training in Jamaica were asked to complete the questionnaire. At the time of this analysis, 160 survey forms from 10 colleges were collected, representing a 32% rate of return. Sixty-four percent of the respondents were female and 36%, male. Seventy-five percent indicated over 11 years of teaching experience.

FINDINGS

Summary

Analysis of the data indicates that most faculty are comfortable with basic computer operations, Windows operating systems (versions 3.1, 95, or 98), and word processing. In addition, most have participated in some training in these areas. However, in the areas of computer graphics, spreadsheet/statistical software, Internet and multimedia, the majority of the faculty reported no confidence and no training. In the final area of technology integration, the results are not quite as clear: Almost half of the faculty indicate that they are not comfortable with integrating technology; but a vast majority have received training, suggesting that a closer examination of this area may be required.

TABLE 1. Teachers Colleges in Jamaica and Returned Questionnaires

Institution	No. of returned questionnaires
Bethlehem Moravian College	0
College of Agriculture, Science, and Education (CASE)	19
Church Teachers College	10
Edna Manley College of Visual and Performing Arts	7
G.C. Foster Teachers College	12
Mico Teachers College	16
Moneague Teachers College	23
Northern Caribbean University	0
Sam Sharpe Teachers College	29
Shortwood Teachers College	18
St. Joseph's Teachers College	20
University of Technology	6
Total	160

A summary of the findings from each area follows. Comfort level/confidence is reported across the scale of not comfortable, fairly comfortable, and very comfortable. Level of training/experience is reported according to Table 2.

Sixty-eight percent (68%) of the faculty reported some level of confidence in their computer operation abilities (fairly/very comfortable). Three-fourths (76%) reported some level of formal training. The majority of the training was at the basic and intermediate level.

A smaller proportion (57%) was comfortable with Windows operating systems, even though more (69%) had formal training in this area. While most faculty had received some level of training in both computer operations and Windows operating systems, more than half had only basic training or no training at all.

Forty-three percent of the faculty reported lack of confidence in their word-processing ability, and 31% reported no training. The responses for word-processing follow an almost diagonal pattern of decline, with 28% reporting training at the basic level, 19% at the intermediate level, 14% at the advanced level, and 8% at the professional level.

TABLE 2. Descriptions of Training Level Responses

Training Level	Description
None	No formal or informal exposure/training
Basic	Up to 15 hours of introductory training, or self-helped basic knowledge
Intermediate (Inter.)	Exposure to courses or short term training up to 30 hours
Advanced (Adv.)	Specialized training and practical experience up to 60 hours
Professional (Pro.)	Training and practical experience with certificate/diploma/degree

Most faculty (69%) lacked confidence in their abilities to use graphics, and almost half (49%) had not had any training in this area. The response pattern for spreadsheet and statistical packages was similar, i.e., two-thirds (67%) of the faculty reported that they were not comfortable with, and over half (53%) had not had any formal training in this area.

Use of the Internet is reported in three categories: Internet communication, e-mail, and online learning materials. Over half (52%) of the faculty reported that they are not comfortable with either Internet communication or e-mail. Forty-one percent had no training in e-mail and the use of the Internet, and another 30% had only basic training. Sixty-two percent of the faculty were not comfortable with online learning materials, and a little over half (52%) of them had received no training in this area.

Most faculty responding to the survey (65%) indicate that they were not comfortable with multimedia, and 60% had no training in multimedia design/presentation.

A little more than half of the faculty (58%) were comfortable (fairly/very comfortable) with technology integration and most of them (83%) had some training in integrating technology in education, mostly at the lower two levels. This result may appear inconsistent with the rest of the findings; the concern is whether the faculty were reporting comfort with the integration of computer technology or with traditional technologies (video, textbooks, overhead transparencies), given their responses to questions about the Internet, spreadsheet, graphics, and multimedia.

In summary, over half of the faculty reported lack of confidence in 8 out of the 10 skill areas measured. Over half of the faculty reported some training in all but three skill areas.

Responses to Open-Ended Questions

Content analysis of the responses to the open-ended questions on the survey revealed the following:

1. Most faculty felt that training in technology was "very important" for a variety of reasons, including enhancing teaching methods and materials, providing competence and comfort, and impacting effectiveness and efficiency at the workplace.
2. Faculty were interested in many different software programs; Windows, word-processing, spreadsheet, and presentation programs were specifically mentioned. Other topics indicated were Web page design and the Internet.
3. Faculty favored hands-on, step-by-step user-friendly training with examples and practical application that are appropriate for their discipline.

These findings from the analysis of survey responses, answers to open-ended questions, and an examination of course syllabi were used to shape recommendations for training topics and strategic planning.

RECOMMENDATIONS

Training

Based on data analysis, it is recommended that a hands-on approach to training be developed. To address the discomfort with computers that many faculty reported, a supportive environment that includes small group interactions, individual attention, and ample time for practice is suggested.

Topics recommended for inclusion in a comprehensive training program are listed below. The order of the topics suggests an optimal sequence for a training program.

Computer operations and Windows operating system. Knowledge of basic computer operations and the Windows operating system can be the first step to understanding the complexities of computer technology. Identifying system information (hard disk size, RAM, disk drives, peripherals, etc.), manipulating files (initializing disks, copying and backing up files, etc.), working with the desktop, using input devices (keyboard, mouse, etc.), and starting up and shutting down hardware are requisite skills.

Because basic skill in computer operation and using operating systems is the foundation from which all other skills are developed, training is especially recommended for faculty who are not comfortable or have had no formal training. However, training in these skills should be tailored to meet the needs of specific groups (e.g., starting with the basics for beginners and providing advanced topics for those with prior training).

Word processing. Word processing can support nearly any kind of task or teaching activity that was previously done by handwriting or typewriter, but word processing offers more capability and versatility than either of these methods. With a word-processed document, the teacher can, before printing, correct errors, insert or delete words or sentences, and even move lines or paragraphs. Once stored or saved, word-processing documents can be changed or reprinted at a later time. Using a word processor can significantly improve a teacher's efficiency. Classroom materials such as lecture notes, handouts, exams, and transparencies prepared with a word processor look more polished and professional than handwritten or typed materials.

A word processor, the most widely used productivity software program, contains many features that are used in other applications, such as copy/paste and formatting text. It is easy to learn, intuitive in nature, user-friendly, and, most importantly, builds confidence. For these reasons word processing is an ideal topic with which to begin training after basic operations are mastered. Because there are so many levels of word-processing techniques, it is also appropriate for advanced study.

Graphics. An advanced word processing skill is the ability to incorporate such graphics as clip art, charts, and line drawings into word-processed documents, adding interest, clarity, and excitement to handouts, slides, worksheets, etc. Computer graphics/illustrations can be treated as an advanced topic of word processing in the training sequence for teachers college faculty.

Multimedia presentations. Multimedia is the use of various formats for the presentation of information, including text, stills, or animated graphics, movie segments, video, and audio. Teacher educators use multimedia to present videodisc, CD-ROM or Internet-based programs, or to develop instructional materials or projects using an authoring program.

Developing multimedia presentations is an advanced skill for most faculty. With the advent of such easy-to-use programs as PowerPoint, faculty can quite easily create multimedia presentations to present interesting and dynamic material in their classrooms.

Spreadsheet. A spreadsheet program is an extremely useful tool for educators. The most common application in the classroom is for assessment activities, including gradekeeping, attendance charts, and performance assessment checklists. In addition, the charting facility enables faculty to graphically depict student progress. Statistical analysis is available through built-in functions such as average, sum, percentile, and *t*-test.

Since using a spreadsheet can improve an individual faculty member's efficiency, training in this program is recommended, but only after he/she is comfortable with computer operations and word-processing techniques.

The Internet. While access to computer technology is a critical issue in technology training and utilization, in teacher training in Jamaica, it takes on a special dimension. If faculty have the opportunity to access the Internet through reliable and speedy connections, there is no limit to the resources at their disposal. Such services as e-mail, instant messaging, professional chat rooms, bulletin boards, discussion groups, lesson plans, clip art, tutorials, curriculum guides, research, and current subject-area content are some of the resources available for faculty.

Because of the vast amount of resources on the Internet, it has the potential to significantly impact teacher education. The effect of increasing globalization on education makes addressing this issue imperative. Training in educational applications of the Internet is essential for all faculty.

Integrating computers into the curriculum. Most teacher educators agree that integrating computer technology into the curriculum is the appropriate strategy for advancing the use of computers in schools. While it is essential that faculty know how to use such tools as word processors and spreadsheets, the next logical step in the utilization of technology is to treat it as an integral part of the teaching/learning process, not as an add-on function.

For example, in primary and secondary teaching methods courses, students can be required to "word process" all written assignments, to include charts in a report, to use the computer for group project presentations, or to use the Internet to identify helpful resources. In addition, pre-service teachers must be taught how to teach with tools (word processor, spreadsheet, graphics) and instructional software (tutorials, drills, simulations, etc.). To illustrate, an appropriate computer integration assignment might be to develop a lesson plan that incorporates student use of a word processor in reading, or a biology tutorial in a science lesson.

Training in this area should be focused on those who indicate lack of experience and confidence and to those who desire advanced assistance in integrating computer technology into the curriculum.

Planning for Information Technology Policy Implementation

A comprehensive professional development program developed from the recommendations herein may be more successful if it is prepared within a rational policy framework. In addition to establishing goals, action plans, and assessment procedures, such a policy should also address the costs associated with adapting to ongoing changes in information technology. These costs include creating and continually upgrading facilities to ensure that they remain state-of-the-art and providing regularly scheduled, on-going training in the latest versions of software.

Because of the rapid rate at which computer technology changes, it is important that faculty workstations and multimedia laboratories adhere to current industry hardware standards and maintain current software titles for productivity tools, integrated software, desktop publishing, Web browsers, and graphics. In addition, speedy and reliable connections to the Internet are a necessity. Most importantly, to facilitate continual use of the newly learned skills, faculty should have access to these resources after training is completed.

As the regulator of teacher education programs, the Joint Board of Teacher Education is in a unique position to play a critical role in facilitating these aspects of policy development and implementation that relate specifically to teacher training in Jamaica. In addition, through collaboration with the Ministries of Education in the Bahamas and Belize, the JBTE can extend its impact to assume a vanguard role in structuring a regional policy for the use of information technology in teacher education.

CONCLUSION

The challenges that developing countries like Jamaica face in keeping pace with the information technology revolution will continue. As fast as technology changes, so will the training needs of the faculty at teachers colleges. Faculty skills will constantly need to be upgraded to keep pace with the demands of an increasing technological society. An on-going, comprehensive program of faculty development is necessary to ensure that all faculty maintain the required skill level so they can provide quality preparation for future teachers. Working together, all stakeholders in pre-service teacher education (as in this case the Joint Board of Teacher Education, the Ministry of Education and Culture, the teachers colleges, and the Jamaica Computer Society Education Foundation) can make progress in meeting the challenges and opportunities posed by information technology.

REFERENCES

Ganske, L., & Hamamota, P. (1984). Response to crisis: A developer's look at the importance of needs assessment to teacher educators in the design of computer literacy training programs. *Educational Communication and Technology: A Journal of Theory, Research, and Development, 32*(2), 101-113.

International Society for Technology in Education. (2000). Available: *http://www.iste.org*

Jamaica Computer Society Education Foundation. (2000). Available: *http://www.jcsef.org.jm/ ourmission.htm*

Osin, L. (1998). *Computers in education in developing countries: Why & How?* (The World Bank Education and Technology Technical Notes Series, Vol. 3, No. 1). Washington, DC: World Bank.

Peart, M. (1998). Essential skills for teachers in the age of information technology and interactivity. In R. King (Ed.), *Institute of education annual* (pp. 194-203). Kingston, Jamaica: The University of the West Indies.

Sheffield, C. (1995). Computer literacy at an historically Black institution: A faculty development project case study report. *International Journal of Instructional Media, 22*(1), 45-58.

The World Bank. (1999). *Educational change in Latin America and the Caribbean.* Washington, DC: World Bank.

APPENDIX A

Technology in Teacher Education–Baseline Survey

Training Needs Assessment (TNA) & Front End Analysis (FEA) of Context

I. Biographical Data:

Name: _____ M/F: _____ Institution: _____

Years of Teaching: _____ Subject: _____

Do you have access to a computer? Yes _____ No _____ Are you computer shy? Yes _____ No. _____

II. Technology Skills Inventory: Use the Key provided to indicate your skill level in each of the following:

Key:

0 = None	(no formal or informal training/exposure in the related area)
1 = Basic	(up to 15 hours of training, or self-helped basic knowledge)
2 = Intermediate	(up to 30 hours of training/exposure to short term courses)
3 = Advanced	(up to 45 hours of training & experience in the specific skills)
4 = Professional	(training & practice up to certificate/diploma/degree level).

Technology Areas–Track I	0	1	2	3	4	Technology Areas–Track II	0	1	2	3	4
a) Using print materials (e.g., textbooks)						j) Basic computing (e.g. keyboard) skills					
b) Using audio tape recorder/player						k) Word processing/desk top publishing					
c) Using videotape recorder/player						l) Basic Windows (3.1/95/98) functions					
d) Graphics (e.g., charts, drawings)						m) Computer graphics/illustrations/clip art					
e) Projected media (film, slide, overhead)						n) Multimedia presentations / software					
f) Non-projected media (e.g., displays)						o) Internet and e-mail communications					
g) Interactive radio, t.v., or telecomm.						p) Spreadsheet and database software					
h) Simulations & games						q) Using online learning materials					
i) Integrating technology in curriculum						r) Courseware/software authoring tools					

III. Comfort Level & Confidence:

How confident and/or comfortable are you when working with each of these knowledge/skill areas ?

Technology	Not	Fairly	Very	Technology Area	Not	Fairly	Very
a) Print materials				j) Basic computer uses			
b) Audio recordings				k) Word processing skills			
c) Video recordings				l) Use of Windows 3.1/95/98			
d) Graphics/illustrations				m) Computer graphics/illustra.			
e) Projected media				n) Multimedia environments			
f) Non-projected media				o) Internet/e-mail communica.			
g) Interactive radio/t.v.				p) Spreadsheets/stats software			
h) Simulations and games				q) Online learning materials			
i) Integrating technology				r) Software authoring tools			

IV. Reasons for Pursuing Training in Technology:
Please check as many of these reasons that directly apply to you.

a) I am required to use technology at work		b) To get better acquainted with technology	
c) Because my colleagues are using IT		d) To upgrade my current knowledge/skills	
e) I plan to or just purchased a computer		f) Training in specific computer applications	
g) For further academic qualifications		h) To enhance my instructional capabilities	
i) To keep up with or ahead of my students		j) Other	

V. Technology Utilization in Work Context:
Please indicate the level of your utilization (Utl) of these technological means/tools in your current work.

Rating Scale:　**N/A** = not available;　**0** = not used;　**1** = used one or two times;
　　　　　　　　　2 = used a few times;　**3** = used most times;　**4** = used all the time.

Technological Means/Tools	Utl	Technological Means/Tools	Utl
1. Textbooks & supplementary readings		8. Teaching computer courses or orientation	
2. Research assignments & book reviews		9. Using computer in lesson presentations	
3. Lectures and information presentations		10. Multimedia presentations without computer	
4. Group discussion/interactions/debates		11. Multimedia presentations with computer	
5. Using charts & illustrations in lessons		12. Using the Internet for classroom learning	
6. Using audio tapes in lesson presentation		13. Using conferences in online learning	
7. Using videotapes in lesson presentation		14. Designing/constructing online courses	
15. Using teaching/learning strategies to integrate technology into curriculum and instruction			

VI. Technology Related Courses/Seminars Attended:

Course Title	Hours	Date	Mode of Instruct	Place/Institution	Sponsor/Facilitator

Key: Mode of Instruction (F/F = Face-to-Face; O/L = Online Learning; M/M = Mixed Modes; OTH = Other)

1. Your Opinions, Needs, and Interests:
Provide a brief answer to each of the following.

Question	Response
1. How important is training In technology to you?	
2. How much technology information can you can? And from what sources?	
3. What specific computer software or application tools are you interested in?	
4. Indicate the amount of time & resources you are willing to spend on the acquisition of these skills.	
5. Give one example of what you would like to get from a course in technology.	
6. How useful or critical is training in technology to your current job, or professional work?	
7. How much guidance or help do you think you will need in order to start and continue with use of IT?	
8. What use do you plan to make of your training in technology ?	
9. Make any other related comment you wish.	

Thomas Fox McManus
Michael T. Charles
Reuben A. Rubio
Ellen S. Hoffman
James S. Lenze

COATT: A State-Wide Initiative to Evaluate and Improve Teacher Technology Education

SUMMARY. Like many other states, Michigan has recently instituted minimum technology standards for pre-service teachers. A group of teacher education institutions decided that that standard needed to be a baseline rather than an end goal. Together they formed the Consortium for Outstanding Achievement in Teaching with Technology (COATT),

THOMAS FOX MCMANUS is Assistant Professor of Educational Technology, Department of Educational Leadership and Services, Saginaw Valley State University, College of Education 160, 7400 Bay Road, University Center, MI 48710 (E-mail: mcmanus@svsu.edu).
MICHAEL T. CHARLES is Assistant Professor, Educational Technology, Eastern Michigan University, Department of Teacher Education, 315 M John W. Porter Building, Ypsilanti, MI 48197 (E-mail: mcharle@online.emich.edu).
REUBEN A. RUBIO is a doctoral candidate, Education Department, Albion College, KC 4743, Ferguson Center, Albion, MI 49224 (E-mail: rarubio@albion.edu).
ELLEN S. HOFFMAN is Assistant Professor, Department of Teacher Education, Eastern Michigan University, Ypsilanti, MI 48197 (E-mail: ehoffman@online.emich. edu).
JAMES S. LENZE is Assistant Professor, Communications Media, Indiana University of Pennsylvania, 129 Stouffer Hall, 1175 Maple Street, Indiana, PA 15705-1087 (E-mail: jlenze@grove.iup.edu).

[Haworth co-indexing entry note]: "COATT: A State-Wide Initiative to Evaluate and Improve Teacher Technology Education." McManus, Thomas Fox et al. Co-published simultaneously in *Computers in the Schools* (The Haworth Press, Inc.) Vol. 18, No. 4, 2001, pp. 165-183; and: *Evaluation and Assessment in Educational Information Technology* (ed: Leping Liu et al.) The Haworth Press, Inc., 2001, pp. 165-183. Single or multiple copies of this article are available for a fee from The Haworth Document Delivery Service [1-800-HAWORTH, 9:00 a.m. - 5:00 p.m. (EST). E-mail address: getinfo@haworthpressinc.com].

165

whose purpose is to set in place a formal process to recognize pre-service, and eventually in-service, teachers for going beyond the mandated standard. Here we discuss both the process of bringing the consortium together and the progress of our students as they applied for the M-COATT certificate. This article discusses the origins of the consortium, the evaluation process, the results of the first rounds of evaluation, and the possible future of the consortium. *[Article copies available for a fee from The Haworth Document Delivery Service: 1-800-HAWORTH. E-mail address: <getinfo@haworthpressinc.com> Website: <http://www.HaworthPress.com> © 2001 by The Haworth Press, Inc. All rights reserved.]*

KEYWORDS. COATT, teacher education, evaluation, technology standards, pre-service, in-service, portfolios

The Michigan Department of Education has established a standard that all entry-level teachers will have "an ability to use information technology to enhance learning as well as enhance personal and professional productivity." A national study published in 1997 (Coley, Cradler, & Engel, 1997) ranked Michigan 44th out of 50 for training teachers in technology. The Consortium for Outstanding Achievement in Teaching with Technology [COATT] was formed in an effort to increase the quality of technology skills of pre-service teachers in Michigan teacher preparation institutions. In its first year, COATT successfully piloted a certificate (the M-COATT) that recognizes pre-service teachers who submit a digital portfolio that demonstrates their use of technology to enhance student learning. Notably, while only a few students applied in this first year, the evaluators were able to come to a consensus on the suitability of the digital portfolios based on an assessment rubric developed by COATT. The consortium has had several positive outcomes, including the validation through real-world testing of the M-COATT certificate. Also teacher educators responsible for preparing students in information technology at very diverse institutions have had a forum to discuss their work as they aim for a common standard. Issues to be addressed in the future include the expansion of the program to meet the needs of practicing teachers and the need to recruit many more applicants from the pre-service population. Those of us who have helped create COATT continue to believe that it will make a significant contribution to long-term efforts to improve the technology skills of Michigan educators.

THE ORIGINS OF COATT

In June 1999, representatives of 10 Michigan colleges and universities joined with Senator Carl Levin of Michigan to announce the formation of the Consortium for Outstanding Achievement in Teaching with Technology (COATT). The consortium is the result of a year-long effort begun by Levin that brought together diverse teacher preparation institutions to find a way to raise the standards for technology preparation for pre-service teachers. Research 1 universities, regional comprehensive universities, and small liberal arts colleges are all members of this consortium.

Each participating institution signed a letter outlining its responsibilities as a member of COATT. The consortium itself will be housed at the College of Education at Eastern Michigan University (EMU). The office at EMU will receive applications, organize evaluation teams, and generally administer the certification. The participating teacher training institutions will assist candidates with the application process. Each school will name a person to act as a point of contact within the institution for potential COATT candidates and to promote COATT to potential candidates through flyers and other communications. Participating institutions will also provide support for candidates seeking COATT certification, such as adequate and relevant learning opportunities in the application of educational technology, and resources for COATT applicants to produce, maintain, and gain access to their COATT digital portfolios. In addition to their responsibilities to support COATT applicants, participating institutions will retain responsibility for seeing to the health of the consortium across the years. Faculty liaisons will participate in an annual review of the COATT standards and will develop policy with other core members of the COATT organization. Faculty and other qualified personnel from participating institutions will be involved in COATT evaluation teams.

EARNING THE M-COATT CERTIFICATE

In the 1999-2000 academic year, COATT began awarding a certificate, the M-COATT (Michigan Certificate of Achievement in Teaching with Technology), to pre-service teachers who demonstrate excellence in the use of technology to enhance student learning. This certificate exists independently of both degree programs and the state certification process. It allows educators to demonstrate their proficiency in this area and helps school administrators who make hiring decisions identify teachers who can be technology leaders in their schools. The certificate also allows students at different institutions of higher education to benchmark their achievements in teacher preparation in technology against an independent standard of excellence. Students attending COATT member institutions who wish to receive the consortium's certificate must submit a digital portfolio for review by a panel composed of representatives of two or more of COATT's participating institutions (other than the student's own institution).

The standards used to award the M-COATT certificate are based on the Michigan Department of Education's (MDE) seventh standard for entry-level teachers. The seventh standard states that all entry-level teachers will have "an ability to use information technology to enhance learning as well as enhance personal and professional productivity." The standard further consists of seven component areas (MDE, 1997):

1. Design, develop and implement activities that integrate information technology for a variety of student grouping strategies and diverse student populations.
2. Identify and apply resources for staying current in applications of information technology in education.
3. Demonstrate knowledge of multimedia, hypermedia, telecommunications, and distance learning to support teaching/learning.
4. Demonstrate knowledge about instructional management resources that assist in such activities as writing and updating curriculum; creating lesson plans and tests; and promoting, reinforcing, and organizing data regarding student performance.
5. Use information technologies to support student problem solving, data collection, information management, communications, presentations, and decision-making including word processing, database management, spreadsheets, and graphic utilities.
6. Demonstrate appreciation of equity, ethical, legal, social, physical, and psychological issues concerning use of information technology.
7. Use information technology to enhance continuing professional development as an educator.

Currently, the State of Michigan asks all entry-level teachers to demonstrate achievement at the "basic" level (2 on the MDE's 4-point scale) in four of the areas and at the "proficient" level (3 on the MDE's

4-point scale) on the other three for minimal, basic, or consistent achievement in all of these areas. We expect the M-COATT standards to set a "high bar" toward which student teachers may aim. Therefore, to be awarded the COATT certificate, candidates need to demonstrate achievement at the highest level (4 on the MDE's 4-point scale) on at least three of the seven components. At least two of the three components must be from among those components most closely linked to enhanced student learning: component area 1, 3, and 5.

THE EVALUATION PROCESS

As mentioned above, all candidates for the COATT certificate are required to submit a digital portfolio for evaluation. The consortium faced the question of just what does a quality portfolio look like? Initially, participants in the consortium offered anecdotal ideas of what they thought would qualify as "M-COATT certified," but actual sample portfolios had not been prepared at the onset of our discussions. The challenge of getting educational technology faculty from diverse institutions to agree on such a standard with the knowledge that a third party would independently evaluate student work was formidable. Eventually a rubric was proposed and agreed upon.

A portfolio is a focused presentation to a prospective employer of one's professional knowledge, experiences, and abilities. Student teachers select important artifacts, the very best and clearest evidences of their growth and learning, to include in a portfolio. Such artifacts can include: a resume and philosophy of teaching; lesson plans and implementations of classroom activities; sample works of their own students; research papers and essays that they have written; video of their classroom teaching; evaluations and letters of commendation about their aptitude with pedagogy or content knowledge; anecdotal records about students or classroom management strategies; or awards of distinction. The portfolio is focused because specific skills and dispositions related to teaching are delineated; for example, one can include specific state or national standards for teacher preparation with corresponding evidence of mastery of those standards. Besides educators, professionals in other fields such as entertainment and the fine arts use portfolios. Doolittle (1994) and Campbell, Cignetti, Melenyzer, Nettles, and Wyman (1997) describe the basic outline of a traditional, or linear portfolio. The design of the portfolio should satisfy three sets of criteria that are not equally weighted:

1. *Pedagogical*: This is related to the quality of the teaching and learning that is presented and is accompanied by the students' reflections. Being astute practitioners of academic technology, we are not distracted from pedagogical substance by style. We have all agreed that substance is to be valued.
2. *Instructional*: Having said that, we do value style. Components of the portfolio such as navigation and aesthetics make an important statement about the student's ownership of his/her technological skills. The portfolio should be structured so that the reader can easily navigate and understand the portfolio.
3. *Functional*: This addresses the simple question, "How *user-friendly* is the portfolio?"

Early in the COATT process, we set a scope for the M-COATT portfolio as something that a student could design in 10 hours, given a basic mechanical understanding of how to construct a hypermedia document. We recognize that not every student-teaching classroom is on a level field insofar as the breadth or depth of available technologies is concerned. While student candidates are expected to be as creative as they wish in applying technology in the service of teaching and learning, those who are in a "technology-poor" classroom can still effectively compete if the degree to which technology is employed is seamless and promotes learning in individual and unique ways.

It is expected that students will include standard fare such as sample units and lessons, artifacts of learning, artifacts of teaching (an electronic gradebook, a classroom presentation, etc.) in their M-COATT portfolio. We also look for evidence of thoughtful contemplation on the part of the student: a summary justification for why the student meets a portion of the standard, a portrayal of the classroom environment, and a reflection on how "well" a particular unit or lesson was enacted and received. The COATT liaison at each member institution is responsible for sensitizing students towards addressing these areas.

We expect submissions to follow good practices of hypermedia and instructional design. The digital portfolio should be *self-guiding*, and organized in a cogent, cohesive manner. Design guidelines for the students' linear portfolio are a good starting point. However, a well-designed digital portfolio also takes advantage of the nonlinear presentation of information afforded by hypermedia. One may use the following pervasive questions (Rubio, Michell, Blackwell, Albery, & Kondelik, 2000) to guide their assessment of how that nonlinearity was utilized: (a) What do I want my reader to know now? (b) What do I want my reader to know next? and (c) How can I take advantage of the multi-media and nonlinearity at my disposal to effectively convey my presentation?

Another important consideration in the first year was when to make the M-COATT portfolios due. We wanted to issue the M-COATT certificate early enough so that recipients would have this certificate in hand for late spring job fairs. But the preparation of a digital portfolio that included actual lessons taught with students was a challenging task, as many of our applicants would only be student teaching in the spring. In addition, the timetable had to accommodate an independent review by university teacher educators. It was decided that there would be two sets of deadlines to accommodate student teachers that taught in fall 1999 or spring 2000. A Web site was set up in early November and was used to begin the application procedure; applications could be made and changed online until January 14, 2000. Candidates from the first group submitted a nominal registration fee and a digital portfolio in Web-accessible format to their COATT liaison, who was responsible for assuring that the portfolios were installed on Web servers that were secured (no further modification) after March 3, 2000. The cooperating teacher was asked to sign the application to signify that the student teacher actually did teach the unit in the classroom.

RESULTS

Our most important result in the first year of operation was that we successfully created a process for reviewing and evaluating digital portfolios on a statewide basis. However, the number of applicants was well below our expectations. In the first year of operating as a consortium, only a handful of students applied to receive the M-COATT. Of the seven applicants, only four qualified for the M-COATT certificate. While this level of participation was well below the rather ambitious goals we had set for our first year, we nevertheless noted a number of encouraging trends.

Another challenge was coming to a consensus on how to interpret and evaluate student performance. While each member institution is committed to applying the state standards, there has been variation in how that is actually applied and interpreted. While the COATT process has brought the member institutions closer together in their understanding of the seventh standard, there was already an awareness from our discussions that we did not all agree on how high performance needed to be for an award. How good was good? These kinds of questions arise in any evaluation but are exacerbated when institutional boundaries are crossed accompanied by rapid changes in technology that make *good* a relative term.

While COATT members discussed a process of peer review similar to the grant process of sending out portfolios, then getting results from judges who knew the field, the final process was more one of building a consensus through joint review followed by an independent judging to test those assumptions. An initial group met to discuss the first round of applications and to ensure that there was agreement about the rubric and the judging tool, including what should be found in an awardee's portfolio. While all the evaluators spent time looking at the portfolios individually during the review session, the initial judging was the result of a consensus discussion, resulting in some changes to the judging process and tool. To test the revised procedure, the rubric and tool were sent to three judges who had not participated in the review session to see if the process could be replicated and to test for issues that might not have been considered. When these judges agreed with the initial group, the first awards were made. The second round again was a process of initial review, and just to be sure, a second round to see if there was agreement. As a result, all the COATT members have come closer to a common understanding of how to interpret the standard and what high performance should look like.

Four distinct criteria emerged from independent analyses of the portfolios as *de facto* gateways to success or failure to achieve the M-COATT. These criteria may be summarized as follows:

How well did the student teacher follow the portfolio submission guidelines or present his/her case? A common characteristic of unsuccessful applicants was that they did not clearly address the rubric in presenting what they did with their students. In some cases, they may have done some interesting and potentially exemplary things using technology with their students and were able to write about what they had done, at some length. However, what all unsuccessful applicants shared in common was that they did not clearly address the requirements of the M-COATT certificate as specified in the rubric. One student teacher who showed some otherwise exceptional classroom artifacts did not receive the M-COATT specifically because of this criterion.

What degree of critical thinking lay behind the technology-based assignment? Taxonomies such as that of Dodge (1999) were considered when we looked behind the technology to see what the students were doing. Teaching experiences that allowed students to synthesize, create, assess, or reflect were esteemed more than those in which students found matched pairs, filled in blanks, or assembled definitions by grouping disconnected facts. Open-ended assignments inevitably produce more variation in student learning and are harder to assess. Thus this criterion is related to the next.

Where was the locus of control? The more successful submissions included teaching experiences where the locus of control was tilted more toward the students. Student teachers had to demonstrate excellence in at least two out of three items from the seventh standard; the three items themselves were classroom based, and two of those were student centered and amenable to student artifacts. While it may have been tempting to only include the "best" student artifacts, we preferred to see a wide range of samples. A wide range of samples that showed a diversity of offerings suggested a student locus; if the offerings were not diverse, it suggested a teacher locus and thus penalized the portfolio's chance of success.

How did artifacts of learning support the claim of excellence? It was up to each student teacher to buttress his/her claim of excellence in meeting a particular standard with student artifacts. In some instances it was highly appropriate to see teacher artifacts that either undergirded the unit or conveyed specific instruction. However, successful portfolios were rich in artifacts. Unsuccessful were not. One student teacher decided to alter the format of the student artifacts rather than leave them in original form, a sacrifice of appearance for space that was not solicited in the submission guidelines and was not well received. Another student teacher described some impressive learning by the students, but did not have supporting artifacts.

A companion list of criteria that had little or no influence on the success of the submissions also emerged:

The technological "wealth" of the school in which the student teacher taught. Successful applicants came from a wide range of different technological environments. Furthermore, in no cases did we find that successful applicants came from unusually rich technological environments. Having one computer in the classroom with no Internet access together with a once-per-week visit to a school computer lab is a very typical level of technological access for K-12 schools in Michigan, and we were encouraged that applicants from that typical setting were successful in earning the M-COATT.

The sophistication of the media employed in the portfolio apart from the artifacts. Appealing aesthetics often augmented a successful submission but certainly did not rescue an unsuccessful one. One of our initial concerns was that, in requiring applicants to write rationales for why they believed their technology-infused units met the criteria of the seventh standard, we would be tempted to recognize writing skills more than technology integration competency. We referred to this as reducing the M-COATT to an essay-writing contest instead of a demonstration of outstanding achievement in teaching with technology. We did not find that to be the case. Again, the rubric furnished clear guidelines about the performance level expected of applicants, and those that qualified were able to write directly to the point. We believe our process allowed us to recognize accomplishments in using technology with students, rather than skills in essay writing.

The content area focus for student teaching and the age of the students that were taught. Successful applicants created their units around a range of topics at the elementary, middle, and secondary school levels. The four successful unit topics were:

1. A creative problem-solving unit for sixth grade students
2. Several interdisciplinary projects in a third-grade classroom
3. A five-week interdisciplinary unit in the humanities at the high school level called Identity and Power
4. A four-week unit that used technology and communicative language teaching techniques to take high school students on a virtual tour of the Spanish-speaking world entitled *Buen Viaje* ("have a good trip")

The size and geographic location of the higher education institution. Awards were given to student teachers from both large and small institutions, all of which were located in different cities throughout the state.

We were also encouraged that successful applicants were able to earn the M-COATT certificate from a variety of mentoring strategies. One real challenge of the M-COATT is that it must be prepared during or immediately following student teaching. Therefore, professors in many institutions cannot arrange to help students prepare their portfolios as part of a typical course.

At one large regional university that prepares a number of teachers each year, the solution to the challenge of supporting students as they apply to reach this higher standard had two steps. First, three group meetings were offered during the evening hours to recruit students for the M-COATT and to teach them particular technical skills, such as logging on to the M-COATT database, and some initial design decisions (e.g., what tool to use to construct their portfolio). Then applicants selected a mentoring professor to guide them individually through the final phases of the application process. The applicants met with the professors in their offices and in the lab, with various lab staff and other faculty helping to assist them in their efforts. This process was not as smooth as we would have liked in its first year, and additional support will need to be provided in the future. However, as a working concept this model of group meetings and individual support appears to be workable for the immediate future.

At another, smaller state university, students used a required course in educational technology to prepare for the M-COATT. As part of this three-credit course, students designed and developed an instructional unit based on one of the benchmarks from the Michigan standards (Lenze, 2000). This unit functions as authentic assessment because it allows the instructor to see how well the student can integrate technology into actual content standards. Students work on that unit throughout the semester, integrating and expanding whenever possible. The final project requires each student to develop a Web site that serves as a template for M-COATT applicants. They utilize the same structure while adding content and learning activities used within their student teaching experience.

Students at a small liberal arts college were asked to create a digital presentation portfolio as part of a seminar course offered concurrently with their student teaching (Albion College, 2000a). Students who wished to apply for the M-COATT simply incorporated the M-COATT portfolio within the other portfolio. They could elect a directed study course, the equivalent of two semester hours, consisting of a working group of several students (some who were not applying for the M-COATT but simply wished to do advance work on their portfolio) and the director of the Center for Technology-Aided Teaching. Last year, because of the pioneering nature of the work, students also gave a presentation at the college's Undergraduate Research Fair on how to make a digital portfolio (Albion College, 2000b). These students received instruction in educational technology as an integral part of different methods courses (Rubio, Michell, Blackwell, Albery & Kondelik, 2000). All of the basic skills needed to begin the portfolio work were thus in place prior to student teaching. During the student teaching semester, all students were asked to consider implementing a substantive technology project. The decision of whether to apply for the M-COATT was made jointly by the student and the director. The directed study course could either be used to prepare the portfolio and the project, or it could be used as a post-process. In either case, it was incumbent upon the student to portray and collect artifacts used to supplement the M-COATT submission.

ISSUES

A number of issues have emerged through the process of creating the consortium and technology certification. These include the marketing of the M-COATT, financing COATT, and the pedagogical basis for this sort of evaluation effort. However, our biggest challenge is to create certificate opportunities for practicing teachers and increase the number of pre-service applicants.

As a consortium, we set a marketing goal that the M-COATT would become a credential valued by both job seekers and those who make hiring decisions in school districts. In order to bring this about, participating institutions have agreed to take a leadership role in promoting the certificate to their students. Senator Levin's office has agreed to work with the K-12 community to market the certificate to schools and school districts. We are also working for the endorsement of the M-COATT certificate by all relevant education organizations in the state. Our marketing efforts will also include working with the news media to publicize this "first in the nation" approach to upgrading technology training standards for teachers.

There is the important question of how will we pay for this "revenue neutral" project. In this era of reduced state budgets for higher education, some creative means will need to be found to support the ambitious goals of the COATT project. The modest application fee ($25.00 per applicant) may one day support this project. However, it does not do so at present. The lack of a funded office and staff to oversee the M-COATT project has hampered our ability to attract as many educators as might be reached. Public and private grant support must be sought to cover the administrative and marketing costs of COATT, and whatever portion of the evaluation costs are not met by application fees. Consortium institutions have given some in-kind support to COATT in its start-up phase, mainly in the form of faculty. However, as the consortium scales up, it will be imperative to fund its efforts on a sustainable basis.

Another issue that periodically appears in our discussions of both the pre-service and the practicing M-COATT is the question of pedagogical expertise and the M-COATT. One possible direction for COATT will be to reexamine the structure of the M-COATT certificate based on some of the research that has been done concerning novice and expert teachers (Livingston & Borko, 1989). Research indicates that there are a variety of levels of teaching expertise between teachers who are novices and experts (Berliner, 1994). Thus far in our efforts, our pre-service M-COATT has served to identify those who can effectively integrate technology into their teaching at the advanced beginner or (arguably) at the "competent" level. We are working toward identifying those at the proficient or (arguably) expert level. Perhaps what we may consider in the future is merging the "pre-service" M-COATT certificate and the "in-service" certificate into one. We are already in a sense developing a tiered rating scale in which teachers who apply for the M-COATT may be certified as "competent" in the early years of their career. As they continue to advance in their practice they could resubmit their portfolio and be recognized at the "expert" level. Thus M-COATT certification could recognize the "wonder of increasing expertise" (to borrow Dr. Berliner's phrase) throughout the career of a professional educator, instead of simply recognizing a set of entry skills, as the pre-service M-COATT now seeks to do. This would be consistent with national technology standards efforts, such as the NETS Standards for Teachers (ISTE, 2000).

While a certificate program for pre-service teachers is in place, an awards process for practicing educators is being rolled out in fall 2000. Modeled in some ways after professional teacher board certification program, the goal is to give teachers both a goal to achieve and recognition for high performance that will have credibility with peers and administrators. Similar to the pre-service program, evaluation will be based on a portfolio that teachers who seek the recognition put together to demonstrate their accomplishments in infusing technology into their classrooms. Over time, COATT may be expanded to recognize high achievement at school and district levels as well as the accomplishments of individual teachers.

Several challenges confront COATT as it moves to recognize practicing teachers. The first is simply the number of teachers who may seek the award. With 97,000 teachers in Michigan, even a program that reaches 10% of the population is a huge undertaking. Based on presentations at statewide conferences to describe the COATT program, such an estimate of potential COATT applicants may not be too farfetched. The response from teachers has been positive, with many asking how they can sign up immediately. For teachers who are already early adopters and high-end users, simply receiving some recognition is enough of an incentive to engender participation. The greater challenge will come later as COATT seeks to reach those who are not already at this level, encouraging them to reach greater capacity. In the absence of formal incentives such as official state certification or enhanced salary for accomplishments, an ongoing question among COATT members is what the enticement will be for that broader participation, particularly given the issues with pre-service application numbers.

A second challenge is determining what standards to apply. Michigan lacks a formal standard for practicing teachers. While some school districts have adopted technology standards, most do not currently have a working model in place. COATT has therefore been placed in a leadership role to produce an appropriate model for the state. After talks with teachers, administrators, and teacher education faculty, the consensus was to use the pre-service standard as a model, with modifications made to reflect differences that would be applicable for ongoing classroom teaching. The result is minor changes to the seven indicators of the seventh standard, but much greater modification of the benchmarks. COATT teachers must demonstrate a higher level of performance on all seven indicators than the pre-service teachers were required to do, with the highest level required on the three that most directly relate to direct learning and teaching. The expectation is that this initial COATT practicing teacher standard will be used for the first year of evaluation, then modified as needed based on the newly released ISTE standards and COATT's experience with the first teacher applicants. COATT is also working with state education leaders to drive a process to incorporate the standards as a Michigan model, with the potential in the future for these becoming a part of official technology policy in the state.

Our most serious concern for us at present is the low number of pre-service teachers who applied for the M-COATT certificate in its first year. In our initial conversation about M-COATT, we often vacillated between concerns about what would happen if too many students applied for the certificate (i.e., "if we build it, and they ALL come!") and what would happen if only a few students applied for the certificate (i.e., "if we build it, and they DON'T come!"). When we started out, we suggested that each participating institution would have at least 5 to 10 pre-service applicants in the first year. Instead we received applications from only seven pre-service educators statewide.

One reason for this became clear this year during our recruitment efforts. There is a shortage of qualified teachers in Michigan at present (e.g., Bondi & Trowbridge, 1999). Thus one of our initial assumptions in this effort–that pre-service teachers would seek out this credential in order to secure a job–has been called into question by the current job market. We believe that the technologically savvy teacher is still very desirable, but the need to "certify" that higher level of achievement through a rather demanding standards-based process has been reduced in our state even as we have worked to create the M-COATT certificate.

A related problem concerns the question of timing. Most of our applicants prepared their portfolios during or immediately following their student teaching experience. Indeed, as the M-COATT evaluation is currently configured, it seems difficult to imagine another time when they could do the bulk of their preparation. A large part of the portfolio is exhibits that cite the applicant's exemplary use of technology with students. For most pre-service teachers, the time in their teacher preparation program when they are fully prepared to do this is during student teaching. But the student teaching experience is a very demanding one for most pre-service teachers, and many of them are actively applying for jobs immediately afterward. Thus there is little time to embark on a project as ambitious as the one we have charted for the M-COATT. There are some alternative teacher preparation programs underway in some of our member institutions that might allow students enough teaching time with students earlier in their program so that they could at least begin to compile their portfolio prior to student teaching. So far, however, we have not received any applications from those institutions.

NEXT STEPS

We are taking steps in this next year to encourage more participation. We are also working to improve the administration of the M-COATT based on our experience of the past year. We believe that, now that we have students who have posted successful applications to M-COATT on the Web, the presence of concrete examples of a successful M-COATT portfolio will be very important in encouraging others to apply. However, we do not believe that better administration and posted examples of M-COATT portfolios alone will increase participation to the levels that we had hoped for when we began.

Thus, as a consortium we have sought to reexamine our original assumptions about the incentives that would encourage pre-service teachers to apply for the M-COATT certificate. Tentatively we are considering four options to increase participation. However, each option is in some way problematic.

1. *Asking member institutions to create an undergraduate credit course that students would take while preparing their COATT portfo-*

lios. This idea has been tested at one member institution already; however, with no success. Many teacher education programs are rather long in terms of the number of courses taken. Indeed, over the years there have been many discussions about making teaching certification a fifth year of college, following a four-year bachelor's program. Therefore, trying to recruit more students by asking them to take an additional course seems unlikely to prove to be a successful strategy. In addition, very few students take any courses during or following their student teaching experience, which is when this "COATT preparation" course would make the most sense.

2. *Adjusting the COATT portfolio review schedule to give students the option of completing their portfolios after graduation.* This would reduce the time pressure of having to complete the COATT portfolio between the completion of student teaching and graduation. However, one of our original incentives for pre-service students was that they would have the M-COATT "in hand" as they went to apply for their first job. Thus, a delayed time frame may not equip the successful M-COATT applicant in the desired way.

3. *Creating a graduate credit course for students who exercise the option mentioned above so that their portfolio work becomes the first step in their professional development in the field.* This again addresses the timing problem mentioned earlier, although this time by preparing the COATT portfolio in the first year of teaching. While relieving the time pressure, once again the M-COATT applicants would not be more marketable as they applied for that critical first teaching job.

4. *Developing a network of school districts that indicate their interest in interviewing COATT recipients for teaching positions.* The point of this approach would be to increase participation by creating a clearer demand for M-COATT recipients. Now that we have our first group of M-COATT recipients, we are in a better position to begin to recruit districts to interview our recipients. One of the original goals that we set was that the M-COATT would become a credential valued by both job seekers and those who make hiring decisions in school districts. Clearly we have a ways to go in persuading both groups of the value of the M-COATT.

CONCLUSION

We have outlined the COATT standard, described the process of applying for the M-COATT certificate, described the results of our first evaluation process, and begun a discussion of some of the issues facing us as we move forward with this task. Thus far our experience with the M-COATT certificate leads us to several conclusions. The standard that we set, while demanding, is at least achievable by some of our students. Our evaluation process, while labor intensive for faculty, is workable and leads to a consensus about who has earned the certificate. In addition, this entire process–the formation of the consortium and the awarding of the first year's M-COATT certificates–has provided an unusual occasion for faculty collaboration. The various members of the consortium represent very different higher education institutions, from small private liberal arts colleges to large public research one institutions to public regional universities of differing sizes. Through a process that has continued over a couple of years we have met often (usually once each month) and agreed to a common standard by which to evaluate our students, and subsequently have met together to examine student work. This is not the norm in our field. Already this consortium has led to a higher degree of statewide professional collegiality among professors who prepare pre-service teachers at these different institutions. Those of us who have helped create COATT continue to believe that it will make a significant contribution to long-term efforts to improve the technology skills of Michigan educators. Our participation in the consortium has led to some important collaborations, one of which is this article.

Developing a parallel certificate for practicing teachers is still under consideration. One of the main questions is whether practicing teachers should be offered the same certificate for the same level of work, or a more advanced certificate that would necessarily reflect a more thorough integration of technology in their teaching methods. It is also recognized that the evaluation methodology we will use in granting the certificate may need to be modified as well.

While some problems with the assessment rubric, the application process, the portfolio instructions, and the judging tool, will lead to minor changes, no major revisions will be necessary to the assessment process or the benchmarks. In fact, what we have is a validation of the state-developed standard through real-world testing that will assist as a new pre-service standard is developed–an activity that is expected to result from the new ISTE standards that will push state reform efforts.

When we started the process, we thought the purpose was to challenge each student to a higher level of performance. What we found was that the higher standard applied more to each institution. We found that we were benchmarking our own performances against the other institutions in the state. Too often in education, this kind of benchmarking does not occur. When it does, it rarely covers the range of institutional types in COATT–large and small, public and private, research one and liberal arts schools. What has happened is a renewed commitment from each of our institutions and faculty for self-improvement, a factor that will positively impact all students in our teaching programs.

REFERENCES

Albion College. (2000a). Albion College Education Department Digital Portfolio Project. [Online]. Retrieved July 28, 2000, from the World Wide Web: http://www.albion.edu/education/fac_educ/dig_portfolio.htm

Albion College. (2000b). Student research abstracts. [Online] Retrieved July 28, 2000, from the World Wide Web: http://www.albion.edu/fac/libr/isaac/abstracts2000.htm#Albery

Berliner, D. (1994). Expertise: The wonder of exemplary performances. In J. Mangieri & C. Collins (Eds.), *Creating powerful thinking in teachers and students* (pp. 161-186). Fort Worth, TX: Harcourt Brace. [Online]. Retrieved July 1, 2000, from the World Wide Web: http://courses.ed.asu.edu/berliner/readings//expertise.htm

Bondi, N., & Trowbridge, G. (1999, June 1). Teacher shortage blocks efforts to improve schools–Metro Detroit's need most urgent in math, science. *The Detroit News*. [Online]. Retrieved July 1, 2000, from the World Wide Web: http://edWeb3. educ.msu.edu/media/news/shortage.htm

Campbell, D. M., Cignetti, P. B., Melenyzer, B. J., Nettles, D. H., & Wyman, R, M. (1997). *How to develop a professional portfolio.* Needham Heights, MA: Allyn & Bacon.

Coley, R. J., Cradler, J., & Engel, P. (1997). *Computers and classrooms: The status of technology in U.S. schools* [PDF document]. Princeton, NJ: Policy Information Center, Educational Testing Service. [Online]. Retrieved January 1, 2000, from the World Wide Web: http://etsis1.ets.org/pub/res/compclss.pdf

Dodge, B. (1999). A taxonomy of WebQuest tasks. [Online]. Retrieved July 28, 2000, from the World Wide Web: http://edWeb.sdsu.edu/Webquest/taskonomy.html

Doolittle, P. (1994). Teacher portfolio assessment. In *ERIC Clearinghouse on Assessment and Evaluation*, April 1994. Washington, DC: Office of Educational Research and Improvement (ED).

ISTE. (2000). *National educational technology standards for teachers.* Eugene, Oregon: International Society for Technology in Education (ISTE). [Online]. Available: http://cnets.iste.org/index3.html

Lenze, J. S. (2000). Addressing content standards in an introductory educational technology class. *The Illinois Association for Educational Communications and Technology Journal, 5,* 178-212.

Livingston, C., & Borko, H. (1989). Expert-novice differences in teaching: A cognitive analysis and implications for teacher education. *Journal of Teacher Education, 40,* 36-42.

Michigan Department of Education (1997, September 8). *Proposed standard with related indicators for the achievement of entry-level skills in information technology for all Michigan teachers.* [Online]. Retrieved November 30, 1999, from the World Wide Web: http://www.mde.state.mi.us/tplan/presrvtech/matrix.shtml

Rubio, R. A., Michell, M. J., Blackwell, C., Albery, B., & Kondelik, J. (2000). Technology in the service of information literacy and writing across the curriculum: Our experience. *Proceedings of the 11th annual meeting of the Society for Information Technology and Teacher Education.* San Diego, CA: Association for the Advancement of Computers in Education.

Dennis M. Holt
Paula McAllister
Erin Claxton Ingram

Technology 2000: Using Electronic Portfolios for the Performance Assessment of Teaching and Learning

SUMMARY. This article describes a collaborative university-school district project for improving teaching and learning by using state-of-the-art educational technologies. The work resulted in the simultaneous improvement of P-12 education and teacher education. The article illustrates some of the important outcomes of a project known as Technology 2000, a collaborative effort between a university, a school district, and a business partner. Through using appropriate educational technologies, pre-service teachers, in cooperation with their supervising teachers in five classrooms at two school sites, engaged in the collaborative alignment of curriculum, instruction, and assessment to facilitate student achievement. The participants believe that the outcomes of this

DENNIS M. HOLT is Professor of Education, Division of Curriculum and Instruction, College of Education and Human Services, University of North Florida, 4567 Street, Johns Bluff Road, S., Jacksonville, FL 32224-2676 (E-mail: dholt@unf.edu).
PAULA MCALLISTER is Educational Specialist/Trainer, Logical Business Systems, an IBM Business Partner, 8301 Cypress Plaza Drive, Suite 121, Jacksonville, FL 32256 (E-mail: Pmcallister@lbs.net).
ERIN CLAXTON INGRAM is personal service representative, Blue Cross and Blue Shield of Florida, Inc., 4800 Deerwood Campus Parkway, Jacksonville, FL 32246 (E-mail: ErinCO401@aolcom).

[Haworth co-indexing entry note]: "Technology 2000: Using Electronic Portfolios for the Performance Assessment of Teaching and Learning." Holt, Dennis M., Paula McAllister, and Erin Claxton Ingram. Co-published simultaneously in *Computers in the Schools* (The Haworth Press, Inc.) Vol. 18, No. 4, 2001, pp. 185-198; and: *Evaluation and Assessment in Educational Information Technology* (ed: Leping Liu et al.) The Haworth Press, Inc., 2001, pp. 185-198. Single or multiple copies of this article are available for a fee from The Haworth Document Delivery Service [1-800-HAWORTH, 9:00 a.m. - 5:00 p.m. (EST). E-mail address: getinfo@haworthpressinc.com].

185

educational technology project have important implications for improving teaching and learning in other schools and teacher education settings. *[Article copies available for a fee from The Haworth Document Delivery Service: 1-800-HAWORTH. E-mail address: <getinfo@haworthpressinc.com> Website: <http://www.HaworthPress.com> © 2001 by The Haworth Press, Inc. All rights reserved.]*

KEYWORDS. Portfolio, electronic portfolio, electronic folder, performance assessment, pre-service teacher education, educational technology, collaboration

The demand for educational technology in our nation's schools has increased tremendously in the last five years. In an effort to meet the demands of parents, legislators, teachers, and others, school districts have spent millions of dollars to put "technology" into schools. In many cases the dollars spent on technology amount to funds for school wiring and computers, with little or no thought given to selecting appropriate software applications, educational technology programs, teacher training, or implementation and evaluation strategies. Today, accountability issues have surfaced and those same parents, legislators, teachers, and others have begun to question the academic results for the huge investment of funds. Following are some of the issues this search for accountability has brought to light:

1. Computer hardware and networks alone make no difference without software applications selected to address educational needs of students in a particular school.
2. Computer hardware, networks, and software alone make no difference if teachers and students are not using them.
3. Computer hardware, networks and software alone make no difference without teaching methods and strategies that give teachers concrete ways to integrate the technology into their existing methods of classroom instruction.

The authors believe that computers and networks are essential, but are simply the basics of an educational technology program. Considerable thought, research, and funds will be necessary to address and resolve the three issues cited, before fairly assessing what positive student learning gains can be achieved through using educational technology.

The Technology 2000 project described in this article was designed to address these issues. Participants in the project were provided with appropriate hardware and grade-level instructional software resources, adequate software and hardware technology training, and methodology for using classroom-based instructional technology for teaching and learning activities. The performance assessment methods used involved the development of electronic portfolios and electronic folders, which in turn provided a means to evaluate the impact of the project on the accomplished practices of pre-service teachers and the academic achievement of their students.

PORTFOLIOS AT UNF

The teacher education program of the College of Education and Human Services at the University of North Florida (UNF) prepares professional teachers to effectively participate in diverse and evolving learning communities. The program emphasizes structured clinical experiences in school settings. The assessment of these experiences by UNF personnel is accomplished through a portfolio process carefully designed by the faculty (Boulware & Holt, 1998).

During the completion of two, two-semester-hour field laboratory courses, pre-service teachers prepare working portfolios through which they document their work with students in classroom settings. The working portfolios are collections of unabridged versions of carefully selected documents used to portray their professional growth (Campbell, Cignetti, Melenyzer, Nettles, & Wyman, 2001).

The culminating experience of the teacher education program is a 16-week internship during which the pre-service teachers produce their professional portfolios. These portfolios are a selective and streamlined collection of teaching and learning materials that reflect their mastery of Florida's 12 Pre-professional Accomplished Practices (Florida Education Standards Commission, 1996). Accomplished Practice 12 is centered on the pre-service teachers' effective use of computers in school classrooms. This article provides the details of an effective means for pre-service teachers and teacher educators to combine the uses of portfolio assessment with the appropriate uses of computers in school classrooms.

RESEARCH ON PORTFOLIOS

During the past five years the interest in portfolio development for teacher education has gained considerable momentum. There are several excellent books and articles that provide comprehensive information on the current state-of-the-art of portfolio development.

Campbell, Cignetti, Melenyzer, Nettles, and Wyman (2001) provide helpful details to pre-service teachers for developing their portfolios. They state that the creation of portfolios is an authentic and holistic way to illustrate the developing professional competence of pre-service teachers. They found that portfolio development enables pre-service teachers to chart their own professional growth while following step-by-step procedures. In another publication, Campbell, Melenyzer, Nettles, and Wyman (2000) provide information for teacher educators on the portfolio development process. The critical elements of a well-designed portfolio assessment system are defined and illustrated. The authors provide directions for teacher educators to tie performance assessment tasks to adopted state and national standards for success in professional education and make them faithful to real-life teaching. They provide specific help with the design and use of portfolio rubrics to assess the performance of pre-service teachers.

Farr and Tone (1998) provide a multitude of illustrations and helpful information on portfolio and performance assessment for improving teaching and learning in the classroom. These authors define portfolio assessment as "the practice of saving lots of things that a student creates so that the student and the teacher can look at the collection and see how the student is doing" (p. 11). Portfolios are viewed as collections "organized in such a way as to reflect, promote, and report a considerable amount of thinking that students have applied to the contents in them" (p. 11). Farr and Tone believe that portfolios should "inform the teacher about the student's progress as a thinker and language user, while indicating how effective the instruction has been and what additional instructional emphases are needed" (p. 11).

Cole, Ryan, Kick, and Mathies (2000) provide definitions, strategies, and details on the uses of portfolios and electronic portfolios across the teacher education curriculum. They define and describe a variety of useful tools for incorporating educational technology into college teaching and learning. They note that "bringing the learning process alive and using portfolios to document the products of this process requires various technologies" (p. 53). They suggest that teacher educators consider incorporating the following with their use of computers in education: local and wide area networks, servers, school networks, online databases, global educational networks, optical media, laser discs, Zip and Jaz cartridges, CD-ROM disks, scanners, digital still cameras and camcorders, and multimedia software.

Barrett (2000) defines several categories for the evolution of electronic portfolios and provides a conceptual framework for thinking about their development. She describes two bodies of professional literature that define the process for developing electronic teaching portfolios to support long-term professional growth: the multimedia development process and the portfolio development process. She illustrates five levels of technology for developing electronic portfolios that are appropriate at each stage of teacher professional development.

After extensive review of the portfolio literature, Read and Cafolla (1999) based their portfolio assessment work on a constructivist theory which "views the learner as actively engaged in the construction of his or her own representations of knowledge" (p. 98). They found that creating professional portfolios requires pre-service teachers to "engage in self-reflection as they select performance items for their portfolios" (p. 99) and is a means for them to provide evidence that they have met national and state professional education standards. Read and Cafolla also found that standardized and criterion-referenced tests fail to reflect the actual learning that takes place during instruction in teacher education. They describe the computer software and hardware used for successfully producing multimedia portfolios in pre-service teacher education programs.

Hartnell-Young and Morriss (1999) offer help to teacher educators interested in digital portfolio development. Their textbook is designed to help teachers "understand ways in which technology can assist them to record and communicate their professional achievements, and how they can share what they have learned with students to help them unlock the secrets of multimedia" (p. 3).

Holt and McAllister (1999) provide a research base for their work with electronic portfolios. They describe the implementation and evaluation of a five-year project with electronic portfolios for pre-service teachers linked to the electronic folders developed by students that feature the accomplishment of some of Florida's Sunshine State Standards (1996). They provide details on how computer software for language arts, mathematics, and science was successfully employed in school-based professional development classrooms through collaboration between a school district, university teacher education program, and business partners.

PROJECT OVERVIEW

The Technology 2000 project was collaboration between the University of North Florida, the Chets Creek and Lone Star elementary schools of the Duval County Public School District, and Logical Business Systems, an IBM business partner. The project was designed to improve teaching and learning through the use of educational technologies.

PROJECT PARTICIPANTS

Participants in the project included a University of North Florida professor who served as project supervisor, a business partner technology trainer; five University of North Florida pre-service teachers, five directing teachers from Chets Creek and Lone Star elementary schools, two school principals, a media specialist; and 110 students from three first-grades, a third-grade, and a fifth-grade classroom.

PROJECT FOCUS

The Technology 2000 project provided five participating pre-service teachers with the educational technology skills necessary to excel in a learning community. Through the project learning activities, they developed the ability to not only use computers and related technology for word processing and recordkeeping of student achievement, but also to use computers and multimedia tools to significantly enhance classroom instruction and student learning.

Participants in the project learned to use multimedia technology, including laptop and desktop computers, scanners, digital still cameras, and video cameras for creating presentations and for instructional activities. They learned to use software, courseware, and related technology-based materials available at the schools for classroom instruction, assessment, and evaluation, with an emphasis on IBM's Teaching and Learning with Computers (TLC) approach to instruction. They became knowledgeable about available technologies for use with a single computer to present whole-class instruction, while successfully conducting technology-infused lessons. They used PowerPoint to create instructional materials that incorporated text, video, sound, and graphics. They used instruction and assessment strategies to assist P-12 students with the creation of electronic folders using PowerPoint.

TECHNOLOGY TRAINING

Enhancing classroom teaching and learning through the use of technology encompassed the following ideas and concepts:

1. *Using technology to present subject area curriculum to students in an innovative, dynamic manner.*

The teaching interns learned to use multimedia computers along with projection devices to display images from their computers onto larger screen classroom televisions. They learned to review the existing software and resources in the school to find computer-based lessons that would enhance or supplement the lessons they were teaching. They learned to use PowerPoint to create their own supplementary lesson materials. They learned to integrate the technology with their traditional instruction by presenting the lessons to the class using the projection devices. They learned to use this method of instruction as a means of teaching their students as a group how to use PowerPoint and other curriculum-based software. This reduced the amount of time needed to work individually with the students to teach them computer basics, and allowed students more time to actually work and create products on the computers.

2. *Using carefully chosen computer-based lessons to supplement and reinforce traditional instruction.*

The interns learned to integrate the technology with traditional instructional methods by creating a variety of cooperative and independent learning centers in the classroom that included computer-based lessons and activities, as well as other "off-line" activities, all based around the goals and objectives for the lesson being taught. These learning/activity centers supported different student learning styles cross-curricular unit lesson planning, and encouraged alternative assessment methods, including the development of electronic student folders. Interns also learned how to organize student groups and manage the movement of these groups through the centers so that every student experienced the learning environment at each center. The technology became an integral part of the classroom instruction rather than a rewards-based, add-on for students who had finished all of their other work.

3. *Using technology to document learning in electronic portfolios and electronic folders.*

Interns learned the basics of PowerPoint so that they could teach their students to create simple electronic folders containing text, graphics, and sound that documented the learning that had taken place during the unit as a culminating activity. Each intern used his/her knowledge of PowerPoint to create an electronic portfolio that contained text, graphics, and sound; documented their experience with the project; and included selected samples of electronic products from their student's folders. They learned how to use technology resources, including scanners, digital cameras, the Internet, clip art, and video cameras, to highlight and bring to life their electronic portfolios.

4. *Using technology as an alternative assessment method to assess and document student learning and progress.*

Interns learned to use product-based assessment methods to evaluate student progress and learning during the learning center activities and through the production of electronic portfolio products.

5. *Directions for interns in the classroom.*

The interns identified an organizing theme for their unit lesson projects and the curriculum areas they chose to highlight. They identified the appropriate hardware and courseware/software resources that were available (such as computers, projection devices, scanners, digital cameras, curriculum-based software, and presentation software (to create unit lesson plans that encompassed whole-class computer presentations, computer, and off-line learning center activities. They divided their classes into student groups for participating in the learning centers and creating electronic folders. They presented their unit lessons. They had their students use the computer resources to create electronic folders to document their learning of subject matter and newly acquired technology skills in creative ways with text, graphics, and sound. The interns used the computer resources themselves to create electronic portfolios that documented their participation and experiences with the technology integration process and included examples of the products produced by their students as evidence of product-based assessment.

ASSESSMENT IN THE TECHNOLOGY
AND LEARNING PROJECT

One of the primary premises behind the project was that networked computers should be an integral part of teaching and learning activities in the classroom. Students worked in pairs, small groups, or large groups in a variety of learning centers (including computers) whose content was based around a specific concept.

Teacher evaluation was integrated as well and included not only a graded assessment of the various product outcomes from the centers (electronic portfolio being one of them) but also assessment based on observation of the learning process. This included teacher observation of such things as teamwork, group cooperation, following of directions, behavioral habits, and so forth. The teacher's role in assessment was ongoing throughout the project and included process and product rather than focusing simply on the final product outcome. The teacher was a guide, facilitator, observer, and evaluator. The student was an active learner as an individual first but ultimately as part of a team of learners.

In this project the pre-service teachers' assessment rubrics were created in advance and included giving points/credit for reaching individual goals in regard to timeliness of completing tasks, individual behaviors in learning center activities, correctness and completeness of work, as well as points/credit for the timeliness, behavior, and final product outcomes of the whole group. All points throughout the work of the projects were totaled for the final grades. The pre-service teachers charted observations and comments regarding the performance of their students during the project. These were combined with the product outcome evaluation to produce the final assessment of student work.

ILLUSTRATIONS FROM A SAMPLE ELECTRONIC
PORTFOLIO

Illustrations from an electronic portfolio provide evidence that students learned the content they were taught and knew it well enough to organize the concepts into a main idea with supporting details using the computer and PowerPoint software. During the unit, the first-grade students learned about reptiles using books, lectures, PowerPoint presentations, Windows on Science lessons, and actual hands-on learning experiences. The students' last assignment during the unit was to write a report on a reptile of their choice. Once the reports were completed, the students typed their reports into a PowerPoint slide. Finally, the students added a graphic to their slide. The students saved their slides to the school network, which then were imported into the electronic portfolio. The following is a slide illustration of student work:

Figure 1 provides the student's information on the habitat of turtles, their diet, and predators. The clip art added illustration for the information. Sound effects, including applause, were included in the electronic portfolio for interest and dramatic effect.

The electronic portfolio provided evidence that students could reproduce their learning at the application level and present it in a totally different format on the computer, using original words and illustrations to document their knowledge. The electronic portfolio proved that students could use the technology (computer, keyboard, and mouse) effectively to complete a task. It also showed that they learned the software sufficiently to be able to produce, format, and edit text on the computer and select and manipulate graphics to illustrate their work. The electronic portfolio was also a valuable learning experience for pre-service teachers, who learned how to create and share instructional presentations using PowerPoint. They also learned how to import graphics and other slides into their electronic portfolios.

FIGURE 1. Example of Electronic Portfolio for Use in Student Assessment

Turtles

≈ My reptile lives in lakes, rivers, ponds, forests, salt marshes, and even in the desert.

≈ My reptile eats living or dead plants and animal matter

≈ My reptile's enemies are alligators and crocodiles.

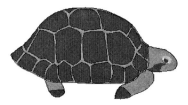

OUTCOMES

Each intern involved in the project presented lessons to his/her respective students, using educational technology resources within the framework of Teaching and Learning with Computers. They created a personal electronic portfolio with PowerPoint, providing information on their intern experiences and displaying examples of technology-based products that their students produced. They facilitated the creation of student electronic folders that displayed knowledge of language arts, mathematics, and science subject matter, and evidence of newly acquired educational technology skills. They developed diagnostic and prescriptive lessons that included educational technologies as instructional and assessment tools. They also created digitized photographs and video clips of their teaching and learning activities using a variety of educational technologies.

ASSESSMENT, REFINEMENTS, AND CONCLUSION

Participants in the project completed an assessment by answering four questions: How did the project work? What worked well? What went wrong? What were the surprises?

1. How did the project work?

The pre-service teachers responded that the technology project worked very well. They learned a lot about using PowerPoint to enhance their teaching and to master technology skills. They suggested more time for doing the project would be helpful, perhaps by beginning the training earlier in the semester. They found that their directing teachers were very supportive and helpful as they knew PowerPoint and could help facilitate the development of the student's electronic folders.

2. What worked well?

The projects worked well because the pre-service teachers carefully organized their units of instruction to achieve goals for mastering the technology they were learning. The organization of students into small groups helped develop a team approach completing the learning tasks. They were able to share information and computer skills with one another. Working on the computer motivated the students to learn the subject matter in a highly engaging manner.

3. What went wrong?

The biggest problem was that the pre-service teachers could not fit enough information on their floppy disks. It was determined that Zip, Jaz, or CD-ROM disks should be employed in the future. It was difficult to decide what to eliminate from the projects as all participants had worked so hard to produce them. Spring term testing of students consumed a lot of instructional time. Another problem developed when one piece of software used in the instruction phase would not easily import into PowerPoint.

4. What were the surprises?

First grade students who were reluctant writers with a pencil readily expressed themselves via the computer. Some exceptional education students initially perceived to be unable to successfully complete the project did as well or better than the regular education students. The novelty, creativity, and variety of learning styles incorporated into the project were believed to contribute to this outcome.

Elementary school students were capable of completing the project with a minimum of actual computer skills being taught. Participants were pleasantly surprised at how readily students acquired the ability to use the educational technology, leaving more instructional time to concentrate on the acquisition of subject matter content. Floppy disks would not hold a lot of multimedia. It was a pleasant surprise for participants to learn how user friendly PowerPoint could be as a tool for creating electronic portfolios and student folders.

REFINEMENTS

The participants believed that there would be value in refining the assessment checklists and rubrics for use in the evaluation of learning-centered projects, electronic portfolios, and folders. The assessments could then be adapted as needed to fit particular grade-level and subject matter needs.

It was agreed that the necessary computer equipment and software for the development of the project should also be provided at the university. The participants believed that the resources available at various schools will vary and that, while some are adequately equipped, others were less so. Having the resources for the project at the university would equalize the opportunity for all participants regardless of their individual school circumstances.

CONCLUSIONS

The professional portfolio is an excellent tool for assessing pre-service teachers understanding and skill to reflect on their own teaching and for providing evidence of their ability to facilitate student learning through the appropriate uses of the computer. The electronic portfolio is an effective means by which educators at all levels can demonstrate that educational technology can improve the quality of education for all students. The creation of electronic folders provides an effective means through which students can display their understanding of subject matter and their skillful uses of the computer to apply what they have learned.

REFERENCES

Barrett, H. (2000, February). Electronic teaching portfolios: Multimedia skills + Portfolio development = Powerful professional development. In D. A. Willis, J. D. Price, & J. Willis (Eds.), *Proceedings of SITE 2000* (pp. 1111-1116).

Boulware, Z., & Holt, D. (1998). Using CD-ROM technology with preservice teachers to develop portfolios. *Technological Horizons in Education Journal, 26*(2), 60-62.

Campbell, D., Cignetti, P. B., Melenyzer, B., Nettles, D., & Wyman, Jr., R. (2001). *How to develop a professional portfolio: A manual for teachers (2nd ed.).* Needham Heights, MA: Allyn & Bacon.

Campbell, D., Melenyzer, B., Nettles, D., & Wyman, R. (2000). *Portfolio and performance assessment in teacher education.* Needham Heights, MA: Allyn & Bacon.

Cole, D., Ryan, C., Kick, F., & Mathies, B. (2000). *Portfolios across the curriculum and beyond* (2nd ed.). Thousand Oaks, CA: Corwin Press.

Farr, R., & Tone, B. (1998). *Portfolio and performance assessment: Helping students evaluate their progress as readers and writers* (2nd ed.). Orlando, FL: Harcourt Brace.

Florida Education Standards Commission. (1996). *Accomplished, professional, and pre-professional competencies for teachers of the twenty-first century.* Tallahassee, FL: Florida Department of Education. (pp. 1-31). [Online]. Available: http://coe. fgcu. edu/Faculty/Honeychurch/ap/apindex.htm

Hartwell-Young, E., & Morriss, M. (1999) *Digital professional portfolios for change.* Arlington Heights, IL: Skylight Training & Publishing.

Holt, D., & McAllister, P. (1999, March) Lone Star 2000: Technology for today. In J. D. Price, J. Willis, D. A. Willis, M. Jost, & S. Boger-Mehall (Eds.), *Proceedings of SITE 99* (pp. 1029-1034).

Read, D., & Cafolla, R. (1999). Multimedia portfolios for preservice teachers: From theory to practice. *Journal of Technology and Teacher Education, 7*(2), 97-113.

State of Florida, Department of State. (1996). *PreK-12 sunshine state standards and instructional practices.* Tallahassee, FL. [Online]. Available: http://www.firn.edu/doe/menu/sss.htm

SOFTWARE SOURCES

International Business Machines Corporation, New Orchard Road, Armonk, NY 10504. [Online]. Available: http://www.ibm.com/ibm/

Microsoft Corporation, One Microsoft Way, Redmond, WA 98052-6399. [Online]. Available: http://www.microsoft.com

Eila Jeronen

Assessing Technology Based Instruction in Biology and Geography

SUMMARY. The article is a report on a development project arising from collaboration between the Department of Education in the University of Oulu, the university training school in Oulu, and some secondary schools in Northern Finland. The key aims of the project have been to promote the use of Information and Communication Technology (ICT) in teacher education and in schools, to develop methods for distant education, and to train student teachers in telematics instruction in biology and geography. The concept of pedagogical action, socio-cultural communicative perspective, constructivist views of pedagogy, ideas of reflective teachers and learners, and new forms of assessment provided the theoretical basis for the project. The main findings were that student teachers are able to plan, conduct, and evaluate telematics instruction. The greatest problems are technical problems and lack of time. Sustained and effective communication between students, local teachers, student teachers, and supervisors is seen to be the key to the successful cooperative work in developing curricula and instructional methods in telematics learning environment. *[Article copies available for a fee from The Haworth Document Delivery Service: 1-800-HAWORTH. E-mail address: <getinfo@haworthpressinc.com> Website: <http://www.HaworthPress.com> © 2001 by The Haworth Press, Inc. All rights reserved.]*

EILA JERONEN is Senior Lecturer in Didactics in Biology and Geography, University of Oulu Faculty of Education, Department of Education, P.O.X. 2000, 90014 Oulu, Finland (E-mail: ejeronen@ktk.oulu.fi).

[Haworth co-indexing entry note]: "Assessing Technology Based Instruction in Biology and Geography." Jeronen, Eila. Co-published simultaneously in *Computers in the Schools* (The Haworth Press, Inc.) Vol. 18, No. 4, 2001, pp. 199-212; and: *Evaluation and Assessment in Educational Information Technology* (ed: Leping Liu et al.) The Haworth Press, Inc., 2001, pp. 199-212. Single or multiple copies of this article are available for a fee from The Haworth Document Delivery Service [1-800-HAWORTH, 9:00 a.m. - 5:00 p.m. (EST). E-mail address: getinfo@haworthpressinc.com].

199

KEYWORDS. Distant education, ICT, assessment, biology, geography, secondary schools, telematics instruction, student teachers

Finland is one of the largest countries in Europe (338,100 square meters), but it only has 5.2 million inhabitants (Kiljunen, 2000, p. 35). Many of the country's rural schools have closed their doors due to the small number of pupils. Many schools are not able to guarantee quality instruction or offer optional courses, especially in languages, science, and mathematics because they do not have professional teachers. Information and Communication Technology (ICT) has been suggested as a key in solving these problems.

Finland is one of the most developed countries in the fields of communication and computers. At the beginning of 1999, about 80 to 90 percent of primary and lower secondary schools, 90 to 95 percent of upper secondary level schools, and 100 percent of vocational schools had Internet access (Tiedolla tietoyhteiskuntaan-tiivistelmä, 1999).

The Finnish national curricula named *Peruskoulun opetussuunnitelman perusteet* (1994) and *Lukion opetussuunnitelman perusteet* (1994), suggest that students ages seven to nineteen should be able to use modern information and communication technologies to find, analyze, and classify information, and to develop knowledge. In the information strategy for education and research, the Ministry of Education has stated the goals for teacher education:

> The departments of Teacher Education have to develop their curricula so that teachers will be able to get the skills in Information and Communications Technology already during the pre-service education, and as a result will be independently able to study the use of new equipment and programs at their work and to develop their usage in instruction. (Koulutuksen ja tutkimuksen tietostrategia, 1995, p. 20. Translation by E. Jeronen)

The Department of Education of the University of Oulu has actively developed the curricula and the use of Information and Communication Technology both in technology education and in integrative ways in different subjects. This article will describe and evaluate a telematics project of biology and geography carried out in 1996 through 2000 as a part of the pedagogical studies with four student groups. With 'telematics' we mean that instruction is real time and interactive, and mediated by computers and telecommunication equipment (Jeronen, 1997).

PEDAGOGICAL BACKGROUND OF THE PROJECT

The teacher education curriculum at the University of Oulu is based on the concept of pedagogical action, which has four principles (cf. Kivela, Peltonen, & Pikkarainen, 1996). The first principle, originally called in German "Bildsamkeit," refers to the initial ability of the student to learn and to develop himself or herself. The second principle, called "Aufforderung zur Selbstätigkeit," means that educators themselves act in a way that later on requires the latter to realize his or her ability. This demand does not have to be a straightforward command to the student, but can take place as a part of his or her whole environment or certain aspects of it. The third principle is that the student acquires awareness about a kind of behavior that he or she cannot spontaneously know. What is rational action in a certain situation depends on the whole cultural context and that is why, in education, we try to get the student to understand this context and to acquire the competence that is needed for it. We call this principle "contextuality." This third principle must be constantly revised because the prevailing cultural context is not unchanging. The direction of development is affected by a multitude of factors. That is why we simply cannot try to prepare our pupils for a certain or an unknown future, but we also have to think what kind of future is worth aspiring to. The fourth principle is called "Bildungs Ideal." It means that in education, we must anticipate a better future and also keep in mind the space for possibilities of contents and competence that will be needed when the students are improving their contexts (Jeronen & Pikkarainen, 1999).

Besides these four main principles, pedagogical studies are strongly influenced by a socio-cultural communicative perspective (Mead, 1909 [as cited in Reck, 1981]; Vygotsky, 1934), constructivist views of pedagogy (Dewey, 1938; Kolb, 1984), and the ideas of reflective teachers and learners (Schon, 1987). The new learning conceptions also include new forms of assessment. The main ideas of the new assessment are: (a) ask students to create, design, produce, perform, or do something; (b) stress complex thinking and problem solving, or both; (c) use tasks that are instructionally meaningful; (d) use authentic or real world applications; and (e) require people exercising judgment, rather than machines, to score. If the assessment is to support attainment of high standards, it must also be fair to all students; use accurate measures; be useful, feasible, and credible; and be aligned with standards or desired student outcomes (Herman, 1997, p. 198).

DESCRIPTION OF THE PROJECT

Elements of the Learning Environment

The key aims of the project have been to promote the use of Information and Communication Technology (ICT) in teacher education and in schools, to develop methods for distance education, and to train student teachers in biology and geography in using telematics instruction and in using the necessary equipment. The resources and tools being used are university e-mail communications, distance education equipment, and the resources provided by the NEttinikkareiden weBEDitori (NEBED) environment at the training school of the university of Oulu. The distance education equipment consists of PictureTel equipment with an Elmo projector camera, a whiteboard, and PowerPoint and LiveSharePlus programs. In addition, there is a camera to transmit images of the telematics class and another camera at the remote class. With these cameras, the teacher can also use a blackboard or an overhead projector. The NEBED system is an open learning environment that was developed by Nettinikkarit Company (Kemppainen, 1996). Students and teachers can access it via the World Wide Web. They have a password that allows them to create simple Web pages and enter messages on a bulletin board.

The cornerstones of the telematics instruction in the project are the learners, student teachers, and tutors (local teachers and supervisors: subject teachers at the training school, and a senior lecturer in biology and geography at the department of teacher education), the technology used, and a certain culture for doing things in the learning community and organization. The elements necessary for learning are built on these cornerstones. These elements can be described in terms of the pedagogical action, appropriate technologies, and social organization of learning (cf. Pulkkinen & Ruotsalainen, 1998).

The pedagogical action includes the activities and methods of instruction. The actual instructional activities in the project were primarily short teaching situations by student teachers via a video conferencing system and individual or group study. Some of the sessions could also be Web and e-mail based situations. The learning activities were mainly self-directed, but local teachers at remote classes and the student teachers at the telematics class guided the pupils or students, if needed. Learning materials and activity guidelines were published on the NEBED Web pages. In addition, the students used textbooks and the Internet to search information. The evaluation activities consisted of validation of information and assessment of the students. The students sent their answers and got feedback partly by e-mail and partly in discussions during video conferences. They also participated in the assessment process by writing in logbooks their opinions, feelings, and observations of individual and group work, and by social interaction, learned facts and concepts, and positive and negative instructional feedback. In distance education, the most important feature is interactivity. In the project, there were two types of interactivity: ISDN video conferencing sessions and the NEBED learning environment.

Each learning community and organization has a culture of its own. Every school is different and has a school culture that is typical for that school. In planning the social organization of the learning, we should stress communicativeness, which means possibilities for a meaningful, transformative communication between different persons (cf. Pea, 1994; Pulkkinen & Ruotsalainen, 1998).

The Participants and the Implementation of the Project

The participants were 14 pre-service teachers in biology and geography from the University of Oulu. Before starting the pedagogical studies, they had studied geography and biology three to five years at the subject departments. The main ideas in the different parts of the project were similar each year. Before the start of the project, the student teachers studied theory of instruction in general pedagogical and subject didactic courses. The theory included (a) growth and development of children and adults; (b) learning concepts; (c) curriculum; (d) lesson planning; (e) communication; (f) instructional material and methods (also ICT); (g) learning environments; and (h) evaluation. The student teachers also visited the distance education schools, familiarizing themselves with the local teacher and the students. At the end of the fall semester, they planned a research project of telematics instruction for their own practice period.

In January and February, the telematics periods were carried out by student teachers in some rural schools. Before the telematics lessons, student teachers planned the lessons and created Web pages using the NEBED system. Some of the materials were sent by telefax or by standard mail to the schools. Distance education lessons were interactive. After the telematics lessons, student teachers collected questionnaires, observation diaries, and logbooks from the students and the local teachers. At the end of spring semester, the student teachers had courses in ethics. They also reported their experiences with telematics instruction and presented reports in seminar sessions. More detailed descriptions of the project follow.

In spring 1997, two of the student teachers worked with the teachers, the seventh-grade pupils (ages 13 to 14 years), and the ninth grade pupils (ages 15 to 16 years) of Toranki yläaste, which is a lower secondary level school in Kuusamo in the northeastern part of Finland (cf. Wedman & Valta, 1997). They conducted two 45-minute lessons by telematics during the next three weeks for both classes. The data collected were based on observations and questionnaires. One part of the questionnaire was multiple choice questions; the other part, open-ended questions. The local teachers gave the questionnaires to the pupils at the end of the lessons. The teachers also completed their own forms. Together, 101 forms were returned to the student teachers: 62 from seventh grade, 33 from ninth grade, and 6 from the local teachers. During the telematics lessons, an outside observer wrote an observation diary in the classroom. The student teachers wrote their own diaries.

One of the student teachers worked with Utajärvi yläaste and lukio (a secondary level school in Oulu region) where he taught three telematics lessons in the upper secondary level (the students were 17 to 18 years old) and three lessons at ninth grade (cf. Oikarinen, 1997). A lesson was videotaped for more accurate analysis of student activity. The students wrote logbooks and used e-mail contacts for communication. All of the upper secondary level students ($n = 12$) and 11 of 12 lower secondary level students sent their evaluations.

In spring 1998, three student teachers taught five lessons to seventh-grade and five lessons to ninth-grade classes in Toranki yläaste in Kuusamo (cf. Karinkanta, Kentala, & Tormanen, 1998). The data were based on questionnaires, observation diaries, and logbooks. During distance lessons, there was also an outside observer in the classrooms. All the pupils sent the questionnaires and logbooks to the student teachers ($n = 17$ from the seventh-grade, and 16 from the ninth-grade).

In spring 1999, two student teachers taught six telematics lessons to two ninth-grade classes in Toranki yläaste (cf. Halkosaari & Mikkila, 1999). After the distance education lessons, the students completed the questionnaires ($n = 98$) and the logbooks ($n = 73$). The local teachers also sent the questionnaires ($n = 6$), which they had completed themselves. In evaluating the concept knowledge of the pupils, the student teachers also used concept maps in this part of the project ($n = 69$).

In spring 2000, six student teachers taught four telematic lessons to three upper secondary level schools: Ruukki and Vaala located in the Oulu region; Rautavaara located in eastern Finland (cf. Haapakari &

Paakkola, 2000; Mantyniemi & Parkkinen, 2000). After the distance education lessons the students ($n = 27$) and teachers ($n = 5$) answered questionnaires. The students also did learning portfolios. The students selected the format (e.g., essays, presentations, reports, article analyses) which they wanted assessed.

Evaluation of the Project and Learning Environment

This evaluation is used to develop the practical arrangements of the pedagogical studies. According to Patton (1980), evaluation research refers to systematic collection, analysis, and interpretation of data on the functions and results of a course or an educational program, so that those interested can determine the value of the essential features of the program that was implemented. This research concentrates on examining and evaluating the project as a case study. The methodological approach is based on qualitative methods. An important feature in this case is the methodological triangulation (i.e., data were acquired using different methods and each complements and validates the other (Patton, 1980; Pulkkinen & Ruotsalainen, 1998).

In this research, data were gathered from the students by questionnaires and logbooks, and from the local teachers by questionnaires and observation diaries. The data contained qualitative items and were divided into three evaluation objects for content analysis: (a) pedagogical action, (b) social organization of instruction, and (c) technical design and reliability. In total, 275 students and 17 teachers took part in the project. Most of the students and all of the teachers had used computers before the project for purposes such as word processing. There were differences among the students in the use of various Internet services.

RESULTS AND DISCUSSION

Pedagogical Action

In this project, student teachers had autonomous roles. They planned the periods themselves, conducted the lessons, and evaluated the processes and products. They had the right to discuss problems and solutions with supervisors before, during, and after the lessons. Most discussions took place at the beginning and at the end of the periods. The student teachers succeeded in their work and, consequently, the local teachers reported that telematics instruction is very suitable in every-day situations in biology and geography. The local teachers were interested in this method themselves–for "the telematics instruction motivates the students and offers variability to the lessons," as one wrote.

Instructional Methods and Activities. Especially in the beginning of the project, most students wrote something about problems caused by the telematics equipment. The reason for problems was incompatibilities in the equipment at different schools. The most serious problem was poor video and audio quality. The sound became better after the student teachers learned to talk smoothly and clearly. Also in the Kilpisjarvi project, it has been observed that the teacher should pay more attention to the style of presentation in telematics instruction (Ronka, 1997). Sometimes the students considered the photos, the diagrams, and the texts blurred. The most common reason was that the student teacher inadvertently moved the pictures or papers. In distance education, it is important to plan written and oral presentations and to consider the facial expressions and gestures even more carefully than in normal class instruction. Both the students and the local teachers liked the audiovisual presentations. They also liked other instructional methods used (problem-based learning, role-playing, demonstrations, and laboratory work). Most of the students wrote that the distance education is more interesting than ordinary class instruction because it is different. Only a few of the students thought the telematics lessons were boring. The reason might be that the project was something totally new for them. Most of the local teachers evaluated the instructional methods and telematics education as effective as the normal class instruction. Only a few of the local teachers thought they were not as good as the teacher-centered method. According to the students, the equipment was interesting. They also reported that the use of e-mail and chat channels was a good idea. In addition, the variety of instructional methods increased motivation. Similar results have been achieved in the TELeopetuksen PEDAgogiikka (PEDATEL) project (1995, pp. 28-31).

Most of the students thought the working tempo was good; however, for some, it was too fast. The latter result is different from that reported by Ronka (1997). In his report he stated that the speed of instruction is slower in telematics lessons than in traditional class instruction because of the equipment.

Content. The local teachers reported that the students were interested in the topics and the phenomena studied. The content stressed biological and geographical concepts and facts. The ethical, social, and economic effects of communication technology were not discussed.

However, it is important to reflect on these areas with students, because the purpose of instruction is to educate students to have critical attitudes about media and its use.

Materials. The student teachers noticed that attractive material on the Web helped teaching and learning processes. There should be short texts, and simple and clearly drawn, large enough slides, diagrams, and patterns (Liflander, 1999, p. 11). The students stated that the materials were "quite common" or "quite nice." Both the students and the local teachers evaluated the level of the materials as suitable for the students. Some of the exercises were easy; some were quite difficult. Both the students and the local teachers reported that the map exercises were difficult.

Tutoring. The students gave positive feedback to the student teachers. They stated that the student teachers succeeded well in motivating and encouraging them. Most of the students were satisfied with the feedback, but some wanted it to be more accurate. Some of the students also stated that they did not get any feedback at all.

Evaluation. Most of the students were realistic in evaluating their learning process and products. They commented that facts and skills were learned as well as in traditional classrooms. Some of the student self-evaluations were not consistent with the test results. The local teachers also stated that the students understood the facts and concepts. The tests before and after the instruction showed that most students were able to describe the important facts and to determine the main concepts at either the "excellent" or "good" level. However, the local teachers noticed that some of the students did not understand the content. The reason was the lack of time and too much information. In telematics instruction, it is important to take care of differentiation more carefully than in traditional class instruction.

Social Organization of Instruction

The students and the teachers were not very familiar with the method of the study in the project. Telematics and student-centeredness were new and strange concepts to most of the students and teachers. Except for the students participating in the project during spring 1997, the students were not self-directed and they did not know how to schedule the working sessions. They also had problems with the multiplication tables–especially when they created Web pages. They were able to do the activities when the local teachers and the student teachers helped them, but they needed more time. Later, the self-directedness increased, and the students were able to work well on their own. At the end of the project, self-directness was at an even higher level than in traditional class instruction. In the Kilpisjarvi project, similar increases of self-directedness in comparison with traditional class instruction were observed (Ronka, 1997).

The students who participated in this study were generally interested in new learning methods, technology, questions of the day, and interactivity (PEDATEL-projektin tutkimusraportti, 1995, pp. 28-31). They also thought that the ICT skills were important in everyday life. These kinds of concepts were strengthened because of some descriptions of the project in the local newspaper. The students were eager to study the topics via ICT methods, although the student teachers were unable to provide individual guidance because student groups were quite large and the student teachers were therefore unable to observe all of the students.

Most students thought that the initial visits of the student teachers to the schools were important for good interaction between them and the student teachers, and reported that these initial visits prevented anxiety, which is typical in a new environment. The rest of the students wrote that it was sufficient for the student teachers to introduce themselves at the beginning of the first lesson. The students reported that the class atmosphere during the telematics instruction was good. The local teachers reported that it was normal, and interaction among the students was at a similar, or sometimes a slightly lower level, than in traditional class instruction. They also stated that the students were more restless in telematics lessons and suggested that the reason for these phenomena was tension when some of the students realized they were appearing on a screen. The local teachers and the student teachers also noticed that the students who met the student teachers beforehand asked more questions from the student teachers than from peers or the local teacher.

Technical Design and Reliability

The possibilities for successful distance education were good. The equipment did not cause any problems the student teachers were not able to solve. The local teachers also reported ease in using the telematics equipment. This result is different from that found in the Kilpisjarvi project (Meisalo, 1996, 3-40). The reason is that in the Kilpisjarvi project, the teachers had the local class and the remote class under instruction at the same time. In our project, the student teachers and teachers had only one class.

The NEBED environment is quite easy to use. Some students created Web pages in the NEBED environment: some had difficulties, created them with other programs, and sent them by e-mail to the student teachers for installation. The equipment and Internet connections were relatively good. Hardware was compatible between the schools but software caused some problems. The image and sound quality were not good. However, most problems could be solved with careful design and training. There are plenty of instructional methods that are suitable for telematics learning and teaching processes. In the future, the application of technology will increase in all areas of everyday life. It is important that the equipment used in instruction is easy to handle and that a variety of methods induces the teachers to use them.

CONCLUSIONS

Assessing the quality of ICT instruction is an important part of instructional projects, and it should be integrated into the teaching, learning and studying processes from beginning to end. In that way, proposals for improvement can be generated. Consequently, students and teachers can manage to avoid old mistakes and benefit from their experience. In addition, the research can become stronger.

The forms of assessment used in this project served their purpose quite well, not only for instruction in schools, but also for the development of the ICT instruction in teacher education. If we evaluate the assessment according to the criteria stated by Herman (1997), we can say that it aligned the students toward desired student teacher outcomes and created goals for their lessons based on the national, school, and classroom standards. The tests and feedback provided information on student progress in relation to goals for student accomplishment. However, in their feedback, the student teachers should handle psychomotoric and affective goals mentioned in lesson plans more than they did. Through psychomotoric goals, children learn to handle equipment and materials and through affective goals, emotional life of children develops. Because the student teachers stressed the cognitive area, all students did not have ample time to solve the complex problems given and create their Web pages because they did not know how to operate the equipment. Although the students wrote learning diaries at home, they did not have enough time to explain their thinking at the expected level. The student teachers were also busy and did not have time to plan and describe the lessons and materials at the expected level.

The language of the activities and the tests was corrected beforehand in discussions among the student teachers, the local teachers, and the supervisors; and it fit the level of the students well. The scoring of the tests was also negotiated, and it fit the goals and was clear. The feedback on lessons from the students, student teachers, local teachers, and the supervisors is very important in improving lessons and telematics instruction, both in schools and teacher education. Use of time is one of the most crucial variables. According to Herman (1997), teachers need time "to become familiar with the new assessments and their administration, understand how tasks are developed and scored, discern and apply criteria for assessing students' work, develop the content and pedagogical knowledge, they need to change their practice, and reflect upon and fine-tune their instructional and assessment practices" (p. 201). We should discuss what kinds of goals and content school curricula and classroom instruction should include from the point of view of an individual, the community, and society, and what kinds of assessment systems are needed. Sustained and effective communication is seen to be the key of such collaboration. The role of ICT is crucial in achieving successful development.

REFERENCES

Dewey, J. (1938). *Experience and education.* New York: Macmillan.

Haapakari, V., & Paakkola, T. (2000). *Biologian ja maantieteen opettajien näkökulmia etäopetuksesta yläasteella ja lukiossa.* (Viewpoints of teachers of biology and geography concerning distant education in secondary level schools.) Paper presented at the Educational Seminar. Oulu: University of Oulu, Department of Teacher Education.

Halkosaari, H., & Mikkila, T. (1999). *Telemaattinen opetus konstruktivistisesta näkökulmasta.* (Telematic instruction from a constructivistic point of view.) Paper presented at the Educational Seminar. Oulu: University of Oulu, Department of Teacher Education.

Herman, J. (1997). Assessing new assessments: How do they measure up? *Theory into Practice, 36* (4), 196-204.

Jeronen, E. (1997, April). *Modern learning environment: experiences of modern information and communication technologies in Finnish schools and teacher education.* Paper presented in Euroland Comenius III In-Service Education Course for Educational Staff. Linz: Pedagogische Akademie des Bundes in Ober-Osterreich.

Jeronen, E., & Pikkarainen, E. (1999, September). Overcoming the gap between theory and practice in subject teacher education: The role of subject didactics, general didactics and the theory of pedagogical action. In B. Hudson, F. Buchberger, P. Kansanen, & H. Seel (Eds.), *Thematic network and European teacher education (TNTEE) Publications, 2*(1). Didaktik/Fachdidaktik as science(s) of the teaching profession? Papers of a symposium of TNTEE sub-network A at the European Conference in Educational Research (ECER) in Frankfurt, 237-247.

Karinkanta, V-M., Kentala, A., & Tormanen, A. (1998). *Eta-vaiko epaopetusta.* Telematiikkaa peruskoulun biologian ja maantieteen opetuksessa. (Distant education in biology and geography in lower secondary level schools.) Paper presented at the Educational Seminar. Oulu: University of Oulu, Department of Teacher Education.

Kemppainen, P. (1996). *Nebed-Nettinikkarien webbieditori.* [Online]. Available: http://norssi.oulu.fi/~pkemppai/telemat/

Kiljunen, K. (2000). *Maailman maat ja liput.* (The countries and the flags of the world.) Keuruu: Otavan kirjapaino.

Kivela, A., Peltonen, J., & Pikkarainen, E. (1996). Lahtokohtia pedagogisen toiminnan teorialle ja tutkimukselle. (Starting points for the theory of pedagogical action.) *Kasvatus 27*(2), 126-140.

Kolb, D. A. (1984). *Experiential education: Experience as the source of learning and development.* Englewood Cliffs, NJ: Prentice-Hall.

Koulutuksen ja tutkimuksen tietostrategia. (1995). (The informational strategy for education and research.) Helsinki: Ministry of Education.

Liflander, V-P. (1999). *Verkko-oppiminen. Yhteistoiminnallinen projektioppiminen verkossa.* (Net learning.) Helsinki: Edita.

Lukion opetussuunnitelman perusteet (1994). (Basics of the curriculum of the upper secondary level.) Helsinki: National Board of Education.

Mantyniemi, V., & Parkkinen, K. (2000). *Telemaattinen oppimisymparisto–muuttuva oppimisprosessi.* Opiskelijoiden ja opettajien nakemyksia lukion telematiikkaprojektista. (Conceptions of students and teachers of a telematics project in the upper secondary level.) Paper presented at the Educational Seminar. Oulu: University of Oulu, Department of Teacher Education.

Mead, G. H. (1981). The psychology of social consciousness implied in instruction. In A. J. Reck (Ed.), *Selected writings* (pp. 114-133). Chicago, London: University of Chicago Press. [Original work published 1909]

Meisalo, V. (1996). *The integration of remote classrooms. A distance education project using video conferencing* (Research Report 160). Helsinki: University of Helsinki, Department of Teacher Education.

Oikarinen, P. (1997). *Konstruktivismi oppimiskasityksena telemaattisessa etaopetuksessa.* (Constructivist ideas and telematic instruction.) Paper presented at the Educational Seminar. Oulu: University of Oulu, Department of Teacher Education.

Patton, M. (1980). *Qualitative evaluation methods.* London: Sage.

Pea, R. D. (1994). Seeing what we build together: Distributed multimedia learning environments for transformative communication. *The Journal of Learning Sciences, 3*(3), 285-299.

PEDATEL-projektin tutkimusraportti (1995). (The research report of TELeopetuksen PEDAgiikka (PEDATEL) project.) *Ammatillisen opettajakorkeakoulun tutkimuksia, 14.*

Peruskoulun opetussuunnitelman perusteet. (1994). (Basics of the curriculum of the primary and lower secondary levels.) Helsinki: National Board of Education.

Pulkkinen, J., & Ruotsalainen, M. (1998, August-September). *Evaluation study of a telematic course for technology teachers (T3 project)*. Paper presented at the Teleteaching'98 Conference of the 15th International Federation for Information Processing (IFIP) World Computer Congress, Vienna and Budapest.

Ronka, A. (1997). Videoneuvottelu koulujen opetuksessa (Videoconferencing in school education). In J. Salminen (Ed.), *Etaopetus koulussa* (pp. 1-18). Helsingin II Normaalikoulun julkaisuja.

Schon, D. A. (1987). *Educating the reflective practitioner: Towards a new design for teaching and learning in the professions*. San Francisco: Jossey-Bass.

Tiedolla tietoyhteiskuntaan-tiivistelma. (1999). (Knowledge and information society-abstract.) Tiede, teknologia ja tietoyhteiskunta. Statistics Finland. [Online]. Available: *http://www.tilastokeskus.fi/tk/yr/tttietoti.html*

Vygotsky, L. S. (1934). *Thought and language*. Cambridge: MIT Press.

Wedman, J., & Valta, K. (1997). *Telemaattisen opetuksen laatu* (The quality in telematic instruction). Paper presented at the Educational Seminar. Oulu: University of Oulu, Department of Teacher Education.

Index

Verbal interactions, 36-37
Verbal messages, 36-37
Virtual classes, 63
Virtual classrooms, 72-73
Virtual office hours, 70-71
Vocal channels, 36-37

Washington, Lisa A., 92-110
Web Course Tools (Web CT), 69
Web tools, 63
Web-based courses, 62-63. *See also*
    Distance education; Online
    distance learning
  assessment strategies for, 67-68
  constructivist theory and, 64-65
  creating rewarding, 74
  designing and assessing, 64
  face-to-face component in, 66-67

for electronic communities of
    learners, 67
  virtual classroom in, 72-73
Web-based testing (WBT), 50
  sources for, 52,53-54
West Virginia Basic Skills/Computer
    Education Program, evaluation
    of, 7
Will, Skill, Tool (WST) Model, 17
  technology integration and, 18-20
Workshops, for faculty development in
    technology, 128-130,143-144
  description of, 130-132
  evaluation of, 132-143
Writing
  computers and, 47
  with pens, *vs.* with computers, 48
Written tests. *See* Conventional tests